¡Ask a Mexican!

Gustavo Arellano

SCRIBNER

NEW YORK   LONDON   TORONTO   SYDNEY

SCRIBNER
1230 Avenue of the Americas
New York, NY 10020

Copyright © 2007 by Village Voice Media Holdings, L.L.C.

The names and details concerning some individuals have been changed.

SCRIBNER and design are trademarks of
Macmillan Library Reference USA, Inc., used under license
by Simon & Schuster, the publisher of this work.

For information about special discounts for bulk purchases,
please contact Simon & Schuster Special Sales:
1-800-456-6798 or business@simonandschuster.com.

Designed by Davina Mock-Maniscalco
Text set in Bulmer MT Regular

Illustrations by Mark Dancey.

Manufactured in the United States of America

1   3   5   7   9   10   8   6   4   2

Library of Congress Control Number: 2006037893

ISBN-13: 978-1-4165-4002-1
ISBN-10:   1-4165-4002-4

Photographs courtesy of participants in the ¡Ask a Mexican! contest.
Winners received a free copy of this book and lawn-mowing services.

To my parents: Papi, who proved you can be an illegal immigrant
and still make something of yourself in this great land,
and Mami, who taught me the alphabet as a toddler despite
not knowing English. *Los amo.*

CONTENTS

¡No contaban con mi astucia!
("They didn't count on my astuteness!")
EL CHAPULÍN COLORADO (THE RED GRASSHOPPER)

¡Ask a Mexican!

Introduction

⚭

Cultural Understanding via Wetback Jokes

Mexicans! Spicy, wabby, drunk, dreamy. The downfall of the United States. Its salvation. Mexicans mow our lawns, graduate from college, fleece us dry. They're people with family values—machismo, many kids, big trucks. Our neighbors south of the border. Our future. Tequila!

Who doesn't love Mexicans? Whether they're family, friends, or the gold-toothed wetbacks you (heart) to hate, Mexicans have been the focus of America's obsession from the days of Sam Houston to today's multinational corporations. We give them jobs, ridicule them, and devour Mexican food as quickly as they do our social services. But we never bothered to *know* Mexicans. There never was a safe zone for Americans to ask our amigos about their ways, mainly because we never bothered to learn Spanish. Besides, how exactly would you ask a Mexican in person why, say, so many of them steal or why they use accents without earning a kick in the *cojones*? A word, by the way, that *no* Mexican uses.

With this in mind, *OC Weekly* editor Will Swaim called me into his office in November 2004. *OC Weekly* is my home: an alternative newspaper based in Orange County, California, that's the best damn rag outside of *Weekly World News.* Seems he saw a billboard on the drive to work that featured a picture of a cross-eyed Mexican DJ wearing a Viking helmet.

"That guy looks as if you could ask him any question about Mexicans and he'll know the answer," he excitedly told me. "Why don't *you* do it? Why don't you ask readers to send in questions about Mexicans, and you answer them?"

My editor is an urbane, tolerant boss, yet he obsesses over Mexicans like all other good gabachos. I had entertained many of his questions about Mexican culture in my five years at the *Weekly,* from why Mexican men live with their parents until marriage to the Mexican affinity for transvestites. Will turned to me not just because I was the only Latino on staff and trim his trees on the side, but because my background—child of Mexican immigrants (one illegal!), recipient of a master's degree in Latin American studies, a truthful beaner—put me in a unique position to be an authority on all things Mexican.

I snorted in disbelief at Will's request: while it was fun to answer his questions, I didn't believe anyone else would care. My boss persisted. We were desperate to fill our news section the week he saw that Mexican DJ billboard. Besides, he promised, it was a onetime joke that we would scrap if no one sent in questions.

That afternoon, I slapped together the following question and answer:

Dear Mexican, Why do Mexicans call white people gringos?

Dear Gabacho, Mexicans do not call gringos gringos. Only gringos call gringos gringos. Mexicans call gringos gabachos.

We named the column *¡Ask a Mexican!* and paired it with an illustration of the most stereotypical Mexican man imaginable—fat, wearing a sombrero and bandoliers, with a mustache, stubbly neck, and a shiny gold tooth. My dad in his younger days. We laughed.

Reaction was instantaneous. Liberal-minded people criticized the logo, the column's name, its very existence. Conservatives didn't like how I called white people *gabachos,* a derogatory term a tad softer than *nigger.* Latino activists called Will demanding my resignation and threatened to boycott the *Weekly.* But more people of all races thought ¡*Ask a Mexican!* was brilliant. And, more surprisingly, the questions poured in: Why do Mexican girls wear frilly dresses? What's with Mexicans and gay-bashing? Is it true Mexicans make tamales for Christmas so their kids can have something to unwrap?

We still weren't sold on the idea until about a month into the column's existence, when we held ¡*Ask a Mexican!* one week because of space constraints. The questions swamped us anew: Where's the Mexican? Why did you deport the Mexican? When will the Mexican sneak back?

The *Weekly* has run ¡*Ask a Mexican!* every week since, and the column smuggled itself across America. Universities invite me to speak about it. I expanded it to two questions per week in May 2005 and began answering questions live on radio. The column now comes out in more than twenty papers and has a weekly circulation of more than one million. More important, questions keep invading my mailbox: Are Mexicans into threesomes? What part of *illegal* don't Mexicans understand? And what's with their love of dwarves?

¡*Ask a Mexican!* has transformed in the two years since its first printing from a onetime joke column into the most important effort toward improving U.S.-Mexico relations since *Ugly Betty.* But there is much work to do. The continued migration of Mexicans into this country ensures they will remain an exotic species for decades to come. Conflicts are inevitable, but why resort to lists and fights when you can take out your frustrations on me? Come on, America: I'm your piñata. As the following pages will show, I welcome any and all questions. Shake me enough, and I'll give you the goods on my glorious race. But be careful: this piñata hits back.

This book offers the fullest depiction of Mexicans in the land— not the same tired clichés of immigrants and mothers but a nuanced, disgusting, fabulous people. I answer not so much to inform but to debunk stereotypes, misconceptions, and myths about America's spiciest minority in the hope that Americans can set aside their centuries-long suspicion of Pancho Villa's sons and *hijas* and accept Mexicans for what they are: the hardest-working, hardest-partying group of new Americans since the Irish.

In this book are a couple of the best *¡Ask a Mexican!*s I've published, along with serious essays and new *preguntas* so that fans of the column will buy this *pinche* book instead of finding them online. And for *ustedes* who have never read the column? Flip the page. . . .

1

Language

Curse Words, Greasers, and Lecherous Whistles

Dear Gabachos: *Bienvenidos* to *¡Ask a Mexican!*, the world's foremost authority on America's spiciest minority! The Mexican can answer any and every question on his race, from why Mexicans stick the Virgin of Guadalupe everywhere to our obsession with tacos and green cards. In the course of his answers, the Mexican will use certain terms and phrases for better-rounded answers. Here are the most used, along with handy Spanglish sentence examples so you too can become a Mexican. Awright, *cabrones:* laugh and *comprende*!

¡: An upside-down exclamation point. Put in front of an exclamatory sentence. *¡Ohmidios, José brought his leaf blower into the living room!*

¿: An upside-down question mark. Put in front of a question. *¿Who gave María my old dress?*

~: A tilde. Put over the letter *n* from time to time to produce a sound like "nyuck." *Candelario sure has a lot of niños.*

Aztlán: The mythical birthplace of the Aztecs. Chicanos use this term to describe the southwest United States. Chicanos are idiots. *Citlali says Aztlán is somewhere in Ohio.*

Baboso: A slug or drooling person. Can also mean "asshole" or "idiot," depending on context. *Don't be a baboso to your baboso son, Josefina.*

Burrito: A flour tortilla wrapped around various goodies. Also a slur used against Mexicans. *That burrito ate a big burrito last night.*

Cabrón: Literally, a castrated goat. Mexicans understand it better as "asshole," or badass.

Chica caliente: Hot chick. All Mexican ladies are *chicas calientes. ¿Where can I meet some chicas calientes?*

Chicano: The poorer, stupider, more assimilated cousins of Mexicans. Otherwise known as a Mexican-American. *George López is such a Chicano with his unfunny jokes.*

Chingar: To fuck up. Its various derivatives are used for a delightful array of insults, such as *chingadera* (fucked-up situation), *chingazos* (punches thrown), and *Chinga tu madre, cabrón* (Go fuck your mother, asshole). *Chinga tu madre, cabrón—if you don't stop this chingadera, I'm going to chingar you with chingazos.*

Chino: Literally "Chinese," but the catchall phrase Mexicans use for Asians regardless of nationality. *Vietnamese food is my favorite chino cuisine.*

Chúntaro: A Mexican redneck. Term used mostly by Mexicans against each other. *Jeff Foxworthy is a white chúntaro.*

Cinco de Mayo: Holiday celebrating an obscure battle between the French and Mexicans in the 1860s that everyone in the United States uses as an excuse to get plastered. Our St. Patrick's Day.

Cochinadas: Disgusting things. Derived from the word *cochino,* which means "pig." *¡Stop seeing those Playboy cochinadas!*

Conquest, the: Refers to the Spanish conquest of the Americas during the 1500s. Centuries later, Mexicans still can't get over it—but having about 100 million of your ancestors slaughtered will do that to you.

¡Cu-le-ro!: The Bronx cheer of Mexico. Means "Asshole!"

Culo: Every Mexican man's obsession.

Estados Unidos, Los: "The United States" in Spanish. Come on—that one's not *that* difficult to decipher, *¿qué no?*

Familia: Guess. You're right: family! If you believe the mainstream media, the most important thing in Mexican culture after tequila.

Frontera, la: The border—specifically, the United States–Mexico border. *¿Why are there so many geezers at la frontera? Because they're Minutemen.*

Gabacho: A gringo. But Mexicans don't call gringos gringos. Only gringos call gringos gringos. Mexicans call gringos gabachos.

Gringo: Mexican slang for a white American. What gringos call gringos.

Guatemalan: The Germans had the Irish; the Irish had the Italians; the Italians had the Poles. Mexicans have the Guatemalans—our eternal punch line.

Güey: Derived from buey—an ox—but means "ass," as in a hoofed ass, not an ass ass. *That asshole is a güey.*

Hombre: Mexico's undisputed rulers.

Joto: Faggot. A preferred male slur.

Madre: Means "mother," but is also one of the most vulgar words in Mexican Spanish. In its various forms, can mean anything from "kick your ass" (*madrear*) to "suck my dick" (*mamámela*).

Malinche: The name of the Indian woman who served as a translator for the Spaniards as they slaughtered their way to the Aztecs during the Conquest. Mexicans turn her name into a noun, *malinchista*—that's a synonym for *traitor*. Typical Mexico—blames everything on women.

Mami: The diminutive of "mother," but also a sexual term of endearment for one's girlfriend. *Ay, mami, give me some of that sweet culo.*

MEChA: Acronym for Movimiento Estudiantil Chicano de Aztlán (Chicano Student Movement of Aztlán), a high school and college group that helps Mexican kids get to and stay in college. And that's why conservatives slur this group and all its members like no organization since the Scientologists.

Mensa: Name of an organization for people with an IQ in the upper

2 percent of the general population. Also the feminine form of "dumb" in Spanish. Mensa members can't be *that* smart given the snafu, no?

Mexicanidad: Mexican-ness. Ridiculous translation for a ridiculous concept.

Mexicano: The greatest race of people in the world—when they're in the United States. In Mexico, they're just Mexicans.

México: Country directly south of the United States with an estimated population of 105 million. America's eternal Paris Hilton.

Migra, la: Nickname for immigration agents. The brownshirts of Mexican society.

Mujer: Mexican worker whose only purpose is to make sure fresh tortillas greet the *familia* daily.

Naco: Mexico City slang for a *chúntaro*.

Norte, El: The North. The United States.

Otro lado, el: The other side. Otherwise known as the United States.

Papi: The diminutive of "father," but also a sexual term of endearment for one's boyfriend. *Ay, papi, give me your sweet green card.*

Pendejo: Literally, a pubic hair. Means "asshole" in Mexican Spanish. So many synonyms for asshole, Mexican Spanish has! *That pendejo should shave his pendejos.*

Piñata: A toy that Mexicans beat so it will spill forth its goodies. Otherwise known as the United States.

Pinche: A short-order cook. Also an adjective meaning "fucking." *Give me a pinche break.*

Pinche puto pendejo baboso: Literally means "fucking faggot pubic hair slug," but understood by Mexicans as "fucking stupid-ass asshole." The best Mexican cursing couplet of them all. *Shut up, you pinche puto pendejo baboso.*

Pocho: An Americanized Mexican.

Por favor: "Please" in Spanish. *The judge said, "Pleas, por favor."*

Puro: Pure. Put it in front of any word to come off as a braggart—a Mexican! *That chúntaro is puro mexicano.*

Puto/puta: The former means "faggot," the latter is "female whore." One of the most popular Mexican-Spanish curse words.

¿Qué no?: Ending phrase used in Mexican-Spanish to denote "right?"

Raza cósmica, la: "The cosmic race." Refers to a movement by Mexican intellectuals during the 1920s arguing Mexicans have the blood of all the world's races—white, black, Indian, and Asian—and therefore transcend the world.

Reconquista: Theory espoused by Chicano and conservative kooks insisting that Mexico is trying to take over the southwest United States, the territory the Yankees took from Mexico as spoils after the 1846 Mexican-American War.

SanTana: Santa Ana, California, from where *¡Ask a Mexican!* originates. The most Latino big city in the United States, according to the 2000 census. Please pronounce the city like the natives: "SanTana," like the famous guitarist, not "Santa Ana," like a combo of Claus and Karenina.

Señorita: A polite lady. Usually coupled with "spicy." *Salma Hayek is one spicy señorita.*

Taco: A corn tortilla stuffed with goodies. Also a slur used against Mexicans. *Tacos sure love tacos, ¿qué no?*

Tapatío: A popular hot-sauce brand featuring a man with a mustache and a sombrero. Drunk by Mexicans from cradle to crypt.

Tejana: A Stetson felt cowboy hat. Refers to Texas, where the hat supposedly originated.

Tequila: Liquor distilled from the agave plant of central Mexico. Also flows in the blood of any real Mexican.

Tortilla: A thin disk of cornmeal eaten by Mexicans since time immemorial. Also great impromptu Frisbees.

Ustedes: A fancy way of saying "y'all." *I'll be seeing ustedes tomorrow in Aztlán.*

Virgin of Guadalupe: The patron saint of Mexico. Appears everywhere in Mexican society, from churches to silk shirts to hubcaps.

Wab: The Orange County version of *wetback.* Spread our hate wide and far, *por favor.*

Dear Mexican: Why do Mexicans call white people gringos?

THE GRINGO-NATOR

Dear Gabacho: Mexicans do not call gringos gringos. Only gringos call gringos gringos. Mexicans call gringos gabachos, which has its etymological roots in the Castilian slur for a French national and does not have anything to do with Don Gabacho, the main character in the classic 1960s Japanese puppet show *Hyokkori Hyotan-Jima* (Happenings on a Gourd-Shaped Island). So, next time you want to look cool in front of your Mexican friends, say, "I don't want that gabacho Mexican food they make at Taco Bell—I want the real *pinche* deal!"

For decades, I've heard *mexicanos* refer to one another as güey. For example, the other day I overheard one *mexicano* refer to his amigo as *"pinche güey,"* and the amigo responded with *"Ay, güey."* What's up with güey?

ANSWER MY GÜESTION, POR FAVOR

Here's my request: I would like to ask for translations of all the smutty street Spanglish put-downs my courtly *maestros de español* wouldn't have dreamed of teaching me. *Pendejo*—I've long assumed it means "hanging one," as in "can't get it up": a pansy, contemptible cake boy. Is that right? What does *gabacho* mean? What does *cabrón* mean? Something relating to a goat?

GRINNING GRINGA

Dear Pocho y Gabacha: Welcome to the wonderful world of Mexican-Spanish swearing, where words assume different meanings according to placement but ultimately reference gonads! *Güey* is derived from the word *büey,* which is an ox but signifies an ass—a hoofed ass, not an ass ass. It's the Swiss Army knife of Mexican-Spanish cussing—we use it affectionately (*¡No mames, güey!* translates as "Don't suck dick, ass!" but actually means "Don't bullshit me, brother!"), in anger (*¡Eres un pinche güey!* is "You're a fucking idiot"), or as a boast (*¡No me haces* *güey!*—"You won't make an ass out of me"). *Pendejo* and *cabrón,* meanwhile, are synonyms for "idiot," but their actual definitions are "pubic hair" and "castrated goat," respectively.

But Mexicans rarely use *güey, pendejo,* or *cabrón* literally—instead, we forge them into some amazingly baroque insults. To wit, when a Mexican tells his friend, *¡Güey, no seas pendejo, cabrón!* we're saying, "Man, don't be an idiot, jerk!" but it literally translates as "Ass, don't be a pubic hair, ball-less goat!" So much better than the English equivalent "stupid-ass fucking faggot," no? As for the meaning of *gabacho,* Gringa . . . to paraphrase Louis Armstrong, if you gotta ask, you're one.

Whenever I hear people whistling at each other across the street to communicate, it always seems to be a Mexican. Is it illegal in Mexico to yell out words too loudly, and whistling is a loophole in the law? Or does the frequency of a whistle carry farther than voice frequencies across a ranch, the desert, or Mexico City traffic jams? Or is it learned behavior from living in an ambiguous environment (immigrant-friendly and -unfriendly) that whistling is somehow more discreet? Or is it cooler to whistle instead of yelling the other person's name?

WHISTLING GÜERO

Dear Gabacho: All of the above. According to *Whistled Languages,* a 1976 book by René-Guy Busnel and A. Classe, which linguists consider the definitive study on the matter, whistled tongues arose in cultures that occupied areas where daunting terrain and distance prohibited easy conversations. Many such ethnic groups influenced the formation of the Mexican nation. Before the Conquest, major indigenous languages such as Nahuatl, Zapotec, and Totonac featured a whistled-only dialect. After the Conquest, migrants from the Canary Islands, home of the world's most famous whistled language, Silbo Gomero, were among the first settlers of Texas. And since the past is ever present for Mexicans, it makes sociological sense to argue that the Mexican propensity to whistle-talk, like our obsession with death and Three Flowers brilliantine, is a (literally) breathing cultural artifact.

But don't think there's some gnostic mystery behind its use, Whistling Güero. There are really just four phrases to whistled Mexican Spanish: a sharp tweet to catch someone's attention, a longer version for showing disgust during performances, and the lecherous, drawn-out double note that plagues so many gabachas. The most infamous Mexican-Spanish whistled phrase, however, is *chinga tu madre* ("go fuck your mother"): five successive, rapid trills that roughly sound like Woody Woodpecker's infamous cackle. The last whistle is our favorite, especially because we can use it in front of unsuspecting gabachos without reproach. But don't use it around Mexicans unless you want a brown fist in your eye and a mestizo foot square upon your t'aint.

Why do Mexicans have sixteen names? Gilberto Sánchez Ramírez De La Lobos Contreras García De La Concha Gutiérrez is a little too much.

NAMES ALWAYS COME OUT

Dear NACO: I tried to believe your assertion for a minute, but it's simply false. In Mexico, we usually go by three names—first name, father's surname, and mother's surname. We shorten that to first and last name in *los Estados Unidos*. But by the time we're scrimping and saving for a new house, we can only afford one name. Think of up-and-coming Mexican celebrities: Pedro, from *Napoleon Dynamite*. Lupe, the maid from *Arrested Development*. Rosie, the maid from *The OC*. The only tongue-twisting name out there right now among famous Mexicans belongs to Los Angeles mayor Antonio Villaraigosa, and Tony cheated: he combined his last name, Villar, with his wife's, Raigosa. Again with the Freud: any Mexican who lengthens his name has father issues—or wants to infuriate gabachos worldwide for daring to have a surname longer than two syllables.

Why is it that when you enroll your non-English-speaking offspring in our school system and they get tested with all the other students, they bring down all the test scores of the school and my kids have to

suffer because your kids don't understand the language? So would you dumb-ass beaners PLEASE learn some goddamn English, for Christ's sake?

PISSED-OFF WHITE MAN IN SAN CLEMENTE

Dear Gabacho: You're one of those parents who hate their kids learning to count up to three in *español,* right? And instead of embracing this confluence of cultures, you'd rather call Mexican kids beaners?! Pissed-Off, stop with the gabacho rage and refry this: the world is shrinking, and people will have to know two languages in the near future just to survive (three if the Chinese continue to pull their act together). But if the many advantages of bilingualism aren't your thing, Pissed-Off, then remember that lower-performing schools tend to get more federal funding and attention. So really, say *gracias* for the current wave of Mexicans moving to your town—they're ensuring your charming town won't become another Detroit.

Why do some Mexicans who speak fluent English without an accent insist on pronouncing their names and Spanish place names with the Spanish pronunciation? Especially reporters: "This is Julio Luís Sánchez reporting from Neek-a-ra-wa." I get that the Southwest was once Spain and Mexico, that many Mexicans here can trace their roots back generations, and that many of the place names are Spanish, but I don't use an Irish brogue to pronounce my last name, we don't say Anaheim with a German accent, and it's Des Moines, not "Day Mwahn." It's fine to say words correctly— La Hoy-a and not La Jol-la—but the overly dramatic accent comes off as annoying and pretentious (same with when someone speaking Spanish comes to an English word and drops the accent as if to say, "Look, I'm bilingual!"). On a related matter, does it piss Mexicans off when non-Latinos who happen to speak Spanish do this too?

A CUNNING YET CLUELESS LINGUIST

Dear Gabacho: Give me a *pinche* break. Everyone wants his last name pronounced correctly, whether you're a Jauregui ("Yah-reh-gwee"),

Nguyen ("Win"), Schou ("Skow," not "Shoe"), or Limbaugh ("Run, reason!"). If you notice Mexican reporters do it more often than other ethnically surnamed scribes, it just means they're not ashamed of actively correcting decades of mispronunciations. Really, Cunning, why don't you lend a lilt to whatever your Irish moniker may be? Afraid the English might trample your potato crop?

"Why do I pronounce my name in Spanish? That's the only way it feels right," says Adolfo Guzmán López, a *chingón* reporter at KPCC-FM 89.3 in Pasadena, California. He frequently encounters strangers who can't understand his name until he Anglicizes it for them ("Uh-doll-phoe" instead of "Ah-dohl-foh"). "If you're bilingual and bicultural, you know how to navigate in those two worlds," Guzmán López told the Mexican. "But I grew up speaking Spanish, and it's never sounded right to pronounce it any other way except in Spanish. Besides, my mom would probably get mad if I did it the other way."

By the way, Mexicans love it when gabachos try to pronounce Spanish correctly. Oh, they usually butcher our rolling double *r* and *n* with the squiggly mark over it, but we respect their effort. Contrast that with my gabacho coworkers, who howl whenever I fumble words like *gamut* (I say "gah-moot," not "gah-muht") and *harpsichord* (I'll spare you the cacophony of spittle and laryngeal scratches). Gabachos can profess all the progressive ideals they want, but put them within earshot of a Mexican gamely attempting to speak the King's English and hear the snickers spread.

What the fucking fuck is up with you border bandit cholos and Old English fonts? They're ugly, just like everything about your culture and people.

REALLY ABHORS CALIFORNIA-INVADING STUPID TOMATEROS

Dear RACIST: The popularity of Old English script is a prison phenomenon that transcends race—just check out some of the tats on your white-supremacist cousins the next time they show up at your family picnic, pit bull and all, or the signs in a town's historic district. But what's up with the gabachos who appropriate gangster fashion for their designer labels? It's impossible to attend an indie-rock show nowadays without some pimply, unwashed gabacho sporting a JESUS IS MY HOME-BOY T-shirt with lettering that seems lifted from the Gutenberg Bible. On the opposite side of the hipster spectrum, princesses proudly tote L.A.M.B. bags from the Gwen Stefani (*puro* Anaheim, *esa*) collection. It's a kind of role reversal, and it's as old as mankind (check out the medieval upside-down celebration, charivari, in which whores dressed as priests and priests as . . . wait a sec, that's the Catholic Church circa 2007). Can it be long before we see Mexicans dressing up as *la migra*?

What do you call a gabacho cholo wannabe like me? *Wexican* sounds pretty dumb. *Wiener* (white beaner) is a lot more insulting than *wigger*. Since I'm the opposite of a pocho, I call myself a *chopo*. Think it'll catch on?

EL CHOPO

Dear Gabacho: No.

Why do Mexicans pronounce *shower* as "chower" but *chicken* as "shicken"?

VIETNAMESE ABOUT TO ORATE

Dear VATO: My column has provided readers with many indicators of the differences between recently arrived Mexicans and *los que* have lived here for generations: skin tone, car purchases, whether the Mexican in question flushes his soiled toilet paper or tosses it in the trash can. Another surefire way is the *ch/sh* phonetic test. Proper Spanish doesn't feature a *sh* sound (known among linguists as a linguapalatal fricative), so most Mexicans pronounce English words with a *sh* sound with the harsher *ch* (known as a lingualveolar affricate). However, many indigenous Mexican tongues use linguapalatal fricatives. The most famous example is in the original pronunciation of *Mexico:* as said in Nahuatl, the word sounds like "meh-shee-ko." The Spaniards couldn't pronounce the middle consonant, though, instead substituting a guttural *j* (as in "Meh-hee-ko") early in the Conquest. They killed most of Mexico's Indians in the ensuing decades, but the indigenous *sh* sound never wholly disappeared; if you do hear a Mexican using *sh,* he or she is probably a Mexican Indian. So next time you hear a Mexican ask for a "Shinese shicken sandwish with sheddar sheese," VATO, *por favor* don't shortle.

A friend of mine calls Mexicans "wabs," but being a dumbshit doesn't even know what it means—except that it's not PC. What's it mean?

THESAURUSAURUS MEX

Dear Gabacho: *Wab* is a slur that assimilated Mexicans use to describe and deride recently arrived Mexicans. It can be used as a noun ("Refugio is such a wab"), a verb ("Look how that idiot Refugio wabbed up his truck with a bull sticker!"), or even an adjective ("Refugio's mustache is so wabby"). The etymology of *wab* is unknown—could be a mongrelization of either *wetback* or *wop.*

But what's most fascinating about *wab* is that it seems to be a distinctly Orange County term. When I asked Oscar Garza, the longtime *Los Angeles Times* staffer who's now editor of the fine glossy *Tu Ciudad Los Angeles,* if he knew the word's meaning, Garza replied it "draws a blank." Freelance journalist Ben Quiñones didn't know what a wab was either. And Lalo Alcaraz, the dean of Chicano comedy and author of the nationally syndicated comic strip *La Cucaracha,* thought it meant "white-ass bitch." *Pinche* racist pocho.

The final word on *wab* goes to Dr. Armin Schwegler, a professor in the University of California Irvine's Department of Spanish and Portuguese who specializes in dialectology and Spanish in the United States. He's taught at the school for twenty years and drops language trivia like some people default on their car payments—did you know, for instance, that the area from Denver to the Pacific Coast is the largest dialect continuum in the world, meaning Western American English is one boring tongue? But Schwegler has never heard of *wab.* He's not surprised the epithet exists, though. "People always think naively that language is just for communication," the good doctor told the Mexican. "But language is so important because it's also an identifier. With *wab*, you can see this tied into the question of nationhood. It's rooted in social discrimination. You coin a word, and it circulates around." So rejoice, Thesaurusaurus Mex! *Wab* is all ours!

Dear Gabachos: After I offered my theory on *wab*—that *wab* is a mongrelization of either *wetback* or *wop* and that it's a slur exclusive to Orange County—readers invaded my mailbox. Theories largely fell into two schools of thought: the Asian and the border.

Here's the Asian:
Mexican, Mexican, Mexican . . . sometimes you really don't need a cunning linguist to know from whence the ethnic slurs flow. It's obvious as a matter of pronunciation, if not spelling: *wab* is a conflation of the classic pejorative *wetback* and the Asian *fob* (fresh off the boat). The OC angle is likely due to proximity of the respective populations, i.e., Garden Grove, Westminster, etc. So how come, you may ask, some white boy in Laguna Beach thinks he's got the 411 on this shit? Let's just say . . . vanilla breaks me out. See also *kike*—before its co-opting by anti-Semites, the epithet of choice for Jews to use on newer Jews. Mmm, Jews!

JESUS ISN'T A REAL NAME

As soon as you said *wab* applied to recent arrivals, I just assumed it was the Mexican version of *fob,* which is what my kids' Asian friends call recent arrivals—it means "fresh off the boat." I bet *wab* is really *wob:* wetback off the boat. Sure beats the dumb etymologies those intellectual types were trying to come up with. Why don't you ask somebody in high school? They'll know.

NO SLURS ALLOWED IN THE CAR POOL

Here's the border approach:
I've always known a *wab* to be an acronym for "walk across the border." [UC Irvine Spanish professor Armin] Schwegler now has some-

thing new to think about—maybe he should publish it so that people will be more edumacated. *¡¡Hasta la victoria!!*

SLEEPS WITH FIVE MEN ON A COUCH

For twelve years, we lived on the west side of Costa Mesa, where the vast majority of residents are Latinos. My daughter heard *wab* from one of her Latino friends, who said it means "walked across the border."

GIMME CHILE

Wab stands for "went across border." Makes perfect sense with his explanation that it is used "to describe and deride recently arrived Mexicans." So now you know.

GIMME NALGAS

One lady claims *wab* isn't an Orange County phenomenon:
About ten years ago, I ran across a piece by William Finnegan in *The New Yorker* about a family in the Yakima Valley of Washington. The parents were Mexican immigrants and true-blue UFW types, and the kids were alienated Nirvana fans who thought all that was crap. And those kids and their pals bagged on wabs throughout the piece. One of their friends never left her daughter with her parents because they dressed her all wabby. Never heard of it before or after. No one ever 'splained the origins, but seems it did have to do with wetback.

WHO ASKED BOBBI

And then there's this prison valentine:
I spent years working in a maximum-security facility and can tell you that, at least from the perspective of the incarcerated, *wab* is an acronym for "wannabe American boy."

OPEN YOUR EYES, ESE

We've been keeping tabs on your wab-ology lessons and were wondering if you've ever heard the term *chunti* (pronounced "chewntee"). It's what people from the Central Valley agricultural mecca in California call the newly crossed, yet-to-assimilate Mexicans or those who haven't quite figured out how to. We're talking a pimped-out '96 Dodge Neon with mexi-chrome hubcaps whose driver wears an air-brushed T-shirt with the Virgin Mary overlooking three gangstas and their lowriders. We don't know if it's unique to the Central Valley, but we haven't heard it since moving to SoCal, and none of our local friends is familiar with the term.

THE POCHO & HIS GÜERA WIFE

Dear Pocho and Gabacha: We Mexican-Americans in Orange County created *wab* to describe our wabby brothers and sisters, and all you Central Valley wabs could come up with to insult your unassimilated *paisanos* is *chunti*?! *Chunti* is shorthand for *chúntaro,* what Mexicans in Mexico call the poorer, rural Mexicans—what wabs call wabs. As a slur, *chúntaro* has never caught on with the children of Mexican immigrants like *wab* or *Guatemalan.* Mexican immigrants, however, toss around the term like tortillas over an open fire—my mom, a native of a poor Mexican village, always warns me not to go out with *chúntaros* since "they dress bad, are dark, and talk stupidly." And ain't that the truth?

Why are Mexicans known as greasers? Is it because they spread rancid lard from their dirty kitchens all over themselves after bathing instead of baby oil or cologne the way clean, civilized Anglos do?

GREASER GREG

Dear Gabacho: *Mira, güey,* the only grease we put on ourselves is the Three Flowers brilliantine Mexican men use to lacquer up their hair to a shine so intensely astronomers frequently mistake the reflection off our heads for the Andromeda Galaxy. That puts us in brotherhood with the 1950s gabacho rebels whom mainstream society also denigrated as greasers. But the reason *greaser* maintains such staying power as an epithet against Mexicans—etymologists date its origins to the 1830s—is because it refers to, as you correctly imply, our diet. Sociologist Irving Lewis Allen devotes a chapter in his 1990 compendium of linguistic essays, *Unkind Words: Ethnic Labeling from Redskin to WASP,* to the predominance of foodstuffs that double as ethnic slurs in American English. "All these slurs in American slang," writes Allen, "indicate a great historical awareness of alien ethnic food, its preparation, and the eating of it—another case of dislike for the unlike." Allen also notes gabachos have called Italians, Greeks, and Puerto Ricans greasers at other times during the American experience. But the food hate goes both ways, Greg—*bolillos* (French rolls) and *mayonesa* (mayonnaise) are what we call gabachos, and in the larger scheme of things, I'd rather people call me something tasteful such as grease or beans than a condiment that always smells like urine.

What's with the Mexican use of the word *mother*?

YO MAMA

Dear Gabacho: While the phrase *yo mama* is used as an insult worldwide, Mexican Spanish is unique in its use of the word *mother* to create some truly vicious vulgarities. Instead of concentrating on traits such as weight and sexual proclivities, Mexican-Spanish syntax uses *mother* in various grammatical forms to mean everything from the threat of physical violence to parental revulsion—the all-encompassing *aloha* of Latino cursing.

As a noun, *madre* can mean anything from "shit," as in *No vale madre* (It isn't worth shit), to "ass," in which *Te voy a partir la madre* translates into "I'm going to split for you the mother" but really means "I'm going to kick your fucking ass."

You can use *madre* as an adverb. *Te voy a dar un chingazo en la madre* translates to "I'm going to give you a fucking blow in the mother" but really means "I'm going to give you a fucking blow where it hurts the most." Or you can tell your closest kith to *Vete a la madre,* which does not mean "Go to the mother" but rather "Go to hell."

Add an *-ar* ending to *madre* and you have the verb *madrear,* which means "to fuck someone up." For example, if you tell your mom *Te voy a madrear,* you're not telling her that you're going to mother her but are letting her know "I'm going to kick your fucking ass." We advise against this.

And a mutation of *madre, madrazo,* denotes "harmful blow." *Te voy a dar un madrazo* is "I'm going to give you a fucking punch."

Saying how you are related to your giver of life is also fraught with swearing. *Hijo/a de tu madre* means "Son/daughter of your mother," but the phrase is uttered by parents to their irresponsible children only when they are disgusted with them. If you try telling that to your mom, she will reward your biological insight with a *madrazo* to the face.

Even the most benign form of mother, *mamá,* can be turned into a crude insult if you don't pay attention. Take off the accent, and you are left with *mama,* the present indicative form of *mamar,* which means "to suck." And when you say that, you ain't telling a baby how to get the milk out of the bottle.

Why don't Mexicans have enough gratitude for America to learn to speak English? Are they too stupid? Too lazy? What—they can't learn two or three words a day? Is this asking too much?

TOOK FOUR YEARS OF SPANISH IN HIGH SCHOOL

Dear Gabacho: The U.S. government shares your concerns, Took Four Years. Its Dillingham Commission released a forty-two-volume study on the waves of immigrants that concluded, "The new immigration as a class is far less intelligent than the old. . . . Generally speaking they are actuated in coming by different ideals, for the old immigration came to be a part of the country, while the new, in a large measure, comes with the intention of profiting, in a pecuniary way, by the superior advantages of the new world and then returning to the old country." The Dillingham report went on to fault the new immigrants for their lack of assimilation and English skills, constantly contrasting them with earlier generations of immigrants, and urged clampdowns on immigration. Sounds familiar, no? That's because the Dillingham report appeared in 1911, and the inassimilable masses at the time were Eastern and Southern Europeans. The Dillingham Commission proves that the time-honored conservative anecdote that earlier generations of immigrants walked off the boats, chopped down their multisyllabic surnames, and learned English immediately is bull-*pinche*-shit. American racism is a carousel—and here we go round again.

You California wetbacks are nothing but a bunch of wannabes. *Aquí en Tejas,* we have the Rio Grande, so *mojado* is a good description. But west of El Paso, there's nothing to get a Mexican wet when he sneaks across the border except a little rain. And, as you keep pointing out, it never rains in Southern California. So *ya no estén chingando*—stop fucking around—and quit using the word *wetback.*

WET AND WILD

Dear Gabacho: Bone up on your racism dictionary, Wet and Wild. Few people call Mexicans wetbacks anymore, or beaners, spics, greasers, Mescans, border bandits, border hoppers, Mexi-can'ts, cockroaches, tacos, burritos, jumping beans, chili chokers, or any of the other derogatory terms gabachos used to smear Mexicans in the past. That *wetback* survives at all is because of American foreign policy. According to a 2003 article by College of New Jersey journalism professor Kim Pearson, *wetback* didn't become nationally popular until 1954, when the Eisenhower administration launched a program to deport all illegal immigrants. But America being America, *la migra* rounded up Mexican-Americans, legal immigrants—anyone who was brown, really. The program's name? Operation Wetback. The American experience is cyclical, of course, so expect Americans to soon begin calling Mexicans Sensenbeaners.

It seems many Mexicans understand a lot more English than they let on. Why do they do this?

NO ESPEAK ESPANISH

Dear Gabacha: Let's start this answer by remembering that English and Spanish are second cousins, children of the Indo-European family of languages; English aligns itself with the Germanic clan, while Spanish sidles up with the Romance *familia,* where Latin is the main *papi.* But English also inherited Latin from the Romans and William the Conqueror, which should make learning English easy for Mexicans, right? But a smart Mexican comes into this country with the understanding gabachos will always dismiss them as idiots. To get ahead, then, many Mexicans pretend not to recognize English so their gabacho bosses can entrust them with all the company secrets—codes, financial figures, and the all-important personal telephone number of the secretary.

Why aren't more migrant Mexicans taking advantage of the English classes made available instead of relying on their children to translate?

NO HABLAR ESPAÑOL BUENO

Dear Gabacho: Trust me, No Hablar, more Mexicans would take English classes if they weren't already crammed with Mexicans. Besides, what's wrong with using kids as translators? By enlisting their *niños* to translate everything from election ballots to dialing 911 to their homework for English-language classes, Mexican parents ensure that their children assimilate quicker *and* become mature, responsible adults. The first generation of immigrants commit themselves to a lifetime of labor, not assimilation—that's the job of the children. Sure, it's dangerous to entrust children with life-and-death responsibilities, and hilarity can ensue when you have an eight-year-old trying to describe a father's diabetes to a doctor, but what better way to teach Mexican kiddies that life in America is brutal but rewarding if you have immigrant parents?

I used to work as a telephone fund-raiser for various charities, and I noticed that when I called someone who spoke Spanish (all Spanish-speaking people are Mexican, right?), they *always* answered the phone by saying *Bueno*. Now, I'm not what you'd call fluent in Spanish, but I'm pretty sure *bueno* means "good." And *hola* means "hello." So why do Mexicans say "Good" when they answer the phone?

PACO BELL

Dear Gabacho: *Bueno* job with your rudimentary Spanish skills! But think outside America; each country has its own *teléfono* greeting. Sociologists have long documented the peculiarities of national telephone greetings—for instance, Germans usually answer the phone by repeating their last name, while Italians say *Pronto* (Ready), and Arabs reply with the wonderfully florid "May your morning be good." Each greeting reflects the culture's comportment—Germans are industrious, Italians are stupid, Arabs overly dramatic (check out Wahhabi Islam). Similarly, the Mexican *Bueno* greeting opens a window into our politeness. It originates from our daily salutations—*buenos dias, buenas tarde,* and *buenas noche* (good morning, afternoon, and evening, respectively), and thus the phone greeting *Bueno* is just a shortened version of the others. And remember that Mexicans are some of the happiest people on earth—and nothing radiates positive vibes like saying *Bueno*.

I was at a Del Taco the other night and noticed two customers speaking Spanish. As soon as they reached the counter, they spoke perfect English—to a Del Taco employee who was clearly a fluent speaker of Spanish. I've seen this before in other social situations. What's the deal?

DAN THE DEL TACO GUY

Dear Gabacho: Thus is the linguistic conundrum of the Mexican in the United States: Speak Spanish, get accused of separatism. Speak English, get laughed at for thick accents and limited vocabularies.

Many Mexicans speak English to Mexican workers out of gratitude—the fast-food counter is the only place Mexicans can feel like Americans by speaking the shared language of haggling with Mexican workers over the cost of fries.

When reading your articles and reviews I imagine the Ricky Ricardo voice (not Mexican, but really, what's the difference to a white guy?). Sometimes I use the "We don't need no steekeen badges" voice. Other times I read your writing in the Speedy Gonzales voice. Once in a while I read it in monotonous high school Spanish-teacher voice. Which do you prefer?

Sí, Señor!

Dear Gabacho: As much as Mexicans love the old Warner Bros. cartoons, that studio can go to *la chingada*. It's this studio's fault that gabachos always try to imitate Mexicans with accents more refried than a Taco Bell special. Not only that, but Warner Bros. inflicted this linguistic plague upon the Mexican nation *dos* times. The first incident came courtesy of voice-over legend Mel Blanc: first as Sy the Mexican in *The Jack Benny Show* (where he popularized the elongated *sí*), then with his fast-talking rendition of Speedy Gonzáles (which, let's admit, was a documentary into Mexican life). The other notorious Warner Bros.-created Mexican accent came courtesy of a real-life Mexican, Alfonso Bedoya, the murderous *bandido* in the 1948 classic *The Treasure of the Sierra Madre*. He's the *pendejo* who uttered the infamous "steekin' badges" line. (Learn your racism, gabachos: the exact quote is "Badges!? We ain't got no badges. We don't need no badges! I don't have to show you any stinking badges!"—a bowdlerization of the line from the original novel's "Badges, to goddamned hell with badges! We have no badges. In fact, we don't need badges. I don't have to show you any stinking badges, you goddamned *cabrón* and *chinga tu madre!*") What's worst about the Warner Bros. accents is that there are real-life Mexican accents even funnier-sounding than those: the vulgar *chilango* singsong of Mexico City, for instance, or the elided sentences of the *ranchos* and the lisped

Spanish of the elites. Warner Bros.—if you're going to be racist, at least do it right.

What's with Mexicans and their abuse of the car horn? Instead of getting out of the car and knocking on the door of someone's house, they use it as a doorbell, as an alarm clock to wake up their car-pool buddy (and the neighborhood), as a toy for their kids who wait in the car while the driver runs in the store *de volada*. And last but certainly not least, instead of using the brakes.

WONDERING POCHO

Dear Pocho: You'd honk like a goose too if you had cool horns like ours. Throughout the barrios of the United States, you can hear us beep with the opening notes of "La Cucaracha," Beethoven's "Für Elise," Usher's "Yeah!"

and the overwrought seventies instrumental "Music Box Dancer." My favorite is the melody gabachos know as "Shave and a haircut, two bits," but which we Mexicans, in our infinite bawdiness, have transformed into *Chinga tu madre, cabrón,* "Go fuck your mother, asshole." Such specialty horns allow Mexicans to distinguish between an angry commuter and a produce truck, between *la migra* and the morning car pool. They are our Navajo code. As for your doorbell complaints, Pocho, let me put it this way: Would you leave your car in the middle of a barrio—where parking is as rare as a mold-free apartment, where cholos skulk behind bumpers ready to pounce on the first available *coche*—just to knock on your friend's door? Or would you punch out "The Mexican Hat Dance" on your *pito*?

Why do Mexicans name their boys Jesús and Guadalupe? Naming your boy after Christ is blasphemous, but calling him after the Virgin Mary is just gay.

CHICHIS CHRIST

Dear Gabacho: What's wrong with calling yourself after your *familia*? Many gabachos name children after their parents—why not after the Son of God and the Holy Mother? But if you don't like such name blasphemy, blame the Mexican's topsy-turvy understanding of the Trinity. The Lamb of God is a minor figure in Mexican Catholic theology; it's the Virgin of Guadalupe—a syncretism of the Aztec mother goddess Tonantzin and Mary of Bethlehem—that's the focus of veneration in Mexican Catholicism. You can see this in many Mexican parishes, where the iconic portrait of *la virgencita*—a pregnant, brown-skinned Madonna shrouded in a green tunic and looking downward toward her children—dwarfs the crucifix, if it's even there. Thus, calling your boy after the Nazarene isn't anything special—it's as common as Juan or Jorge. But, conversely, Marian worship is so ingrained in the Mexican psyche that many families name their *niño* after Guadalupe, much as many Muslim families name their boys Muhammad (pbuh). Mexican families shorten "Guadalupe" for boys to "Lupe" out of respect to Guadalupe and to spare their boys the tough life of "A Boy Named Sue." And before you accuse Mexicans of faggish behavior, remember that gabachos name their boys with fey names like Taylor or Kelly, so there.

I like to speak Spanish, but it seems that if I do, I am committing a political act endorsing some Hispanic agenda, which I do not support. If I speak Spanish to an undocumented worker, does that mean I support his illegal presence? Is it all right for me to speak Spanish whenever I want to?

NEED TWO DAY LABORERS FOR TOMORROW

Dear Gabacho: First off, what's with this "Hispanic" agenda you speak of? The right to become an American? The right to work? Our plot to fry gabacho brains with salsa? Speaking Spanish supports no agenda other than ensuring your future and getting your order right at the taquería. Spanish is no longer a subject juniors sleep through in high school; it's the fourth most spoken language in the world. It's the language of choice in the western hemisphere and an increasing necessity in our modern world of open borders and NAFTA. So better practice Spanish as *mucho* as possible to ensure your future. Besides, wanting to learn only one language is shared by one other culture on earth—the Taliban.

I caught your appearance on *The Colbert Report*. I admire your insight and cultural references, but I noticed you mispronounced the Spanish word *patience*. You told Colbert that the word was *pacencia*, instead of the correct word, *paciencia*. Why do assimilated Mexicans lose their language and find Spanglish acceptable?

EL ERUDITO

Dear Wab: Indeed, I did appear on the *pinche* hilarious *Colbert Report,* and I did indeed pronounce *patience* as *pacencia* instead of the formal *paciencia.* But I'm not a *pendejo;* I merely practiced elision, the linguistic phenomenon where speakers drop consonants or vowels from words. Hispanic elites have long considered Mexicans the Eliza Doolittles of the Spanish-speaking world for their tendency to elide and epenthesize (add vowels or consonants), much as gabachos ridicule the sons of the South for their Dixie dialects. Examples of elision in Mexican Spanish abound—*pa'* instead of *para* (for), *apá* instead of *papá* (father), SanTana instead of Santa Ana, *pos* instead of *pues* (well), and my supposed gaffe. Elision is most common among the working class and poor, so any Mexicans who talk that way aren't butchering the language of Cervantes; they're probably of rural stock like my parents, natives of Zacatecan mountain *ranchos.* You might frown upon elision, Erudito, but that's the beauty of language—it doesn't give a shit what you and other self-appointed language guardians think. It doesn't conform to ideas of purity or uniformity, and anyone who tries to squeeze languages into finite linguistic boxes is ignorant of the human condition—or is a member of the French Academy.

How come U.S. Mexicans get pissed when you assume they are Mexican and talk to them in Spanish?

SPANISH-SPEAKING MEXICAN FROM MEXICO

Dear Wab: They don't want to be accused of being Mexicans.

Your English is great. Why do your compadres choose to not adapt to an American accent when speaking English?

NACHO MAMA

Dear Gabacha: What the hell is an American accent, anyway? The drawl of the South? The lazy *uh*s of beachside Southern California? It's difficult enough to learn a second language, and now you want Mexicans to adopt a mythical "American" accent?! When a Mexican keeps his accent, he's just continuing the proud American ethnic tradition of allowing one's native tongue to influence a region's cadence—examples include the Scandinavian singsong common to Minnesota and North Dakota, the Irish brogues of Boston, the hurried Italian of Philadelphia, the Jewish nasal inflections of New York City, and so on. Even the slow English of Mexican learners is just emulating the laziness of California—itself a by-product of stupid Okies. To lose your accents would be to turn your back on assimilation. So when Mexicans speak their bad English, they're just following the American way—another gooey nacho in the melting pot.

Why don't Mexicans ever drop their Spanish? Even third- and fourth-generation Mexican-Americans still speak the language to some degree or another. I speak Japanese, but I'm losing it quickly, and when my mother passes on, so will my language. The typical Asian-American kid may attend Chinese, Korean, or Japanese school on Saturdays, but guess what? They do it because their parents force them to attend, and I bet they speak English during recess.

FEELING A BIT NIPPY

Dear Chinita: Still haven't assimilated into North America, eh? Spanish has kept a constant presence in the United States since even before English. The oldest city in the United States is St. Augustine, Florida, founded by Spaniards in 1565, twenty-one years before the English crown ever bothered to explore the Americas. The oldest American capital is Santa Fe, founded in 1609, over 150 years before the United States *was even born* and almost 250 before the United States eventually conquered what's now the Southwest from Mexico. Spanish is the native language of this massive swath of land, encompassing California, Utah, Nevada, Arizona, Texas, Florida, and Colorado, has a presence in various geographical names, *and* has continuously been spoken all these centuries—and you want Mexicans to drop this language, Nippy? Chinita, Spanish *is* the most American language—English is just an intruder that Mexicans were gracious enough to allow to exist.

Okay, so I got it that the World Cup was a huge deal and everyone gets excited, and so I also get why whenever anyone hits a goal, the announcer drags out the *¡¡¡¡¡Goooooollllll!!!!!* part for, like, five minutes. But what's with ALL the drama? Because it never stops. Why do ALL Mexican radio and television announcers make even the simplest phrases like *five minutes* (*ciiiiinnnnncooooo minuuuuutooooossss*) sound like the end of the world?

SHADDUP, SUCKERS!

Dear Gabacho: My theory regarding our overexcited *locutores:* it's a habit borrowed from real life. Resourceful Mexicans already stretch out everything in their lives—under-the-table salaries, privacy in houses shared with seventeen other people, fake Social Security cards passed around dozens of friends—so why not vowels and consonants? Not only that, but Spanish is the most fun language outside tongue-click-heavy Xhosa to pronounce: full of fricatives, affricates, and diphthongs; palatal nasals (the infamous *ñ* sound) and lateral approximants (the *ll* that sounds like the gabacho letter *y*); deep *ooooooooooooo*s, high *aaaaaaaaaaaa*s and *iiiiiiiiiiiiiiii*s; and the alveolar trill, the double-*r* roll that sounds like a Harley rumbling through a suburban morning. English's most enjoyable sound? The gnashing of teeth whenever a Mexican takes the job of another lazy gabacho.

2

Cultura

Chickens, Dwarves, and
the Soccer-Osama Connection

Dear Mexican: How come Mexicans are always so damn happy? There could be ten of them in the bed of a beat-up pickup in hundred-degree heat, and they're all smiles. Are they always drunk or something?

LOOKING FOR MEXICAN DRINKING BUDDIES

Dear Gabacho: You remind me of my *papi*'s favorite song—"El Muchacho Alegre" (The Happy Boy), a *ranchera* tune popularized by Francisco "El Charro" Avitia that begins, *Yo soy el muchacho alegre / Que me amanezco cantando / Con mi botella de vino / Y mi baraja jugando* (I'm the happy boy / That wakes up singing / With my bottle of wine / And playing cards). "El Muchacho Alegre" should be the Mexican national anthem because it has everything a Mexican needs for fun: boozing, whoring, gambling, singing, gunplay, anal—what psychologists call escapism but I call Tuesday night. Besides, what's there *not* to be happy about, gabacho? Everything is great in the Mexican universe! Fucked-up Mexican economy! Exploitation in *el Norte*! Endemic diabetes and alcoholism! HR 4437! Underachieving Mexican soccer team! Lou Dobbs! Whether it's music, booze, gambling, work, or nibbling on cricket quesadillas, we're happy at all times lest we remember life's one unfortunate wrinkle: we're Mexican.

Dear Mexican: I worked in a department store this past holiday season. Every day, without fail, whenever I heard a kid crying or screaming or saw a kid running in the store, it was always a Mexican kid. I saw kids shrieking like banshees with parents who pretended to be oblivious. And get this, I'm Mexican and would have gotten a *patada* (kick) upside the head from my parents for just talking loudly in the store when I was a kid! Chihuahua, when did the rule change?!

SHUT UP YOUR MOUTH

I work in retail, and I deal with people from all over the world. Everybody speaks to me in English no matter where they're from, except Mexicans. Mexicans will walk up to me and speak Spanish. Why do Mexicans assume that everyone knows how to speak their language?

ENGLISH ONLY, POR FAVOR

Dear Pocho y Gabacho: Shut Up, I have to disagree with you—it ain't just *mexicanos* who let kids run around in stores nowadays as if a border were constantly in front of them, resisting the parental urge to smack some sense into them. Consider a 2002 ABC News poll that revealed that 65 percent of American adults approve of spanking kiddies, down from the 83 percent in a similar 1986 Gallup poll. I tried to gather a focus group of the gabacho-est gabachos I could find for comment, but Pat Boone and Jerry Falwell weren't available. But the fact remains that huarache-to-*nalga* discipline is going the way of legalized immigration. As for the second question, English Only, I have two words for you: Chinatown.

What is it with Mexicans and firecrackers?

BLOWN AWAY IN THE BARRIO

Dear Gabacho: Mexicans have better access to cherry bombs, is all. The world's finest black market for firecrackers, Tijuana, is in Mexico. But who's saying *cuete*-popping is an exclusively Mexican thing? Gabachos have their own boom-boom fetish too—it's called the Iraq War.

Why is it that when you invite Mexicans to a party, they feel compelled to bring along thirty of their relatives?

NOT ENOUGH FOOD FOR EVERYONE

Dear Gabacho: Mexicans and parties—was there ever a coupling more spectacularly grotesque? We drink *mucho,* we eat *mucho,* we fight *mucho,* we love *mucho,* we *mucho mucho.* Examining the Mexican propensity to party, Mexican Nobel laureate Octavio Paz wrote, "The explosive, dramatic, sometimes even suicidal manner in which we strip ourselves, surrender ourselves, is evidence that something inhibits and suffocates us. Something impedes us from being. And since we cannot or dare not confront our own selves, we resort to the fiesta."

But one thing we don't do anymore is swarm parties with our extended family, Not Enough Food. Time was when Mexican immigrants would rent out labor halls to throw massive weddings, quinceañeras, and baptisms and invite the entire *rancho* to invite everyone—more than a thousand people attended my baby brother's christening reception in 1992, even *norteño* star Juan Zaizar! But the Mexicans of my generation prefer subdued celebrations—invite-only, no kids, with lame, sobbing testimonials by the best men and bridesmaids and no *banda sinaloense* to deafen guests with its brass-band roar. For instance, my cousin held his wedding reception a couple of years ago at a country club with an MC and a guest limit of 250 (considering that's about the size of the Miranda clan, there were some angry *primos* that night). Mexican parties are turning into prim-and-proper, gabacho-fied affairs, Not Enough Food—so we're working on being as boring as you are.

I am a *mexicana* who is dating a gabacho. My gabacho always asks me why you see Mexicans lying in the grass under a tree. It never fails—if you drive by a park in Anaheim, there are Mexicans lying under every tree in the park. *¿Por qué?*

UNIVERSITY CHICANA

Dear Pocha: Dick Nichols was right. In 2003, the Newport Beach, California, council member riled up every Mexican from El Salvador to SanTana after he told a newspaper reporter too many Mexicans claim the grassy area in Corona del Mar State Beach "as theirs and it becomes their personal, private grounds all day." Nichols never apologized for the statement, and he didn't have to—because he was right. Mexicans continue to loll on the Corona del Mar State Beach grass and every green patch in the world as if it were outside a Home Depot. Mexicans, unlike gabachos, are good public citizens who know that parkland is best used for whiling the afternoon away underneath an oak, a salsa-stained paper plate and an empty six-pack of Tecate tossed to the side.

Toilet Matters

Why do Mexicans like to spit everywhere?

LOOGIE LAD

Dear Gabacho: While we can hack phlegm with the best of them, spitting isn't exclusively Mexican. My gym used to have a sign in English, Spanish, Korean, Vietnamese, *and* stick-figure-ese warning patrons not to spit on the jogging track. But if you insist, Loogie Lad, blame pollution. Last year, the Environmental Protection Agency reported that Californians breathe the second-dirtiest air in the country, and that Orange County residents are almost twice as likely as other Americans to suffer from cancer because of it. Other world cities notorious for spitters, such as Mexico City, Mumbai, and all of China, are similarly polluted. The body's natural response to irritated lungs and throats is to expunge excess saliva, but our lungs and throats are already so blackened that we don't even notice the cancer air anymore. Many Mexicans, on the other hand, come from the countryside, where the air is as pure as their daughters. Want to cut down on public spitting? Easy: urge Congress to support the Kyoto Protocol.

What is it with Mexicans' avoidance of handkerchiefs? It is not uncommon to see a Mexican walking down the street suddenly stop, pinch his nose between thumb and forefinger, take a deep breath, and eject huge gobs of *mocos*. Is this a common practice for those just off the *ranchos*?

Loco Moco

Dear Crazy Booger: It's true that Mexicans from the countryside are the most notorious nose-pickers south of the border, but I'd be careful to assign Mexicans all the public-booger blame. First off, the only gabachos who nowadays use handkerchiefs are dandies and Oscar Wilde imitators, so why should Mexicans? We do carry bandannas, but those are to wipe sweat from our moist brows, not to deposit mucus or saliva in them. No straight man I know, whether Mexican, *chinito,* gabacho, or *negrito,* carries around tissue paper for his effluvia. And if anyone is disproportionately responsible for flicking boogers in public, it's commuters. Ever get stuck on the freeway and see someone pinch his nose between thumb and forefinger, take a deep breath, pick out a nostril nugget, and flick it out of his car? Mexicans at least have the decency to clean their noses on their hands.

What's up with all of you Mexican men pissing in public?! Don't they have toilets in Mexico? And please don't compare homeless white bums pissing on the street to what you guys do all the time.

Don't Piss in My Pool

Dear Gabacho: Only manly men dare whip out their wangs in public and tinkle. But it's more than that, Piss. Many cities are shockingly lacking in public restrooms—no grand, sterile lavatoriums à la those of imperial Rome or even like those found in all major Mexican cities. Instead, Mexicans—who usually live on the toughest side of town— must relieve themselves when away from home in graffiti-infested, never-cleaned, rancid, no-doors park restrooms where the possibility of a mugging or rape is always a pee away. *Meando* in public isn't some disgusting Mexican trait—it's a means of hygiene and survival.

Why do Mexicans love public restrooms so much? It seems like any one you visit has a minivanload of Mexicans waiting to get into it. Also, why do Mexicans wipe after a No. 2 and then throw the crappy toilet paper into the trash can rather than flushing it away? So gross! Let's try to put an end to that madness.

ANÓMINO

Dear Gabacho: ¡*Felicidades!* You have just stumbled upon the most surefire way to tell if a Mexican is fresh from the border —or, as Mexicans who have lived in this country for years like to describe them, *si tienen un nopal en la frente* (if they have a cactus growing from their forehead)! See, flushing toilets remain a novelty in rural Mexico, so Mexicans new to this country treat public restrooms with the same anticipatory awe Japanese tourists save for Disneyland's Matterhorn— hence, the long lines. Regarding the *popó*-gunked Charmin: those precious few *ranchos* that do have indoor plumbing suffer from inferior pipes installed on the cheap by Mexico's government. Anything heavier than last night's menudo would rupture the sewage system and ruin the *rancho*'s water supply, so used toilet paper must go in the wastebasket. *Nopal*-wearing Mexicans keep this tradition long after emigrating here, though . . . can you do me a favor, gabacho, and tell *nopaleros* that here in *los Estados Unidos,* we're much more sophisticated with our No. 2—we flush it into the ocean.

Politics

When all those Mexicans marched last year for amnesty, why did they wave Mexican flags? If they want to become Americans, why didn't they wave the American flag?

OLD AND TAINTED

Dear Gabacha: You're right—waving the Mexican flag won't get you anywhere, and that's one of the main criticisms of the great immigrant-rights marches that swept the country during the spring of 2006. But really, what else could the Mexicans do? When many of them waved the American flag during the May 1 rallies held concurrently across the country, gabachos accused them of crass opportunism; if they wave the Mexican flag, they're accused of being separatists. But let's not forget what these people are first and foremost—immigrants. Contrary to this country's assimilationist myth, immigrants didn't cut off all ties to the motherland immediately—what else explains the immediate birth of fraternal organizations right after the immigrants got off the boat and supposedly became Americans? That the immigrants so proudly displayed the flags of their mother countries during the marches or continue to do so in their neighborhoods is a good thing—it's a final death throe of their former nationality as they march toward becoming Americans.

Why do more Mexicans than Argentines worship Che Guevara? I don't think we even give a shit about him.

MARADONA MAIDEN

Dear Gabacha Wab: You're one to trash Mexicans for revering a long-dead Argentine—how's Evita's corpse holding up these days? Besides, we suffer from the same condition—*caudillismo,* a sociological phenomenon that sees nations fall under the sway of a charismatic individual who promises to deliver power and wealth to the masses, then gets powerful and wealthy as the masses starve and the opposition disappears. Historians love to pin this malady exclusively on Latin

America, but gabachos suffer from it as well—nothing else can explain why George W. Bush is president. Che worship amongst Mexicans, however, features a few more wrinkles than the usual *caudillismo* causes. Guevara, for one, was an emigrant—left Argentina for revolution—who remade his life in Mexico when he met Fidel Castro. He died young, like all good Mexican men. Che was a romantic—can't tell you how many pro-immigrant-activist e-mails end with Guevara's supposed quote "At the risk of seeming ridiculous, let me say that a true revolutionary is guided by great feelings of love." More important, Guevara wasn't afraid to use violence as a method in the pursuit of his love, the love that dare not speak its name except through the barrel of a gun. Don't believe Chicanos: while César Chávez advocated nonviolence, Mexicans like their leaders armed to the gold teeth—think Emiliano Zapata, Pancho Villa, Subcomandante Marcos. And now you know why democracy has never existed in Mexico.

Why do you portray Mexicans as liberals when the majority are conservative?

JORGE P. BUSH

Dear Half-Wab: Don't you read my column? Week in and week out, *¡Ask a Mexican!* portrays Mexicans as perfect Republicans: homo-hating, Jew-baiting, Negro-bashing, *chino*-trashing religious fanatics who believe in free markets and self-determination and want to wipe Guatemalans off the map. Various polls identify this Mexican GOP gene. The most comprehensive, a 2003 survey by the Pew Hispanic Center, found 80 percent of Latinos disapprove of abortion, 40 percent think divorce is unacceptable, and 72 percent hate gays (by comparison, 60, 24, and 59 percent of gabachos felt the same regarding each respective topic). But even the most Neanderthal Mexican becomes a Democrat once Republicans start babbling about immigration restrictions. See, Mexicans support open borders not because they want to take back the Southwest, but because they're students of American history. They know that *los Estados Unidos* exploits wave after wave of immigrants, and that these immigrants willingly suffer through the toil with the understanding that America will allow their children a chance at better lives, a chance at becoming Americans. Stop Mexican migration, and the children of Mexican immigrants remain Mexicans—and what Mexican in his right mind wants *that*?

Why don't Mexicans want to assimilate and accept our way of life? All I see them do is wave their flag and put stickers with the name of their home state on their cars.

STUCK IN THE MIDDLE WITH TÚ

Dear Hick: Where have you lived your life? One of those Arizona Mormon towns where men have thirty wives and the kids are retarded 'cause cousins marry cousins? Ever been to a city? You know, one of those newfangled things with asphalt and streetlights? You should visit. You'll find there are a lot of immigrants, and they all maintain ties to their mother country—*because they're immigrants*. But do you make the same anti-assimilation charge when gabacho households fly the Irish tricolor in the weeks leading up to St. Patrick's Day? How about the European fraternal organizations that rent booths during street fair? Your sentiment is just another manifestation of American exceptionalism, a syndrome Alexis de Tocqueville noted in his 1840 classic, *Democracy in America,* which argues this country is unique from every other nation and therefore can do whatever the fuck it wants—violate international treaties, invade sovereign countries, ignore the FIFA World Cup. In the case of reverence for one's roots, it boils down thusly: gabachos long-removed from Ellis Island can love their ancestry without shame because they're the descendants of immigrants, and immigrants made this nation great; Mexicans can't because they *are* immigrants, and immigrants are turning America into the Third World.

The Mexican presidential elections were a freaking mess. I voted for the conservative candidate, Felipe Calderón, who almost everyone agrees won the election. But the leftist Andrés Manuel López

Obrador is making a mess out of this by claiming electoral fraud. Does the Mexican have an opinion of Mexican politics? Or do you—as many *pochos* I know—not give a shit about what happens in Mexico?

A MEXICAN IN MEXICO CITY

Dear Wab: *Sí y no.* On one hand, Mexicans in the United States care even more about the goings-on south of the border than Mexicans in Mexico—why else would we send billions of dollars in remittances, the country's second-largest source of revenue after oil, to bolster the lives of lazy *pendejos* like you? But the recent Mexican presidential elections revealed a fascinating paradox: despite our investments in *la patria*, we don't care much about Mexico's emerging democracy. Polling revealed that out of the 4 million eligible Mexican voters who live in the United States, only twenty-eight thousand cast a ballot—a woeful seven-tenths of one percent. And out of those who did vote, 58 percent sided with Calderón, the free-market proponent, over the populist Obrador, who rails against the *yanquis* and seeks to take our billions in remittances and hand them out to idiot Mexicans who haven't got the good sense to flee for *el Norte.* Mexico's election results prove again what the Mexican repeats, mantralike, to the Sensenbeaners and Gilchrists of the world: not only do Mexicans in the United States not care about Mexican politics (as long as the government keeps its hands off those billions, that is), but the United States transforms even the wabbiest wab into an individualistic, laissez-faire lover of liberty who hates the welfare state. And the United States wants to alienate these dyed-in-the-wool conservatives *why*? Besides, not voting in elections is as American as Old Glory.

Transportation

Why do Mexicans always cram into a small car?

BABA LOUIE

Dear Gabacho: Because a burro can't support more than three people.

Why do Mexicans drive so goddamned slowly?

VIEJA GRINGA

Dear Old Gabacha: You realize my column is ¡Ask a Mexican!, right, not ¡Ask a Geezer!? Accuse Mexicans of any other driving sin—accuse us of lowering cars until the steering wheel scrapes asphalt, of adorning windows with Pissing Calvin decals, of driving without insurance. But don't say we drive slowly. Vieja Gringa, why do you think Mexicans make the sign of the cross before starting the car? When I learned how to drive on the mad streets of Tijuana, my father taught me a simple rule: if you brake, you die. Mexicans learn to drive with finesse but also with speed in Mexico's hairpin *glorietas* and epic boulevards lest a VW Bug taxi rear-end us straight to hell. That mentality carries over to the United States—just look at Santa Ana, which has one of the highest pedestrian fatality rates in Southern California, if not the nation. If you think Mexicans drive slowly, then there's some beachfront property in Mexico City I'd like to sell you.

Why do Mexicans feel that it's their privilege to take home the grocery cart they used from the supermarket, abandon it, or use it for their own personal toiling?

THIS LOAD OF LAUNDRY BROUGHT TO YOU BY STATER BROTHERS!

Dear Gabacho: It's not just Mexicans who do this—retailers report thefts of grocery carts to the tune of $800 million a year. They didn't break the stats down by ethnicity, but Mexicans do love grocery carts—it's our buffalo. We use the grilles as support for blooming vines, the wheels to transport heavy stuff, the handles to stir pots. In its rolling form, Mexican women use them to troll around their kiddies and carry their groceries—impromptu minivans, if you will. Markets might fret about the lost revenue, but better that markets allow Mexicans to keep the grocery carts—otherwise, they might start to steal real cars.

What is it about the operation of light-controlled intersections that your brethren on foot find so difficult? I understand their sensitivity about crossing against a red light or when the don't-walk sign is flashing on a green light because some cops may use that as an excuse to question them. But would you mind pointing out that when it's necessary to activate the walk sign, *one* push on the button is sufficient? Okay, a second one maybe to make sure, but *it's not necessary to keep pushing the damn thing until the light changes!!!*

PUSHED TO THE LIMIT

Dear Gabacho: Wait a minute, Pushed—you think the walk button actually works?! Do you also believe man walked on the moon, Lee Harvey Oswald acted alone, and that there's such a thing as a frigid Mexican hombre? Modern walk buttons are like nipples on men— vestigial, a diversion for idle fingers. Most traffic signals became automated long ago and rely on sensors that recognize traffic flow, not the needs of pedestrians, to decide when the little *gabachito* lights up and allows us to legally cross. And I don't know what Mexicans you roll with, Pushed, but Mexicans are people on the go—lawns to mow, houses to build, entire regions to take over. No buttons will ever dictate our day. And now you know why Mexican pedestrian deaths are so endemic that the U.S. Federal Highway Administration commissioned a 2004 study titled *Hispanic Pedestrian and Bicycle Safety* just to deal with our impatience.

Why do Mexicans park their cars on the front lawn?

MIGHT EVEN NEED SOME OAXACANS

Dear MENSO: Where do you want us to park them, MENSO? The garage we rent out to a family of five? The backyard where we put up our recently immigrated cousins in tool-shacks-cum-homes? The street with the red curbs recently approved by city planners? The driveway covered with construction materials for the latest expansion of *la casa*? The nearby school parking lot frequented by cholos on the prowl for a new radio? MENSO, the lawn is the only spot Mexicans can park their cars without fear of break-ins, drunken crashes, or an unfortunate keying. Besides, what do you think protects us from drive-bys? The cops?

What is it with Mexicans and jaywalking? No crosswalks in Mexico?
RUN, DON'T WALK

Dear Gabacho: Try no streets. Although the number of urban Mexicans immigrating to *el Norte* is on the rise—Tulane University sociologist Elizabeth Fussell estimated in her 2004 paper, "Sources of Mexico's Migration Stream: Rural, Urban, and Border Migrants to the United States," that 61 percent of Mexican immigrants in 2000 came from cities with populations of at least fifteen thousand—most streets in Mexico still lack such amenities as stoplights, stop signs, or even lanes. Mexicans learn to navigate these mean *calles* from a young age and keep this mentality upon sneaking into the United States, where they find everything so orderly, so preplanned, so . . . lame. We ignored the jagged fence, deserts and Minutemen that separate the United States from Mexico—what makes you think we're going to obey a *pinche* YIELD sign when we're driving?

Media Matters

I'm a culturally sensitive, PC Asian-American who laughed my head off at Jack Black's imitation of a Mexican in *Nacho Libre*. Is this wrong?

VIETNAMMY MAMMY

Dear Chinita: Wrong? Of course not. While Latino activists weep and moan about how gabachos like Jack Black reduce Mexicans to stock characters with mustaches and bad accents, real-life Mexicans not only don't care about those stereotypes, they *embrace* them. Visit your local

Mexican restaurant, and its logo is most likely the Mexican that American consumers have demanded from Hollywood for over a century—a fat greaser sleeping under a cactus or burro. Check out the real-life portrait that runs with my column. And did you notice that many of the Mexican fans who attended the 2006 FIFA World Cup in Germany dressed in ponchos, fake mustaches the size of black kittens, and sombreros large enough to use as a raft? Mexicans know that caricatures are just that—exaggerated depictions based on a kernel of truth that no one should take seriously. Besides, Mexicans love to offend as much as gabachos: switch on Telemundo or Univisión, where hilarious caricatures of *jotos, negritos, chinos,* gabachos, *indios,* fat people, the rich, the poor, *chicas calientes,* dwarves—everyone and anyone—prance across the screen as often as Mexicans on burros in American television. So laugh away during *Nacho Libre,* Vietnammy Mammy, but remember this: if you laugh at Mexicans, you also better laugh when we depict your race as buck-toothed, slanty-eyed, rice-rocket-driving dog-eaters in the next hot *telenovela.*

The last two movies I attended were rated R. Sitting around me were Mexican families with young children. Why do Mexicans bring their eight-year-old kids to see a movie like *Hostel*? Plus, the Mexicans let their kids kick my seat.

CONFUSED MOVIEGOER

Dear Gabacho: The only sin I see here is *anyone* forking over cash to watch *Hostel,* the 2005 horror turkey whose main claim to fame was casting handsome wab Jay Hernández as a character with the *retre-*gabacho name Paxton. As for your question, the Mexican refers you to the late *New Yorker* film critic Pauline Kael, who famously quipped, "The words 'Kiss Kiss Bang Bang,' which I saw on an Italian movie poster, are perhaps the briefest statement imaginable of the basic appeal of movies." Nowhere is that nugget more applicable than with Mexicans. Mix gore, boobs, popcorn, and the occasional midget or gay guy, and you can occupy a Mexican for two hours. See, violence and Mexican cinema go together like refried and beans—it's been one prolonged shoot-out that started with the 1919 silent classic *El Automóvil Gris* (*The Gray Automobile,* which dramatized the real-life exploits of Mexico City's murderous Gray Automobile Gang and included actual footage of their executions), continued through the urban dramas of the 1950s and various 1960s sci-fi/Aztec mummy/*lucha libre* super-hero follies, and reached its zenith with *narcopelículas* (drug dramas) that Spanish-language television channels have broadcast without pause for the past three decades. The Mexican love for filmic blood isn't a pathological cultural trait, though; as any Hollywood executive will tell you, violence is a universal tongue that needs no subtitles. That's why Mexican parents take their kiddies to see such films—as the children become Americans and the parents remain stuck in remedial English classes, sometimes the only way to communicate is to speak the language of Charles Bronson. And the kid behind you? Just practicing his *Death Wish* moves so he can kick your ass.

Why don't Mexicans like science-fiction movies?

JUAN SOLO

Dear Gabacho: One of my favorite ethnic jokes goes like this: "Why aren't there any Puerto Ricans on *Star Trek*? Because they don't work in the future, either." But Mexicans don't like alien films because they're always thinly veiled allegories about Mexicans, if you believe University of Texas professor Charles Ramírez Berg. In a fascinating essay included in his 2002 anthology, *Latino Images in Film: Stereotypes, Subversion, and Resistance,* Berg wrote that a gabacho film such as *Alien* "now symbolizes real-life aliens—documented and undocumented immigrants who have entered, and continue to attempt to enter, the United States." He goes on to use the examples of Superman, Spock, and the replicants in *Blade Runner* to conclude that the "cultural tension" brought about by immigrants becomes cinematic "fear that transforms the greaser bandit into a terminating cyborg, the Hispanic harlot into a fertile, black Alien mother, menacingly reproducing monsters down in her lair." But if you actually *talk* to a Mexican, you'll discover Mexicans love their aliens, Martians, and brains that won't die. Just look at the canon of Santo, the legendary silver-masked *luchador* (wrestler) who starred in fifty-five films throughout the 1960s and 1970s. The superhero—he even wore a silver mask with a cardigan sweater—fought brains (*Santo Contra el Cerebro del Mal,* Santo Versus the Bad Brain), zombies (*Santo Contra los Zombies*), Martians (*Santo Contra la Invasión de los Martianos,* Santo Versus the Martian Invasion), Aztec mummies, vampires, the daughter of Frankenstein, even infernal men (*Santo Contra los Hombres Infernales*). Mexican science-fiction films are among the world's weirdest—*and* Ricardo Montalbán played Khan. I knew there's a reason why gabachos call Mexicans illegal aliens. . . .

As a *pocho,* I can relate to countless cultural things related to my rich Mexican culture. However, there is one thing I can't understand: why do Mexican women, including my *vieja,* need to spend innumerable hours in front of the idiot box watching *pinche telenovelas*? Those *chingaderas* are merely repeat versions of the same tired formula. Is there a way to put an end to them?

EL POCHO ENCABRONADO

Dear Fucking Angry Pocho: Unfortunately, the plague of the *telenovela*—the weepy Spanish-language soap operas that invariably place big-breasted women, machine guns, and dwarves in sexy situations involving mistaken identity, marrying cousins, class conflict, and death at childbirth—shows no sign of containment. Spanish-language *telenovelas* are now a worldwide phenomenon, with huge fan bases in Russia, Israel, Lithuania, the Philippines, and even Japan. Miami-Dade College offered a writing course in the *telenovela* genre for the first time in 2005, and more than forty-four hundred students from twenty-six countries applied for just thirty slots. But it's not just women who watch, Pocho Encabronado. A 1998 study, *Los Medios y Mercados de Latinoamérica* (The Mediums and Markets of Latin America), revealed nearly 40 percent of Latin American men in the key eighteen–thirty-four demographic watched *telenovelas* regularly, a figure not far from the 54 percent of women in the same category. There's no shame in watching: while our old ladies lose themselves in the fantastic plotlines of the typical *telenovela*—you watch the one on Telemundo a couple years back that involved Lebanese and the Mexican Revolution?—we can admire the prettiest petites Latin America has to offer. And the ladies aren't bad either.

Why is there no intelligent programming on Spanish-language stations?

MEDIA MARICÓN

Dear Media Fag: You're right—Mexicans demand fluff just like Americans. And we have some of the fluffiest fluff in the world—shows like *Cero en Conducta* (Zero in Conduct), where adults wear school uniforms and pretend to be first-graders, and *Sábado Gigante* (Giant Saturday), a Saturday-night variety show, hosted by a Chilean Jew named Mario Kreutzberger who calls himself Don Francisco, that combines weird hats with girls in bikinis and couples popping balloons to win cars. And every Mexican child knows the work of Chespirito (Little Shakespeare), the stage name of Mexican comedian Roberto Gómez Bolaños. He gave birth to El Chapulín Colorado (The Red Grasshopper, a superhero who dressed as a grasshopper and whom Matt Groening acknowledges is the inspiration behind Bumblebee Man in *The Simpsons*) and *El Chavo del Ocho* (The Boy from Flat Number Eight), which dealt with a boy who lived in a barrel. All these shows might sound like lunacy, but Mexican television producers continue to suck from the teat of Charlie Chaplin, who knew that the best vehicle for transmitting class critiques was the simplest. Gabacho fluff, on the other hand, deals mostly with sluts.

What is the deal with Mexicans and Tweety Bird? I don't understand why Tweety is so appealing to Mexicans and shows up on their trucks, cars, and tattoos. Was it because the Tasmanian Devil was taken by dumb rednecks?

SPEEDY GONZÁLES

Dear Pocho: Tweety, along with Bugs Bunny and Speedy Gonzáles, always maintained a large following among Mexicans because he personifies the Trickster, the universal archetype who uses mayhem and wits to wile his way through tough situations. Nowadays, however, slapping a Tweety sticker on your truck or *carro* also signifies allegiance to El Piolín ("Tweety Bird" in Spanish). He's the Los Angeles–based Spanish-language DJ who used his nationally syndicated show to help organize the immigrant rights marches that gripped the United States in the spring of 2006. Born Eduardo Sotelo, El Piolín's nickname (which came from his Tweety-like frame and big lips) is appropriate. Contrary to popular opinion, Tweety is *muy macho* and definitely not a pussy. Consider Tweety's constant escapes from Sylvester the Cat's jaws a metaphor for the Mexican immigrant experience, with Mexicans assuming the trickster Tweety role and gabachos personifying the clueless fat cat who fails to stop his short, colored antagonist again and again.

On a recent trip to San Diego, I heard numerous radio ads for Mexican wine, chocolate, and even a public-service announcement encouraging the younger generation not to sniff paint. All of the ads were credited to the Mexican Chamber of Commerce. Why would they broadcast Mexican propaganda in the United States in English?
WHITEY FRIEDMAN

Dear Gabacho: Business savvy, Whitey. The Mexican government knows gabachos will never bother to learn Spanish outside of the words *pinto, Mexico,* and *Drinko por cinco.* So when Mexican companies want to do business in *los Estados Unidos,* they create English-only ad campaigns. For instance, the Mexico Tourism Board launched an $8.2 million ad campaign in 2004 to entice gabachos down south. The Mexican actors in these commercials, according to *Advertising Age,* invited American tourists to their weddings, worked as caddies, or led tours, all in the name of displaying what the board described as "the country's unmatched hospitality." They were pretty fascinating commercials, and not just because *Amores Perros* director Alejandro

González Iñárritu directed three of them. The Mexicans spoke almost no Spanish—about as much as a gabacha housewife uses to boss around María, actually. Same thing with those San Diego commercials. Mexico is a wonderful country with amazing produce and people—so why would Mexican companies turn off American consumers by reminding them that Mexicans live there?

Why aren't there more Mexicans on television? George López and Eva Longoria don't count.

THE CISCO KID

Dear Gabacho: There's no need: we already have *The Simpsons,* the most-watched television show in Latino USA and most-watched American show in Mexico. Surprised? Don't be: *The Simpsons* is the most Latino show on television, depicting the urban reality of America's largest minority.

At first glance, the only constant Latino presence in Springfield seems the inept Cuban Dr. Nick Riviera and Bumblebee Man. Beyond these obvious characters, though, are subtle yet crucial incidents in the show that expose Latino Springfield.

Referents to Springfield's Latino life are everywhere. The town's main movie palace is the Aztec Theater and is resplendent with pre-Columbian motifs. Springfieldites can also partake of *lucha libre* matches at the Springfield Memorial Stadium (in one episode, Marge and her friends invest in a Mexican wrestler known as El Bombástico). In the world of crime, Springfield's only soccer riot occurred after a match between Mexico and Portugal, and Snake once shared a cell with a Colombian drug lord in Springfield Penitentiary. And let's not forget the great hero of the doorbell industry, Señor Ding-Dong, who single-handedly saved the entire town from Marge's broken doorbell and its repetition of "Close to You." Or Señor Spielbergo, Steven Spielberg's "nonunion Mexican equivalent," whom Mr. Burns hires to film his hagiography.

Cultural values espoused by members of the Simpson family themselves also suggest a substantial Latino influence on Springfield that could only arise from daily interaction with Latinos. Bart's catch-phrase "Ay, caramba!" is impossible to imagine without Bart hanging around Mexican kids who taught him Spanish swear words or expressions. Meanwhile, Lisa is Chicana-conscious enough to care to point out the difference between Olmec and Mayan to Maggie after Mr. Burns gave a giant stone head of the Olmec war god Xtapalatecetl to Bart. And noted dolt Homer is not immune to the spell of Latino culture, owning a battle scar from the time a lunch truck door slammed on his head after he demanded a burrito, and once imagining himself as "Evil Homer" playing maracas over his grave.

Even Dr. Nick and Bumblebee Man are nuanced. Dr. Nick is an immigrant, having to take an immigrant test to remain in the country after the passing of the anti-immigrant Proposition 24 (more on that later). Though hilariously inept, Dr. Nick operates a free clinic in the poor section of town that advertises itself as *Se Habla Español*. This little touch both alludes to the reality that Latino immigrants face in obtaining health care and suggests that Latino immigrants in Springfield are recent arrivals—and poor. And their only form of diversion outside soccer matches and *lucha libre* is their idol, Bumblebee Man, the Spanish-speaking Mexican in a bee suit who overshadows even Krusty the Clown and newscaster Kent Brockman. To the Simpson family and their friends, Bumblebee Man is just (as Bart once said) "unpredictable Mexican sitcoms." But Pedro (Bumblebee Man's real name) is so popular that he and his network, Channel Ocho, beat Krusty the Clown in the ratings. His network is so important (having its own production studio) that when Sideshow Bob threatened to blow up Springfield, Channel Ocho was one of the "distinguished representatives of television" that met with Mayor Quimby to decide the fate of television in Springfield. And eventually, Bumblebee Man defects to Channel 6 in an apparent move by Springfield's English networks to attract Latino viewers by hiring one of their own (a rough parallel to the ABC sitcom *Ugly Betty*).

Since all of Bumblebee Man's skits are in Spanish (albeit a horribly corrupted version), his ratings power indicates a large, unassimilated Springfield Latino population. This same population also explains why Springfield felt it urgent in one episode to pass Mayor Quimby's

Prop. 24, an anti-immigrant measure eerily similar to our nation's anti-immigrant wars.

Latinos should claim *The Simpsons* as their own and encourage the show's writers to fully develop the large Latino community already established as a major component of Springfield. This doesn't involve a threat of boycott or creation of the implausible situations that *The Simpsons* writers have unfortunately grown fond of. By demanding a fuller depiction of Springfield, Latinos could give *The Simpsons* the biggest Latino presence on television outside of *Cops*.

Sports

How come Mexicans play soccer and not a real sport like hockey or football?

ICE-COLD LINEBACKER

Dear Gabacho: Because soccer involves more running, and how else will we train for the midnight run across the U.S.-Mexico border?

Why do Mexican soccer fans chant "Osama! Osama!" when their side plays the United States? You don't hear American soccer fans yell *"¡La migra!"*

WHITE BOY DASH

Dear Gabacho: You think hurling bin Laden's name is tasteless? How about the *Daily Mail* columnist who, on the day England faced West Germany in the 1966 FIFA World Cup final, wrote, "West Germany may beat us at our national sport today, but that would be only fair. We beat them twice at theirs"? Or the hooligans who greeted Jewish fans during a Lazio-AS Roma Italian-league match with a banner that read "Auschwitz is your town, the ovens are your houses"? This is soccer we're talking about, not Wimbledon. Offensive jeers are part of the game, and anyone who can't take the heat should leave *la cocina*. Jingoism is the main reason *fútbol* is the world's most popular sport: countries and regions can spill their aggression toward one another out on the pitch and in the stands instead of on the battlefield. That's why Mexicans love to trash the United States when the two countries play. *Ustedes* exploit us, humiliate us, dominate us in every socioeconomic category, even beat us in soccer—the United States has triumphed over Mexico in seven of their last ten matches, including a 2–0 shellacking in the second round of the 2002 World Cup. So instead of wielding knives, our best revenge is the clever insult, the well-timed *Chinga tu madre* whistle, and some beer poured upon Landon Donovan as he triumphantly exits the stadium. All the great soccer-playing nations draw rabidly nationalistic fans, and the United States will remain a third-rate country until Americans cry "Tacos!" next time Mexico's squad invades *el Norte*.

What is it about a pirate-themed football team from Oakland, of all places, that makes Mexicans so crazy? Okay, so they used to have a Hispanic coach and a Hispanic quarterback. Any other reasons?

CLEVELAND BROWNIE

Dear Wab: All Mexicans like the Raiders? Tell that to the cholos that sport the jerseys of the Dallas Cowboys or Cleveland Browns (get it? Brown? Mexicans? Yep, cholos have great irony), or Joe Kapp, the tough-as-nails quarterback who led the Minnesota Vikings to their first Super Bowl and thus made the cover of *Sports Illustrated* in 1970 underneath the headline "The Toughest Chicano." But, yes, the most popular football team for wabs by far remains the Oakland Raiders. Even though they haven't won a Super Bowl since 1984, even though they've suffered through four straight losing seasons, Mexicans worship the Silver and Black as if the team fielded the Virgin of Guadalupe at nose guard. One of the reasons is the Raiders have always drawn a working-class, multiethnic fan base drawn from the team's Oakland roots. Another possible cause for their huge Mexican fan base, as you point out, is that Raiders owner Al Davis hired the league's first Mexican coach and quarterback—both of them, incidentally, Tom Flores. Another answer lies in the fact that the Raiders played in Los Angeles, capital of North Mexico, from 1982 until 1994, a time when millions of Mexican immigrants came of age and the Raiders enjoyed just three losing seasons. This is also why the Los Angeles Lakers and Los Angeles Dodgers are so popular among Mexicans—both became winners when Mexicans migrated en masse to California, and Mexicans are as much a bunch of front-runners as gabachos. But the best explanation comes courtesy of the late, great Hunter S. Thompson, who described the Raiders Nation as "beyond doubt the sleaziest and rudest and most sinister mob of thugs and wackos ever assembled in such numbers under a single 'roof,' so to speak, anywhere in the English-speaking world"—words of love that also accurately apply to Mexicans.

The only thing I don't like about the Mexican culture is their apparent attraction toward fighting animals (dogs, cocks, bulls). I don't understand how any human being can gain enjoyment out of watching two dogs rip each other to shreds.

LOVE EVERY VIABLE ANIMAL

Dear LEVA: California state senator Nell Soto (D-Pomona) agrees with you, LEVA. She's the author of SB 156, a 2005 California Senate bill that sought to toughen already existing laws against cockfighting by making repeat offenses punishable as felonies. Its biggest opponent: Nativo López, a longtime Orange County Chicano activist. In July, as president of the Mexican American Political Association (MAPA), López pushed through a resolution opposing SB 156 on the grounds that it was "completely oblivious to the cultural, economic, and social realities of our community." This coming from a *pendejo* who confessed to the *Socialist Worker* in 2004, "I still covertly like cockfighting."

But I'm not going to defend cockfighting by citing its deep roots in

Mexican society. Pitting animals against each other is disgusting and cowardly, LEVA, but all sports are inherently violent. The difference between sports involving animals and humans, of course, is that the latter participants are voluntary, but it's the specter of injury or death that attracts so many to most pastimes. Why do you think the NHL makes millions packaging vicious hits into DVD specials? How can Mike Tyson—a boxer fifteen years past his prime—continue to sell out matches? And what about the popularity of the Oakland Raiders, the team that elevated dirty play to an art? Animals mauling each other for human entertainment is bad, but remember, one man's barbaric sport is another man's NASCAR.

Miscellaneous *Cochinadas*

Bored one night a few days ago, I was flipping channels and noticed for the first time that Mexicans are obsessed with dwarves— as guests on talk shows, as crime-fighting little superheroes, and always, always chasing women whose breasts are as big as the dwarves. *¿Qué pasa?*

EL GABACHO GIGANTE

Dear Gabacho: *Enanos* dominated the imaginations of Mexicans before Mexico existed. Both the Aztecs and Mayans associated little people with rain gods, while the Olmecs believed they held up the sky, according to authors Mary Miller and Karl Taube in 1997's *An Illustrated Dictionary of the Gods and Symbols of Ancient Mexico and the Maya.* "At the time of the Spanish Conquest," the two write, "Moctezuma . . . kept a troop of dwarves to entertain him and sometimes to advise him on matters of state and religion." The ancients also thought *enanos* were human manifestations of the Trickster, which explains their continued role as the id of Mexican society. Mexicans adore little *gente,* especially in movies: after all, wouldn't you love to wield guns, leap across wrestling rings, imitate celebrities, and pinch a buxom woman on the *nalga* cheek and have the spicy *chica* turn the other one?

Why is it that many of us in our culture tend to live at home until we get married?

STAY-AT-HOME SLACKER

Dear Wab: Gabachos view this strange facet of our culture as a sign of immaturity, but it's really the wisest thing a young person can do. It's a good deterrent against premarital sex, you get free room, board, and cable, and your doting mother will ensure your underwear is ever clean. Parents get the added benefit of incorporating their child's salary into constant home renovations *and* get a bit of rent. Let gabachos have their starving student years—I'll take the comfort of *mami* any day.

What's with the Mexican need to display the Virgin of Guadalupe everywhere? I've seen her in the oddest places, from a sweatshirt to a windshield sticker. As a Mexican, I find it a little offensive and tacky to display this religious symbol everywhere. You have all these fuck-ing *persinados* who do their shit in front of the image of the Holy Mother.

FOXY MUJER

Dear Pocha: Among Mexicans, Virgen de Guadalupe product-sighting is a pastime as popular as sneaking illegals into the United States. The beautiful 2002 pictorial anthology *Guadalupe* shows Mexico's patron saint on bandannas, booze bottles, and car hoods; as tattoos, key chains, and even soccer jerseys. I've seen her painted on murals, woven into fabulous silk shirts worn by Stetson-sporting hombres, and—one holy night—in my bowl of guacamole. But while I share your disdain for the hypocrites who cross themselves in Her presence before they sin, Foxy, I don't find public displays of the Empress of the Americas offensive at all. Mexican Catholicism is sublime precisely because it doesn't draw a distinction between the sacred and the profane. We can display our saints as comfortably in a cathedral as we do on hubcaps. Besides, the brown-skinned Guadalupe is a divine *vete a la fregada, puto* (Go to hell, fucker) to the gabacho rulers of the world. Remember from the Sermon on the Mount that God loves the wretched—and what people are more wretched than Mexicans—besides the Guatemalans, I mean?

Are all Mexicans Catholic? If so, why?

SAINT BIG GUT

Dear Gabacho: Not all Mexicans are Catholic, but about 90 percent are, a number that has dramatically decreased in the past couple of decades due to the rise of evangelicalism and—as in the rest of the world—exasperated congregants who want a church for the twenty-first century and not one that continues to build gaudy churches and little else. So why do Mexicans follow such a faith? Blame our *papi* and *mami:* the Spanish friars who imposed the word of Christ with the sword of Man, and the Indian woman who succumbed. But the Indians had the last laugh—Mexican Catholicism is Catholicism in name only, with many adherents still clinging to indigenous traditions, mixing many of the saints with former local gods (best example is the Virgin of Guadalupe) to create a mestizo religion that infuriates the Vatican but is their only salvation.

I would really like for you to explain the great popularity of quinceañeras. Especially since I don't think this was a Mexican custom, but rather a manifestation of *cultura* born in the United States. Am I right?

CURIOUS COUTURE

Dear Gabacha: Wrong. All cultures have their female coming-of-age rituals, and Mexico's version involves church services, fluffy dresses, and waltzes derived from the Hapsburg invasion of Mexico during the 1860s. But while the quinceañeras in Mexico are generally modest affairs, those parties in the United States make the episodes in *My Super Sweet 16* seem as humble as a catechism paschal play. The reason they're so extravagant is because the Mexicans here quickly learn it's not the religious ceremony or coming-of-age message inherent in a quinceañera that's important—it's how deep you can put yourself in debt to show the world how rich you once were.

What's the deal with Mexicans and their fear of banks? In my neighborhood, a home invasion netted the robbers $2,000 that the Mexican victims were using for their next mortgage payment. When I mentioned this to a *mexicana* friend, she told me she was once robbed of $15,000 that she kept at her apartment. Doesn't word reach the wabs from their relatives in *el Norte* that American bank accounts are insured to $100,000?

GÜERO IN THE BARRIO

Dear Gabacho: Mexicans have distrusted American banks for generations—because of bad experiences with Mexico's shaky financial institutions, because American banks wouldn't allow nonresidents to open accounts, and because many Mexicans are paid by their tax-dodging gabacho employers in cash. Hence, a gray-market financial system based on mattresses, tomato cans, and cacti. But that's a habit nowadays practiced by only the wabbiest Mexicans because, in 2001, Wells Fargo, Bank of America, Citigroup, and other major American banks received approval from the U.S. Treasury to accept Mexican identification cards (known as a *matrícula consular*) as proof enough for illegals to open bank accounts. The underground money of illegal immigrants soon flooded American bank vaults and continues to do so. A July 18, 2005, *BusinessWeek* article forecast that "half of all U.S. retail banking growth is expected to come from new immigrants over the next decade." Critics (see AmericanPatrol.com, for instance) accuse Wells Fargo and Bank of America of pandering to illegals, but remember this, Güero: the influx of Mexican money into American banks means that, like the U.S. economy itself, your life savings will soon depend on Mexicans.

Why don't Mexicans ever go to the doctor?

EL BLANCO BORRACHO

Dear Gabacho: No need to. *Primeramente,* we're too hardworking to allow something as inconsequential as a cold or a ruptured spleen to make us take a day off. And when we do get ill, we chiefly rely on ourselves. A 2001 *Journal of Immigrant Health* article noted the popularity among immigrants of self-medicating and argued that "low-income groups may self-medicate to avoid the cost of seeking medication." Another answer, though, lies in the fact that Mexicans continue to use millennia-old organic medicinal traditions. Mexican women, for instance, keep gardens full of natural medicines such as aloe vera, epazote (good for a sore tummy), yerba buena (mint), and many others. All barrios have at least one *botánica,* an underground health clinic that sells herbs, amulets, and other Catho-indigenous remedies. And when all else fails, many Mexicans along the border drive to Tijuana, where the pharmacies stock powerful antibiotics and other medicines next to deodorants and gossip rags. Self-medication is risky, Blanco Borracho, but as the *Journal of Immigrant Health* piece pointed out, many Mexicans simply can't afford to rely on the American medical system—not only are the costs prohibitive, but most stateside hospitals and doctors are overrun with Mexicans.

3

Sexo

Dirty Sánchez, JuanGas, and Indomitable Sperm

Dear Mexican: My friend and I were wondering why Mexican girls are so beautiful when they are teenagers, then over the years, they become fat, old bags?

NO MORE FAT CHICAS

Dear Gabacho: Get your facts straight. Women raised in Mexico who migrate here maintain their beauty forever—check out pictures of silent-film goddess Dolores Del Río, who gave men *palos* even into her seventies. Their *hijas,* on the other hand, are the ones who blow up into blimps. The difference? A Mexican mom's eighteen-hour workday—the mopping and kid-rearing for other families and hers, the factory-working, and the husband's lunch preparing—keeps the flab off; any thickness is muscle earned from repetitive work that would crumble a weight lifter. The daughters, meanwhile, are as American as you, gabacho: they're spoiled, fat asses who party hard, overeat, and don't do *quehaceres* (chores) after coming home from a day at the office or Chicano Studies class because they have a Mexican to do it—their *mami.*

Why do Mexicans have so many babies?

ONE IGNORANT GABACHO

Dear Gabacho: The anthropological response? Poor people need large families to bring in more income. The theological answer? Mexicans don't believe in contraception because the Catholic Church considers it a sin. But there's a reason why the American media constantly casts Mexican actors as Latin lovers or spicy señoritas and gives them thirty siblings, and it ain't the salsa. Ever had *sexo* with a Mexican? No prophylactic in the world can hold back a Mexican spermatozoon during coitus—those little hombres rip through your average condom like an Aztec tearing up a conquistador's sternum. As for oral contraceptives? I have many Mexican friends who were born while their *mamis* were on the pill. The Border Patrol can't hold us back from starting a new life—what makes you think a puny pill can?

I love Mexican hombres! They treat their women like queens. But my friend disagrees—he says Mexican husbands make their wives sleep on the floor. Who's right?

NUBIAN NOVIA

Dear *Negrita:* Both of you. All cultures vacillate between two archetypes in how they treat women: the saintly Madonna and the Great Whore. But few societies have institutionalized this Manichaean duality like Mexico. Consider the country's founding mothers—*la Malinche y la Guadalupana.* Malinche (alternately known as Malintzin and Marina) was an Indian maiden who served as translator and mistress for Cortés on his bloody march to Tenochtitlán during the Conquest. Mexico has reviled her ever since—indeed, the term *malinchista* is a synonym for *traitor*. Twelve years after the fall of the Aztec empire, on December 12, 1531, another brown-skinned woman changed Mexico's course: Our Lady of Guadalupe. Whereas *la Malinche* brought the sword of Spain to the *indios* of America, Guadalupe rewarded Her children with salvation by fusing the Catholic Virgin Mary with the Aztec earth goddess Tonantzin. Freud might say that these two epic *mujeres* appearing so early in Mexico's gestation explains why they're seared into the Mexican psyche. Would that also explain the extreme positions Mexican men take toward their women? But really, every woman has a bit of Mother María and a butt slut in her—men just react accordingly.

My friend told me that Latinas believe in being virgins until marriage, so if they decide to have sex before . . . they take it up the ass. He said this is a common practice and quite a pleasurable one if you're a back-door man. Is this a myth?

LARRY THE LIAR

Is it true that in Latin cultures it is considered gay to take it in the ass, but it's not gay to give it to another guy in the ass? In other words, catchers: gay; pitchers: not gay. What's the deal with that?

GABACHO GARY

Dear Gabachos: I was ready to dismiss both of your inquiries as little more than American stereotypes of lusty Latins along the line of the notorious Dirty Sánchez, the sexual peccadillo whereupon you stick a finger up the *culo* and smear feces on the lips of your beloved. But medical journals teem with studies documenting ass love in Latin America. *Por ejemplo,* the Global Campaign for Microbicides, a pro-contraceptive organization, notes on its Web site "the frequency of anal intercourse has . . . been documented among heterosexuals in Latin America [in other scientific publications]."

Gary, you're right: I own a 1989 University of California, Irvine–produced comic book that lectured immigrants on the dangers of AIDS and featured a man wistfully recalling a Papa Bear among a lineup of señoritas from his immediate sexual past. Mexican men are manly men, and they'll stick their *pitos* inside anything that's warm and available (see the Edward James Olmos prison-love tale *American Me* for further detail). But Larry, you're wrong: the everything-but-vagina virgin myth is something I've also heard of Afghan, Persian, Jewish, and Indian girls. If you believe gabachos, seemingly every woman from a patriarchal, repressive culture loves ass play. Consider a 1994 report by Dr. Ineke Cunningham disclosing that 34 percent of female Puerto Rican college students reported practicing anal sex. "When we wrote questions in our second survey asking why this was so, some of our colleagues belittled the idea," wrote Cunningham. "'That's already known,' they said. 'In a Latino culture, women engage in that practice to avoid pregnancy and maintain virginity.'" But Cunningham discovered that 56.2 percent of women indicated they had anal sex because their partners liked it, personal pleasure accounted for 16.5 percent of the cases, "while birth control and the maintaining of virginity together came to less than 10 percent." And, yes, this is *¡Ask a Mexican!* not *¡Ask a Boricua!* but everyone knows Puerto Ricans copy Mexicans *porque* they want to be us—even when it comes to the butt.

I'm twenty-two. My question is, why is it that I always get whistled at by Mexicans who are gardeners and in their late forties? I don't do anything to attract their attention, and yet I can't walk past them or even drive by them without being hollered at. No amount of dirty looks deters them. What gives?

LA GRINGA

Why are old Mexican men the ones that gawk at young girls walking down the street, but you never see an old white man do the same?

WHITE EYES AND THIGHS

Why do Mexican men insist on hanging out of their truck windows and honking, whistling, and catcalling at women who walk down the street? Do they know how incredibly disgusting it is to hear a *woo-*

hoo and look to find a dirty gardener looking at us through his side-view mirror?

WHALE TALE MADEMOISELLE

Dear Gabachas: Public lechery among immigrant men isn't limited to Mexicans in America—have you forgotten the Vikings, the Spaniards, Gauguin in Tahiti, and study-abroad programs? Men pillaging foreign villages for their women is a time-honored tradition, maybe even the foundation of civilization, so be happy Mexicans here are merely wagging their tongues and making kissing sounds rather than kidnapping you in the middle of the night and setting your hut on fire. These immigrants leave home, family, and church to become agents rather than subjects of history, and the world moves forward as a result. Any man who breaks the shackles of propriety and chivalry and grabs his crotch at a gal is the type of immigrant we want, the type of immigrant that makes America great—visionary, innovative, horny. Wolf-whistling Mexican men are our modern pioneers, and gabachas are their new frontier, their virgin soil.

Why does every Mexican man I meet want to invade my ass? I'm a straight-acting gay male who works at a restaurant. When the busboys and cooks aren't grabbing each other, they go out of their way to grab my ass or dick, or to just plain eye-rape me. These experiences are not limited to the kitchen staff. A couple of weekends ago, I went to a Día de los Muertos event, and a greasy churro vendor asked me point-blank if I wanted to suck dick. Are all Mexican men secretly gay?

JIZZ OMELETS TODAY ONLY

Dear JOTO: Maybe you're not as straight-acting as you think. But your question reminds me of a funny joke repeated by many Latino comics but usually attributed to César Chávez: "What's the difference between a straight Mexican man and a gay Mexican man? About two beers." In all seriousness, *mariconismo* is the apex of maleness regardless of ethnicity. It's well documented that such manly men as football players, soldiers, and longshoremen are habitual ass grabbers and cock flashers. But Mexican men—the manliest of all men—are more open about their hombre love than tight-ass gabachos. Many Mexican bars boast a lively transsexual and transvestite scene, where glamorous divas bust balls as easily as they nibble on them. And in those bars, the *ranchera* music crying from the jukebox glorifies the JuanGa, the *ranchera* archetype immortalized by singer Juan Gabriel that creates the cultural space in which macho wussies can flourish. And every mariachi ensemble includes a fey chap who croons in a blaring falsetto, flutters around like Harvey Fierstein, and eventually snuggles in the lap of a pretending to-be-outraged man, much to the delight of the audience. Mexican men embrace their inner queer, *¿y qué*, JOTO? Just means more potential brown boyfriends for you.

It seems every weekend I see a twenty five-year-old wab with a fourteen-year-old girl. Why are wabs always after the little girls? Don't they have any laws against pedophilia in Mexico? Where are the parents?

ONE CONFUSED POCHO

Dear Pocho: Along with tuberculosis, poverty, and bubbly sodas, Mexicans also import their sexual mores to this country. The age of consent in Mexico is twelve, and girls can marry at fourteen. Call it the lively hand of history: the idea of bedding pubescent maidens is as much a part of Mexican morality as calendars with religious figures—even *ranchera* idol Pedro Infante winked at the trend in his classic *canción* "El Gavilán Pollero" (The Chicken Hawk). The quinceañera, that much ballyhooed party parents throw to mark a girl's entry into womanhood—at fifteen—is really just a cattle call: by holding a lavish ceremony, Mexican fathers announce to the world their daughters' availability. The parents don't have a problem with it—most of them married young too. Gabachos like to use this phenomenon as proof of Mexican men's inherent perversion, but what's the bigger crime against nature, Confused Pocho, twenty- or thirty-some-year-old Mexican men lusting after a girl who just broke open her first box of tampons, or a moneyed octogenarian leaning on his latest prep school graduate?

Why do Mexican boys prefer their prospective wives virginal when they themselves are more broken-in than a construction worker's boots?

CHERRY-POPPIN' PAPI

Dear Gabacho: The obvious answer comes courtesy of my dago cousin Mario Puzo. In his 1969 novel *The Godfather,* Puzo describes how, after Michael Corleone makes his Sicilian bride, Apollonia, a woman, Michael "came to understand the premium put on virginity by socially primitive people. It was a period of sensuality that he had never before experienced, a sensuality mixed with a feeling of masculine power." But another theory comes courtesy of the December 2004 issue of the *Journal of Marriage and Family.* There, University of Texas–Austin professor Gloria González-López examined why Mexican fathers in the United States wanted their daughters to remain virgins until marriage. Contrary to myths about machos expecting their daughters to be forever maidens, González-López argued, Mexican dads "expect their daughters to practice sexual moderation and to delay premarital sex. For them, this is a strategy that their young daughters may use to attend and complete college, and thus improve their living conditions and socioeconomic future as they survive in an increasingly competitive society." Mexican men want their women to remain pure, therefore, because that shows a committed, serious lady who, unlike men, has mastered her libido.

Why is the Dirty Sánchez called a Dirty Sánchez and not, say, a Filthy Hobsbawm or a Grimy Kierkegaard? Is it because Mexicans invented it?

SOILED SCHLIEMANN

Dear Gabacho: I assume you refer to the sexual proclivity whereupon a man sticks a finger up his beloved's butt during intercourse and smears feces on her upper lip, and not the same-named lame band from northern California, the 1999 film, or the 2002 British television show that prudish MTV execs renamed *Team Sanchez* when it aired in the colonies. The answer is obvious—upon completion of the Dirty Sánchez, your *ruca* sports a *mierda* mustache, and Americans nowadays associate thick, bushy mustaches with Mexicans. But the Dirty Sánchez is just one of many sex acts named after a locale or ethnicity, in a subgenre of slurs linguists call ethnicons. These are insults meant to comment on an ethnic group's supposed depravity that become popular shorthand for said characteristic—for instance, we call vicious people *mongols, welsher* is synonymous with *swindler,* and the hip kids yell "Guatemalan!" whenever their friends do something *estúpido.* Other famous sexual ethnicons, as listed in the Rotten.com library's "Rolodex of Love" section, include the Cleveland Steamer ("the act of leaving a shit stain on the rib cage of a woman while receiving penile pleasure from friction between the mammaries"), a Dutch Oven ("entrapping an unsuspecting sleeping partner in a world of ass odor by farting under the covers and pulling them over her head"), and the mysterious Greek ("the act of using your 'glue stick' and gluing your gal's eyes closed with your man seed").

But do Mexicans invoke the Dirty Sánchez during sex as much as they do the name of the Santo Niño de Atocha? No. Although Mexicans are fond of anal, poop porn is the domain of your culture, Soiled Schliemann. Gentle readers, go to your local porn store and rent a *scheizer* ("shit" in German) film. The mixture of genitalia and excrement in those movies makes a Dirty Sánchez seem as chaste as an exposed ankle.

I am obsessed with Mexican women—however, I am married to a gabacha. My wife wants to indulge my rampant fantasies by looking for a Mexican *mujer* to have a threesome with us. But we can't seem to find anyone willing. We've had better luck finding white participants, but I am not interested in them. Are threesomes not a Mexican thing?

MÉNAGE A TRES

Dear Gabacho: I asked ten Mexican women and ten males whether they enjoy the occasional group grope. *Y el* survey says . . . negatory for the ladies, *sí* for one guy (with my gabacha ex, it turns out—oh, the curses and *putazos* exchanged after that surprise!). "Threesomes with Mexicans? Hell, I have a hard enough time getting into a two-some with any race" went the typical response. The results didn't surprise me. Don't believe *Y Tu Mamá También:* threesomes just aren't part of the Mexican sexual vocabulary. Blow jobs (also known as *soplazos*)? Sure! Anal? Of course! Infidelity? See below! But not threesomes, Ménage—*perdónanos.* If you want some brown sugar to sweeten your relationship, buy a bag of C&H Hawaiian Sugar and dump it on your bed.

Why is it that from my personal, thoroughly unscientific observations it seems blue-collar, illiterate Mexicans are more prone to cheating on their wives than other races?

CHEATIE CHEATIE BANG BANG

Dear Gabacho: You're right—sort of. In the monumental 1994 *Sex in America: A Definitive Survey,* researchers from the University of Chicago interviewed a random sample of thirty-five hundred Americans and found that 25 percent of married men had strayed from their vows. Latino rates of infidelity were about the same, and lead researcher Edward Laumann told *Hispanic Magazine* that "he believed the stereotype of Latinos being more unfaithful than other people was overstated." But there weren't enough funds to create a Spanish-anguage questionnaire, meaning most of the three hundred or so Latinos surveyed were pochos and not immigrant Mexican men. In the mother country, though, male infidelity is as Mexican as the tricolor—condoned by the church, tolerated by women, lionized in song. My favorite paean to cheating remains "Las Ferias de las Flores" (The

Flower Fairs), a Chucho Monge composition immortalized by Trío Calavera, which uses flowers as metaphors for *mujeres* and includes the immortal verse "And although another wants to cut her / I saw her first / And I vow to steal her / Even if she has a gardener." So the question isn't why Mexican men cheat, Cheatie, but rather why we tone down our tools upon immigrating to this country. Notch another victory for Manifest Destiny, which since the days of Cotton Mather has labored long and hard to turn this nation's virile ethnic men into pussy Protestants.

Thirteen years old, and I'm jacking off, not knowing I left the bathroom door ajar. Just as I blasted onto the shower curtain, my mom walked in. Aghast, she shouted, *"¡Cochino, te vas hacer ciego y se te va enchocar el pito!"* (You pig! You're going to go blind, and your dick will get crooked!) Scared the hell out of me, and I stopped choking the chicken for at least a month. Is the threat of going blind from jerking off purely a Mexican belief, or is it universal? *Gracias a Dios por* laser eye surgery.

PITO CHUECO

Dear Crooked Dick: All American boys have pickle-pulling hang-ups, but Mexican *chavos* suffer doubly *gracias* to two antimasturbation schools of thought: the Puritan view that monkey-spanking is dirty because it leads to pleasure, and the Catholic insistence that wanking is a mortal sin because it doesn't lead to life. For a history of the former, the Mexican recommends Thomas W. Laqueur's fine 2003 book, *Solitary Sex: A Cultural History of Masturbation,* an academic tome with many interesting tidbits—for instance, did you know the Protestant war against beating your meat didn't begin in earnest until the 1712 publication of *Onania: or the Heinous Sin of Self-Pollution, and All Its Frightful Consequences in Both SEXES, Considered, With Spiritual and Physical Advice to Those Who Have Already Injur'd Themselves by This Abominable Practice*? Catholic theologians, on the other hand, have maintained for millennia that masturbation is evil incarnate: Augustine of Hippo railed against it, St. Thomas Aquinas claimed in his *Summa Theologica* that dancing the one-fisted tango is worse than rape because rape can at least lead to pregnancy, and the *Catechism of the Catholic Church* describes rubbing your rocket as "an intrinsically and gravely disordered action."

But thanks for sharing your plight, Pito Chueco; it's further proof Mexicans can assimilate into this great land. The dual dogmas of Protestantism and Catholicism, America and Mexico, old and new countries, truly screw with a horny brown boy's mind. The *International Encyclopedia of Sexuality* says "self-pleasuring is still one of the most anxiety-provoking of all sexual issues" for Mexicans, and I can attest to that—I continue to promise God that the last time *really was* the last time, that I defile myself because I'm a sinner. And then I do it again. *Gracias a Dios* for His eternal forgiveness.

Why are Mexican women so incredibly hot in bed? There seems to be an absolute animal hunger that manifests once the lights go out. Please explain.

PLEASE ANNOUNCE NEW OFFER CONCERNING HOT ASS

Dear PANOCHA: I wanted to rip your *culo* apart for believing gabacho stereotypes of spicy señoritas—all the Mexican women I know are either twenty-seven-year-old virgins, married *mujeres* who don't masturbate, or my sister—but you're on to something. A Pfizer survey once ranked Mexican couples as the most sexually satisfied people on earth, with 74.5 percent of respondents declaring their love for *el sexo*. So who's right? Both of *nosotros*. You can reconcile my findings and Pfizer's by remembering the infamous duality with which Mexican men imprison their women: the Madonna and the Puta. It's a psychological split noted even amongst sexologists (the *International Encyclopedia of Sexuality* noted Mexican women "were dichotomized into the two double-moral-standard subtypes of the princess and prostitute") and one that assimilation can never fully erase from the Mexican psyche—and there's nothing wrong with that at all. Mexicans want womenfolk to remain virgins as long as possible, not because of a repressive patriarchal system, but because *everyone* should delay sex until physically and emotionally mature enough to deal with the consequences. Once some *pendejo* works his *pito* into a woman's *panocha*, however, Mexican ladies take the flip side of purity to heart and aspire to become whores. They're no longer Marian; they're free from machismo's ridiculous restraints.

Why do wabs, regardless of age and body size, always have one hand rubbing their bellies under their shirts? Because they all do it, especially the "fresh from the border" ones. They all look so fucking stupid doing this. Just go to Home Depot and watch them.

POCHO WITH ALBÓNDIGAS GRANDES

Dear Pocho with Big Meatballs: What's with the *panza* hate? In previous eras, girth was a sign of bounty and promise—I'm thinking Santa Claus, William Howard Taft, and the Earth Mother. That's still the case in Mexico: next to a broom-thick mustache and a gray Ford truck, a glorious, well-rounded stomach is our ultimate proof of machismo. A *panza*'s layers of fat fuel our insatiable work ethic; its orbital shape is a testament to the wives we keep in kitchens at home. Gabachos might work out, but taut muscles cannot compete with the centripetal force of a *panza*. Kids flock to it; crowds stare in jealousy when a magnificent specimen passes by. So when we rub our *panzas*, we pat the larded treasure that brings us success, popularity, and prosperity—recall how Buddhists massage Siddhartha's plump belly for luck. And, in an amazing coincidence, Theravada Buddhists celebrate a mid-July holiday called Khao Pansa, in which the faithful live in monasteries for three months and conclude with a gluttonous festival of food—all in the name of expanding that sweet, sweet *panza*.

I am a nice-looking white girl with a great job and life. I recently starting seeing a Mexican guy, and I'm pretty certain I scare the crap out of him. He has never dated a white woman before and seems nervous around me. He also asks me about the education and status

of my ex-husband and previous boyfriends. I really feel like he thinks he is not good enough for me, although I don't know why. He is gorgeous, hardworking, and so kind. I have never been one to care about what someone does, where they are from, or how much money they make. How can I get this guy to see that I really like him as a person and just relax?

ENAMORADA GABACHA

Dear Gabacha in Love: The first draft of my answer to your question ended this way: "You want to soothe your Mexican man's frayed nerves, Enamorada? Give him a blow job." Thinking this was too glib, I wrote a second draft in which I explained the minefield of race and class that you and your beloved will have to cross. I noted that dating a gabacha is the pinnacle of a Mexican man's sexual life, proof that he can navigate bedrooms as easily as borders. I cited the Orson Welles classic *Touch of Evil* (notice white-hot Janet Leigh is married to protagonist Mexican Mike Vargas—Charlton Heston in brownface), and I considered *norteño* supergroup Los Tigres del Norte's "El Mojado Acaudalado" (The Wealthy Wetback): "*Decía una güera en Florida /* 'I love you Mexican men' " (Said a white woman in Florida / "Amo a ustedes hombres mexicanos"). By the time I'd worked through all of that, I concluded that my first answer was best: nothing eradicates ego and all of its clunky superficialities (race, class, culture), nothing says I love you, nothing says "Welcome to America," like an old-school blow job.

Why do we always think Mexican men drink tequila and sing mariachi tunes, while the women are pretty señoritas?

VIVA MEXICO

Dear Gabacho: You can blame gabachos for perpetuating various Mexican stereotypes of Mexicans over the centuries, but a big part of the blame also falls on the Mexican government. During the Second World War, a time when Mexico's film industry experienced a renaissance that film scholars refer to as *la Época de Oro* (The Golden Age), Mexican filmmakers produced great films. But the ones that stuck most in the mind were the *comedia ranchera* films, starring matinee idols such as Pedro Infante and Jorge Negrete, who meted out frontier justice and wooed underneath sombreros while always drinking tequila and riding horseback. This image came directly from the state of Jalisco, birthplace of mariachi and tequila. "Needing a people who could personify *hispanismo*," wrote Joanne Hirschfield in "Race and Class in the Classical Cinema," an essay in the anthology *Mexico's Cinema: A Century of Film and Filmmakers,* "its proponents found them in Los Altos de Jalisco, the isolated northwestern mountain region of the state of Jalisco. The mythology of Los Altos created a horse-riding people who were devoutly Catholic and capitalistic, had never intermarried with Indians, and played Mariachi music." Mexico thought Americans would think better of Mexicans if they thought of beaners as devoid of Indian roots, but Hollywood didn't care—they inverted the Jaliscan tropes and created the fat, drunk, gold-toothed greaseball who sleeps under a cactus and gets up only to drink and write columns about Mexicans. As for the Mexican women being sultry and spicy—that's all documentary, baby.

Are there any signals in Mexican culture that indicate sexual interest? I noticed my Mexican friend pops his lips to make a sucking sound. Is this some sort of signal you're aware of?

HORCHATA GAL

Dear Gabacha: Signal? How about just *breathing.* Every moment in a Mexican's life is a chance for some sexy results—don't you see all the kids we have? But there are various ways we express interest. We grab asses, wolf whistle, issue a loud kissy-kissy—those gestures are the ones we use but are also common to immigrant-male culture. Better are the come-ons expressed in Mexican song, where sex takes on the metaphors of flower beds. One of my favorite examples is in the classic *corrido* "Juan Charrasqueado" (Johnny Scarface), which describes the terrors Juan inflicted on a poor town where "there were no more flowers"—the polite way of saying Johnny banged his way through many a poor woman. But the best way to know if a Mexican man is sexually interested in you? If he asks whether you're a citizen wanting to marry.

I have traveled all over the world and had sex with women from many countries. Mexican women are some of the sexiest and most erotic anywhere. My question is, why do these beautiful women fuck with unabashed passion but give the worst oral sex?

MORAL ORAL

Dear Gabacho: As with *gabachos*, fellatio is a time-honored insult in Mexican Spanish, with various slurs originating from the act. We differ, however, in the inventive ways we describe the act. If we want to say that José sucks, we'll say *"¡José pela!"*—"José peels," with the peeling referring to a man's foreskin. There's also the earthier *"Chupa verga"* (Suck dick) and *"Lamamela"* (Lick my [dick]). The creepiest slur, however, involves your mother. As I've noted elsewhere, many Mexican swear words originate from the simple *mother,* and the most notorious derivative is *mamar*—to suck. It obviously came from the maternal act of breast-feeding, but is understood in Mexico to mean "suck dick." The most curious form is *"No mames,"* which means "Don't suck dick," but is known as "Don't fuck around"—suggesting that fellatio isn't treasured in Mexican society, for the same reason masturbation is such a dirty secret: it doesn't lead to procreation, and Mexicans are Aquinists who feel any sexy deed that doesn't lead to *muchos* babies is grounds for eternal damnation.

How come all my friends want a BMW (big Mexkin woman)?

BABY GOT CULO

Dear Gabacho: Who doesn't want a chubby? Everyone knows fat chicks try harder, and it's doubly true when it's a Mexican *gordita* (fatty). What makes them even more appealing is that the rolls on a Mexkin aren't born from fatty foods but from the traditional, protein-rich Mexican diet of beans, maize, and rice, which leads to healthy, sturdy women perfect for bearing children or working long hours without breaks. When famine and depression finally hit the United States, those big girls will be the salvation of us all.

Why do Mexican couples call each other *mami* or *papi*? That's really perverted.

SPANK ME, DADDY

Dear Gabacha: Remember the most important feature in Mexican society: *la familia*. Just as our Puritan *papis y mamis* addressed each other as Goodman and Goodwife, Mexicans refer to each other by their primary roles in life—in this case, continuing the family tree. By calling all males *papis* and all females *mamis,* we remind each other of our duties to procreate. Besides, all cultures have a bit of an oedipal thing in them—Mexicans are just less ashamed of it.

Why don't Mexicans marry outside their own group? Whenever I see the wedding announcements, they're always two Hispanic surnames together. Don't they want American kids?

THE GORDA DIVORCÉE

Dear Fat Gabacha: Ha! You're asking this question to a Mexican who so far has bedded only one *mexicaliente* girl and whose sister is dating a roly-poly gabacho. Getting a gabacho or gabacha is a badge of honor for Mexicans, but a difficult achievement because who in his or her right mind would want to marry a Mexican? Nevertheless, it's happening. According to the 2000 census, the number of households where Latinas married gabachos totaled 766,819, while 656,269 Latinos snagged a pretty gabachita (disclaimer: while the census has categories for race, income, and size of household, it has yet to include bubbles for hotness, so the "pretty gabachita" comment is pure speculation). Men from different cultures stealing women from each other is a pastime as old as the Bible, and gabachos are beating Mexicans at the moment, frankly because the gabachos like to snap up Mexican women in the belief they'll cook and clean and be good Mexican housewives for them—and, frankly, that's why Mexican men marry Mexican women *también.*

Why are Mexican men always portrayed as hot in the movies?

LOOKING FOR SOME CHORIZO

Dear Gabacha: Duh—because we *are.* The Latin Lover is a stereotype played at least once in TV and film by every male Mexican actor, including the Taco Bell Chihuahua. The Latin Lover talks like Ricky Ricardo (played voluble and apoplectic by Desi Arnaz), lives like Mr. Roarke (Ricardo Montalbán on the palatial estate of *Fantasy Island*), and loves to sing and dance (Ricky Martin). It's not necessarily a good stereotype, though. Consider the incarnations in three high-profile 2001 bombs: *Original Sin, America's Sweethearts,* and *Crazy/Beautiful.*

In *Original Sin,* Luis Vargas (Antonio Banderas) reflects the traits middle-aged audiences have been conditioned to expect from their on-screen Hispanics: aristocratic lifestyle, cold heart, and white-hot phallus honed by almost constant practice; when they're not frowning and fighting, these guys are frowning and fucking. Thus, Banderas's Vargas is a rich plantation owner in late-nineteenth-century Cuba who is an atheist when it comes to romance. Then he meets Julia Russell (Angelina Jolie). Disguised as a mail-order bride, she has come to Cuba with a sanguinary assignment: kill Vargas. But—*sopresa*—Vargas seduces her so thoroughly that she finds a way to remain with Vargas and his white-hot appendage.

Original Sin's technical aspects (hot salsa music and Spanish guitars for the ears, native dances and lush and luxuriant scenery for the eyes) accentuate the exotic appeal of Luis, who spends what time he has—when not making love to Julia—in either fighting men or plotting to kill them. His dialogue is classic Latin Lover, ranging from the insincere "I love you" to the more sincere "I'm going to kill her." Banderas is a talented actor (see his work with Spanish director Pedro Almodóvar—please!), but for Hollywood and American audiences, he is a Spanish sex machine.

The Latin Lover is one of the few roles Hollywood offers Hispanic men. The other is the *bandido*/cholo/drug dealer, and they are not mutually exclusive. The actor portraying the Latin Lover doesn't have to be Latin (witness Charlton Heston's brownface turn in *Touch of Evil*), but he must act on a hair-trigger temper (Al Pacino's Tony Montana) and, of course, get any woman he wants (Rudolph Valentino).

Hank Azaria's portrayal of Héctor in *America's Sweethearts* reveals other characteristics of the Latin Lover: destroyer of happy white couples. As vain as Paris Hilton, Azaria's Latin Lover is also unintentionally funny: Azaria cannot decide whether to employ the lisp native to Madrid or a guttural Castilian. But in his jealousy and obsession with penis size, Héctor is true to type, even calling Eddie Thomas (John Cusack) "Pussy Boy" to provoke a fight.

Some people might dismiss Héctor as just another unfunny joke in an unfunny movie. But Hollywood's historical cultural myopia suggests otherwise: Héctor's mangled lisp is universally derided in the Hispanic world, where critics have wondered why Azaria threw in overenunciated h's and g's. We can tell them: because in Hollywood, every Hispanic character is a universal spic.

There is hope, though, for a more nuanced Latin Lover, and that came courtesy of another little-seen 2001 film. *Crazy/Beautiful* stands as a beautiful antithesis to the lazy caricatures of *Original Sin* and *Sweethearts*, subverting all the Latin Lover traits. Yes, Carlos (Jay Hernández) speaks in an "exotic" accent, but it's the street-smart argot of East Los Angeles. Yes, he is eye candy, and Nicole (Kirsten Dunst) originally treats him as her little Hispanic pet (early in the film, she wants Carlos to talk in Spanish because "it's hot"). But his main allure is that he's a multidimensional success. Most surprisingly, *Crazy/Beautiful*'s Latin Lover is not a purely European type but a Chicano with brown skin.

Although *Crazy/Beautiful* is a teen flick, it's extraordinary in its depiction of the Latin Lover and of the interethnic relationships that today's youth view as the norm rather than as bizarre anomalies.

Hollywood's original fascination with the Latin Lover was largely based on barely repressed fears of miscegenation and the seduction of white women. But Carlos does not conquer the white woman; the white woman conquers him. And he does not ruin Nicole's life; instead, she nearly ruins his, but he ends up saving her nevertheless. Most remarkably for any Hollywood film, let alone those with Latin Lover roles, the pair builds a relationship based on love rather than mere lust. Hernández and Dunst have eaten a fruit forbidden to our parents, but not to us: we recognize the couple as partners in a relationship based on real affection—and therefore truly as America's sweethearts.

Who's the hottest Mexican woman in history? Don't tell me it's Frida Kahlo.

HUNGRY FOR PINK TACO

Dear Gabacho: Gabachos drool over Salma Hayek, their maids, and that hot chick with the great ass in the next cubicle, but no one matches Mexican screen goddess María Félix. Incredibly beautiful even in advanced age, Félix not only was Mexico's greatest movie star but also used her influence to create a fiercely feminist persona that redefined how a woman should act. Félix, who made all of her films during Mexico's *Época de Oro,* was an icon for women and men (for wildly different reasons) worldwide, except—surprise, surprise!—in the United States. She never bothered to learn English and go Hollywood such as contemporaries Dolores Del Rio and Katy Jurado because she knew that American producers would invariably typecast her as a hot señorita.

She didn't have a problem being a hot señorita; indeed, it became her trademark character. But Félix did it her own way, emphasizing not mindless female passion but a proud independence that owed nothing to men.

One of Félix's best performances was in *La Diosa Arrodillada* (The Kneeling Goddess, 1947), in which she played a woman who so entrances her lover that the man gives his wife a nude statue of Félix's character. Not satisfied with merely antagonizing the woman, Félix insists that her lover divorce and then forces him to marry her after the wife dies under mysterious circumstances. This performance and many others bring to mind those of her closest Hollywood contemporary, Marlene Dietrich: both were self-confident women with such stunning looks that they literally drove men insane—both in film and in real life.

Félix was more than just an actress or harlot in the Mexican imagination, though. Men as varied as Octavio Paz, Carlos Fuentes, and Diego Rivera (who drafted Frida Kahlo to write Félix a letter urging her to marry Rivera) cited her as inspiration for their masterpieces. But perhaps her greatest influence was on Agustín Lara, the legendary songsmith and main force behind Mexican cinema's *cabareta* genre.

The genre had as its principal setting a nightclub where songs, most penned by Lara, were sung about the perfidy and beauty of womanhood. These films cinematically articulated Mexican men's love-hate relationship with women, and we can indirectly thank Félix, who starred in such Lara-penned films as *La Devoradora* (The Devourer), for this spectacular but ultimately damaging genre.

But María Félix made no excuses for her career; she always made sure men understood that women were not to be dismissed or mistreated. "I cannot complain about men," the eternally quotable Félix once said. "I have had tons of them and they have treated me fabulously well. But sometimes I had to hurt them to keep them from subjugating me."

Why isn't there any good-quality Mexican porn?

HORNY HUNGY

Dear Gabacho: We don't need it. Granted, there are some Mexican porn classics, such as 2000's *Platillos Violadores* (Flying Saucer Rapists), and Russ Meyer ultravixen Kitten Natividad is a Juárez native best known for hard-core features such as *Cum to Dinner* and *Thanks for the Mammaries.* But pornography's primary purpose is to titillate, to provide a simulacrum of the real thing, and Mexicans don't need aids to get off—look at all our babies! If you're in the mood for Latin lechery, though, I recommend Justin Slayer's *Mami Culo Grande* (Big-Assed Honey) series, in which the African-American porn star does his part to end simmering Mexican-black tensions by deep-dicking Mexican gals in all three inputs as they moan in English and *español*. And for the ladies: nothing cools down your hot, hot heat like twiddling to the little hombre in the hat on the Tapatío bottle.

Speaking of porn, I also think it's the best way to keep Mexican boys occupied. I grew up in a neighborhood that had long ago been overrun by gangs. The cholos ignored me at school because, well, everyone ignores nerds. But summers were trying. My parents—both hardworking nine-to-fivers—couldn't take care of me, so they dropped me off every day at my cousin's house in the heart of slummy Anaheim. We were five barely teenage Latinos—cousins, friends, and me—with nothing to do, starving for acceptance by our peers. We should just have lined up against the wall and let the notorious Anaheim police whale on us. But salvation came in the form of a dirty young man and his obsession with double penetrations.

One day at my friend's house, we broke into his uncle's room looking for cash to steal. We found something better: pornos stacked as high as our heads. The uncle had moved back to El Salvador but left his most prized possessions—by mistake? Or providence? Because this was our deliverance. The gangs were only a few steps outside our front door, but we soon stopped caring about hanging out with them. Every weekday for the next five summers was spent watching, talking, breathing, and buying porn. I'd be dropped off at my cousin's house at 6 a.m., sleep for two hours, have breakfast, pick up our friend, and then we'd walk to another friend's house. At noon, we'd take a break for an hour to eat lunch, then go back to work for the rest of the day. And the rest was porn. Any slivers of time not spent watching pornos were spent discussing them or trying to get more of them. Forget the cholos on the street; we had a new lifestyle all our own.

That treasure trove of trashy threesomes had everything: Traci

Lords when she was sixteen, rape fantasy clips, a guy duct-taping his balls into a makeshift dick and then using his new appendage to butt-fuck Nina Hartley. We can tell you exactly when Ron Jeremy became truly ugly, what made Savannah a better slut than Jenna Jameson, and the physics involved in quadruple-dong sex. And as the gang lifestyle became more tempting, we began to explore other aspects of pornography to stay out of trouble. We'd find magazines in bushes, *Hustler* trading cards at 7-Eleven, even dig videos out of strangers' trash. Once, my cousin found a *Penthouse* that helped him earn A's on *two* class papers due to fine investigative pieces on corruption in boxing and Howard Stern—true story. I even started a porno repository at my house: anyone who liked porn but couldn't keep it in his house could leave it in my care for a nominal fee. And through it all, our good citizenship—and our fierce teenage hard-ons—never faltered.

And now? All of us are doing well. We attribute our success to porn—we'd probably just be a cluster of statistics if it weren't for our pubertal passion for watching tit fucks. Most of our peers joined gangs or got into some sort of trouble, mostly through friendships formed during those summers. But none of us ever crossed paths with the law. And we still remember those summers fondly: our favorite titles (*The Best Rears of Our Lives, White Trash Whore #7*), actors (who has the better cunnilingus form: TT Boy or Tom Byron?), even magazines (does *Penthouse* still have those piss pictorials?). Our idea of a romantic evening now is not an interruption-free masturbation session; regular porno viewing for all of us ended upon graduation from high school. But it's a phase in our lives that's nevertheless sacred and close to our hearts. To this day, we thank God for introducing us to the likes of John Holmes, John T. Bone, and *Bone Appétit.* You see, porn kept us off the streets. And I can't help but think, if the Boys & Girls Club really cared about keeping kids safe, they'd give out free porn.

A Spicy Timeline of Sexy Mexicans in the United States

1838: "In point of chastity, the most important and influential qualification of Northern nations, we are infinitely superior to you—Lust is, with us, hateful and shameful; with you, it is a matter of indifference. *This* is the chief curse of the South: the leprosy which unnerves both body and mind."
—*Mexico versus Texas,* Anthony Ganilh, one of the first novels to dramatize the tensions between gabachos and Mexicans

1884: Helen Hunt Jackson's weepy novel *Ramona* idealizes the California Mission days and blesses Mexican ladies with the spicy-señorita stereotype—never mind that Ramona is part-Scotch, part-Indian.

1908–18: *Broncho Billy and the Greaser, Broncho Billy's Greaser Deputy, The Girl and the Greaser, The Greaser and the Weakling, The Greaser, Tony the Greaser, Greaser's Palace, Lone Greaser, Ah Sing and the Greasers, The Greaser's Gauntlet, Guns and Greasers, The Greaser's Revenge,* and so many more. Hollywood discovers the Mexican. Bandito hilarity ensues.

1920: *The Mark of Zorro.* Gabacho Douglas Fairbanks dons the brownface, introduces the Latin Lover to the American public.

1930s: *The Mexican Spitfire* series: real-life Mexican Lupe Velez stars in many B-grade shorts, but most gabachos remember her as the starlet who died by drowning herself in a toilet after taking too many sleeping pills. America's perception of Mexican women goes down the loo as well.

1948: *Treasure of the Sierra Madre:* John Huston classic immortalizes the bandito stereotype with one line: "Badges!? We ain't got no badges. We don't need no badges! I don't have to show you any stinking badges!"

1950s: A heady decade for Mexicans. Katy Jurado brings dignity to the spicy señorita with her role as Gary Cooper's former lover in 1952's *High Noon.* The following year, Speedy Gonzáles—Academy Award–winning mouse who outwits gabacho cats and bandits and espeekies likee dees—debuts in *Cat-Tails for Two.* Decade ends with Charlton Heston slapping on the brownface for Orson Welles's tawdry 1958 noir *Touch of Evil.*

1967–71: The Frito Bandito threatens to "steel" Frito chips from innocent gabacho households. Gets the ax after Latino advocacy groups begin a boycott. Latino advocacy groups have no sense of humor.

1970–93: Erik Estrada stars on *CHiPS,* plays paunchy "Ponch" Poncherello. Makes Mexicans hot again. Too bad he's Puerto Rican.

1978–84: Ricardo Montalbán earns fame in *Fantasy Island* by playing a mysterious Latin gentleman with a gabacho last name.

1986: Congress passes Simpson-Rodino Act, which grants amnesty to 4 million illegal immigrants. The Mexican rides again.

1995: Salma Hayek's breasts appear in *Desperado,* and America loves Mexicans. . . .

1996–FOREVER: Until Congress takes up the issue of Mexican immigration, a subject they've yet to drop. The greasy bandit rides again.

4

Inmigración

More, More, and More

Dear Mexican: As a Mexican, aren't you embarrassed and ashamed that probably the number one dream of people in Mexico is to sneak illeagelly [*sic*] into the United States, a gringo gabaucho [*sic*] society that is probably not one-tenth as corrupt as Mexico, which enables it to have an economy which has so much wealth even the poor people here have twenty-seven-inch color TVs?

BORDERING ON INSANITY

Dear Gabacho: As an American, aren't you embarrassed that you can't write proper English—or as you may spell it, Inglich? "Illeagelly"? "Gabaucho"? *Cabrón*, what country are you from? I know teenagers fresh from Jalostotitlán who spell better. And as a Mexican, I am ashamed—ashamed that more of my *paisanos* haven't moved into gabacho neighborhoods and scared *pendejo* gabachos like you off to South Dakota, just as we did in California. And Colorado. And Arizona. And North Carolina. And . . .

I've often wondered how Mexicans would react if 25 million piss-poor Chinamen snuck into Mexico and took up residence. Would they be greeted with open arms? Or would they be greeted by armed men? And I'd bet a sack of pesos they wouldn't be given free health care, free schooling, and Mexican driver's licenses either.

BI-COASTAL CURIOUS

Dear Gabacha: Damn straight we'd kick those *chinos* down to Guatemala. In fact, Mexican-on-Chinese violence is one of Mexico's darkest legacies, on par with the Conquest and the donkey show. Mexican government officials used the pandemonium of the Mexican Revolution to discriminate against, evict, and sometimes even massacre entire Chinese communities in a strategy known as *el movimiento anti-chino*. "Leaders of the anti-Chinese movement promulgated a wide array of invidious legislation, including discriminatory labor laws and public health circulars, anti-miscegenation laws, and residential segregation laws," writes Dr. Robert Chao Romero, a Southern California attorney, professor at the University of California, Los Angeles, and the country's leading authority on the Chinese in Mexico.

The Mexican anti-Chinese movement was understandable—Chinese immigrants worked hard, built successful businesses, established themselves in civic life, and made the natives in their adopted country look like the lazy *pendejos* they were. So what I'm trying to say, Bi-Coastal Curious, is that I get why you and so many gabachos hate Mexicans.

I am awestruck by the lack of anger from Mexicans for the Mexican government. Mexican leaders have forced Mexicans from their land. Mexico degrades its citizens like no other country in our hemisphere. The Mexican government and aristocrats despise the majority of Mexican people. The demonic lack of respect shown to Mexicans by Mexico should be shouted from the rooftops! Instead, all we hear is anti-American tripe. Why don't Mexicans embrace the country that is their salvation?

EVERY ZEITGEIST LEVELS NIMRODS

Dear EZLN: Which Mexicans do you knock back Cazadores with, EZLN? No Mexican I know—and I know more Mexicans than the Border Patrol—ever bad-mouths *los Estados Unidos.* Sure, most of them express a blind, chauvinistic nationalism for a homeland that screws them over again and again, but Mexican pride doesn't translate into "anti-American tripe."

But if you want Mexicans to trash their government, then I urge patience: you will get all the Mexican-against-Mexican anger you desire in 2010. That's when the cycle of revolution will sweep across Mexico again, as it has during the same denary year for the past two centuries. Father Miguel Hidalgo y Costilla clanged the bells from his church in Dolores, Guanajuato, in 1810 to signal the start of Mexico's War of Independence from Spain. One hundred years later, Francisco Madero provoked the Mexican Revolution with his Plan de San Luís Potosí, a call to arms against the dictatorship of General Porfirio Díaz.

Who knows what awaits Mexico in three years? But the Mexican can guarantee you two things, EZLN: it'll be bloody, and even more Mexicans will stream across the border than in the previous two wars.

How come all the Mexicans who came here two or three generations ago look like "almost-white" people while the ones coming now look like those little guys who live naked in the Amazon and kill things with blowguns?

No Indios Need Apply

Dear NINA: Chalk the phenomenon up to the natural unfolding that is the American immigrant experience. Countries tend to dump their upwardly mobile, lighter-skinned natives on the United States before the shoddier, darker folks show up in the steerage of rusting freighters—remember that northern Italians arrived at Ellis Island before their swarthy Sicilian *paisanos*. That's what's happening with Mexico, NINA. In his 1983 study, *East Los Angeles: History of a Barrio,* historian Ricardo Romo cites a 1922 demographic survey that showed almost two-thirds of the Mexican community of Los Angeles at the time originated from just four states: Chihuahua, Durango, Jalisco, and Zacatecas. These states are in north-central Mexico, where the conquistadors spread their seed farthest and most vigorously. As the twentieth century progressed, however, Mexico's poorer, more indigenous states in the south tumbled like dominoes as they sent their populations to *el Norte,* subsequently ratcheting up the brownie mixture in the Mexican-American pot. Michoacán and Puebla (next to Mexico City) didn't start sending their residents en masse to the United States until around the mid–twentieth century; Guerrero and Oaxaca followed around the 1970s; our Central American colony, Guatemala, now follows. The push continues even in Mexico—in a 2004 *Orange County Register* piece, staffer Valeria Godines described the tensions among the *güeros* of Arandas, Jalisco, and Chiapan immigrants, showing Mexicans can be as race-obsessed as their gabacho oppressors.

What is it about the word *illegal* that Mexicans don't understand?
MINES, NOT FENCES

Dear Gabacho: Take your pick, Mines. Mexicans don't understand the word *illegal* because (A) when paying their gardeners, nannies, busboys, and factory workers in cash (and forgetting to withhold payroll taxes), U.S. employers don't seem to understand the word *illegal,* so why should Mexicans? (B) The Anglo-American trappers and traders whom you and I were taught to admire as tough, self-sufficient frontiersmen and pioneers were among the American Southwest's first illegals. Who are you calling illegal, gabacho? (C) Presidente Bush's proposal to offer amnesty and a guest-worker program to all illegal immigrants—a move designed to appease his supporters in the business community—means even Republicans don't understand the word. (D) Whether they buy a fake passport or take a citizenship oath, Mexicans will never be more than wetbacks in the eyes of many Americans, so why bother applying for residency? (E) The stylebook for daily newspapers across the country reportedly requires its reporters to describe as *undocumented workers* the men and women you call *illegal.* (F) Little-known fact: the fragment of poetry on the Statue of Liberty ("Give me your tired, your poor, your huddled masses yearning to breathe free," etc.) does not, because of a French engraver's error, include Emma Lazarus's rarely cited footnote: "No Mexicans, please." Fucking French. But the real answer is the word itself. *Illegal* is an English word; Mexicans speak Spanish—yet you never hear Mexicans whine that their bosses don't understand such easy Spanish phrases as *pinche puto pendejo baboso,* do you?

What is it with you Mexicans who want to take back California? Is it that conquistador blood that's driving you?

GO BACK TO GRANADA

Dear Gabacho: Besides beards, light skin, and bad wine, the Spanish conquistadors brought with them to Mexico the legacy of *reconquista,* which has replaced WMDs as the *número uno* doomsday conspiracy espoused by conservatives. Originally, *reconquista* was a specific period of Spanish history (about the eighth century AD to 1492) in which Spain's Catholic nobles united to expel the North African Muslims (they called them Moors) from the Iberian Peninsula. Today, *reconquista* refers to a hypothetical master plan by Mexican officials to reconquer the southwestern United States—territories lost in the 1848 Mexican-American War. Their ostensible weapon is unlimited migration. It sure seems *reconquista* is a reality, what with bilingual ballots, Spanish-language radio stations topping the Arbitron ratings nationwide, salsa supplanting ketchup as the top-selling condiment in U.S. supermarkets, the Aztec prophecy that the People of the Sun would return to their northern ancestral lands—and a 2002 Zogby poll showing that 58 percent of Mexicans believed that the U.S. Southwest rightfully belonged to them.

But as a member of the invading army, the Mexican can say without a doubt that *reconquista* is a myth. *Primeramente,* the Mexican government is incapable of formulating a sound economic policy; can we really expect it to successfully take over former territories not named Guatemala? Those who insist *reconquista* is real also forget American history, which time and time again shows that immigrants in America plan the takeover of their *mother* countries, not their adopted nations. Prominent examples include José Marti (Cuba), Garibaldi (Italy), and Ahmed Chalabi (you shouldn't need me to tell you "Iraq"). If there's a *reconquista,* it's working in reverse: Mexicans in the United States make their fortunes here and send money (along with toasters, big-screen televisions, monster trucks, and democracy) south. As a result, Mexico is freer than ever before.

So why does a concept as loco as *reconquista* earn such an enthusiastic reception among conservatives? Simple, it's easier to point at Mexicans for the problems of illegal immigration than to critique the American economic and political structures that require cheap labor. If conservatives believe in *any* gospel in these days of international aggression and ballooning federal spending, it's this: when all else fails, blame the Mexicans.

Whenever I bad-mouth illegal immigration at work, many of my Latina coworkers automatically assume I'm bad-mouthing Mexicans. Why do Mexicans always think that when a gabacho expresses dislike toward illegal immigrants, they're talking about Mexicans?

FENCES MAKE GOOD NEIGHBORS

Dear Gabacho: Where to begin . . . where does Bush want to deploy the National Guard? To the *Mexican* border. What pissed off the Fox News nation last year? A *Spanish*-language version of the national anthem. What was gabachos' biggest complaint during the March marches and student walkouts last year? All those damn *Mexican* flags. What immigrant group does influential neocon and

Harvard historian Samuel Huntington argue will destroy the United States? *Mexicans.* Which country do many conservatives accuse of trying to take over the southwest United States? *Mexico.* You can argue that Mexicans warrant the attention since they constitute more than half of all illegal immigrants in *los Estados Unidos,* Fences, but you gotta ask at some point, why don't the Michelle Malkins of the world rail against the Guatemalan aliens among us or the non-Mexican illegal immigrants who came here legally but overstayed their visas? Simple, because none of those groups are *Mexican.* You can talk about fences making good neighbors, Fences, but your anti-immigrant amigos don't like barriers put between *Mexican* and *illegal immigrant.*

Why do Mexicans always find the need to cut in line? I see this happening in *la carnicería,* the airport, and everywhere else there are Mexicans.

A DISAPPOINTED *MEXICANA*

Although I have great empathy for the plight of illegal aliens and their families, their illegal "cutting in line" ahead of others has resulted in depriving other law-abiding families waiting to legally immigrate from the same entitlements, opportunities, and citizenship they so righteously and aggressively defend. At its core, it just isn't right and cannot be justified with hard work or innocent children. My wife's brothers and sisters live in near poverty in the Philippines, but they're waiting so they can become *legal* immigrants.

WAITING AND WAITING

Dear Wab and Gabacho: I get this question asked every week, so to Disappointed, Waiting, and all other curious minds: grow some *huevos.* Mexicans cut in line not because they're rude but because they have lives to live and places to go. Disappointed, are you going to patiently stand there like a *pendeja* as Mexican after Mexican cuts in front of you? Do what Mexicans do: cut in front of them. Or at least slash their tires afterward. And, Waiting, let's be realistic. The only reason Mexicans come into this country illegally is because it's easy for them—just one hopped border and you're here. If the Philippines weren't thousands of miles away, your impoverished in-laws would swim over faster than Mark Spitz. Why wait years and years just because it's the right way? Waiting to immigrate legally won't calm those hunger pangs. Besides, entering America illegally, agitating for rights, and watching as a foreign government grants you recognition under pressure isn't a sin: it's called the Declaration of Independence.

Why shouldn't the United States adopt the same type of anti-illegal immigration laws that Mexico keeps on its books? Illegal aliens in Mexico are felons—so why do Mexicans complain if the United States wants to do that as well? Mexico deported hundreds of thousands of Central Americans each year—so why do illegal aliens from Mexico complain if the United States deports a few? Foreign nationals in Mexico can't stage massive marches in the streets of Mexico waving the flags of their home countries—in fact, Mexican law prohibits such tactics under penalty of jail time. So how does "The Mexican" respond?

VERY HYPOCRITICAL

Dear Gabacho: Why in God's good name would Americans *ever* want to follow Mexico's example? Mexico experienced boom times when it welcomed immigrants, and much of what passes for Mexican culture today came courtesy of these late-nineteenth- and early-twentieth-century influxes—*banda* and *norteño* music (German and Czech), *al pastor* meat (Arab), Frida Kahlo (Jews), calling all Asians *chinos* (*chinos*). But once Mexico began cracking down on immigration after the drafting of the 1917 Mexican Constitution, which forced every foreigner to "strictly comply with the conditions established for him in the immigration permit and the dispositions established by the respective laws," this once promising country stagnated. A more liberal immigration policy is one of the things that distinguishes the United States from Mexico—that and flushable toilet paper. Like France, Mexico worries about the "purity" of its "national identity"; our Founding Fathers understood that immigrants enrich us with their customs, numbers, and, sure, cheap labor. We agree on one thing: like Mexico, we should deport more Central Americans. The Guatemalan menace must be stopped at all costs.

If, as I have heard a million times, Mexicans come to the United States to make a better life for themselves, due to the poverty in Mexico, why don't they stay in Mexico and try to make their own homeland a better place?

CONFUSED CABRÓN

Why don't Mexicans stay put and develop their own land into what they want? Why don't "they" bring themselves up like "we" did by doing what it takes to build a country like "we" did? It seems that Mexicans want a ready-made modern democratic country, but don't want to work for it themselves "back home." It really pisses me off and seems lazy to me. Get educated (you *can* learn anywhere there is a library and at least one person willing to teach), get a backbone, and get to business in your own country.

JOHNNY REBEL

Dear Cabrones: *Gracias* for illustrating the great double standard in America's immigration policy, what I call Mexican exceptionalism. Centuries of immigrant waves chose not to improve their homelands and to try their luck in a new land, and we rightfully celebrate their pluck as pioneers. Yet when Mexicans follow in the footsteps of our gabacho forefathers, we accuse them of lacking self-motivation and want to shut down the border. You call these migrating Mexicans invaders; I call them the vanguards of innovation. It's these restless individuals that propel history, the crazies not content with their lots in life that transform society for the good. And Mexicans in the United States are about the boldest innovators yet—not only do they improve life in Mexico by sending billions of dollars in remittances each year, they also sacrifice their sweat and children to the American way. If those Mexicans actually stayed in Mexico as you prefer, Cabrón, the United States would lose both its cheap labor and taco-and-enchilada combos and the one thing that keeps Mexico from turning into Guatemala-by-the-Pacific. So which do you prefer?

How am I supposed to like Mexicans that come here by just jumping a fence and running or sneaking onto a transport truck entering this country illegally when you have law-abiding immigrants working their ass off to come to this country legally?

LOVE THE MEXICANS BUT HATE THE BORDER-HOPPERS

Dear Gabacho: Wait a minute, you don't like your first-world life? How about clean offices? One-dollar tacos with free horchata? All come courtesy of our free-market economy, which demands cheap labor and thus requires workers that undercut established workers. Sure, illegal immigration is a crime, but let's put it this way: if all those illegals waited in line like their idiot legal-immigrant cousins, Big Business would lose millions of low-wage workers and be forced to significantly increase wages for menial jobs—after all, no American in his right mind would pick strawberries for $7,000 a year like illegal immigrants. But Big Business doesn't like that—they'd rather pay Lupe nothing than Mary something. So Big Business would then relocate to Mexico—and when those Mexicans began demanding higher wages, then business would relocate to India or Suriname or some other country with lax regulations and a government willing to stay mum as the companies pay no wages. American life would, meanwhile, suffer from lost jobs and other inconveniences caused by our vertically integrated way of life. So be happy for the illegal Mexicans among you, Love the Mexicans—otherwise, you'd be competing with felons for the right to pick rhubarb.

Would Mexicans ever return home for good?

PRAYING FOR A MILAGRO

Dear Gabacho: Sorry, Milagro, but Mexicans are already home in the United States. That's why they're *immigrants*—immigrants leave the poverty and anguish of their former countries for the New World. No immigrant group ever left the United States for their mother country— not the Pilgrims, not the Poles, and definitely not the Mexicans. But the most deluded people in this matter aren't gabachos like yourself but the Mexican immigrants themselves. Take the story of my dad, who first sneaked into this country in 1968 in the trunk of a Chevy along with three other men. He played a cat-and-mouse game with immigration authorities for the next decade—they would deport him, he would sneak back in—until the 1986 amnesty put my father on the path to citizenship. Shortly after taking his citizenship oath, he bought a house in his hometown of Jerez, Zacatecas, in central Mexico. My father sent money and appliances back to the house over the next fifteen years—in the hope he'd soon move back with his four children. Last year, my father sold the house. He said he wanted to use the money to build a new kitchen in our Anaheim home. And, on top of that, he now hates illegal immigrants—says they ruin the economy. And if that's not assimilation, I don't know what is.

Why are Mexicans so casual about sharing the information that a friend or acquaintance is living here illegally? Don't your people know that if I was a nasty person, I could make the life of this third party much more difficult by disclosing this information to their employer or *la migra*?

MIGRA MAN

Dear Gabacho: Either you're lying, or the Mexicans you hang out with deserve to be deported for stupidity. First off, no Mexican in his right mind would ever admit to being illegal—why do you think fake driver's licenses, Social Security numbers, and birth certificates are as common among illegals as piñatas? And even if nefarious assholes called immigration officials to deport illegals, they won't do a damn thing. Why do you think there are now so many illegals in the United States? Because the Border Patrol not only isn't doing its job securing our borders, but also doesn't bother to go after the problem internally. Illegal Mexicans walk with little or no fear because they know the Border Patrol is too busy trying to nab Mexicans at the border to pay any attention toward the Mexicans already prancing in the United States. I'm not blaming the Border Patrol, mind you; my cousin once worked for *la migra*. But let's be realistic—if the United States *really* wanted the Border Patrol to capture and deport Mexicans, Los Angeles would be a ghost town tomorrow. But it doesn't, and thus the illegals spread.

If everyone in Mexico has the right to be a U.S. citizen, can U.S. citizens all apply to be Mexican?

ENSENADA MAMA

Dear Gabacha: You can try, but good luck. Article 30, section B, paragraph *dos* of the Mexican Constitution and articles 17, 19, and 20 (paragraph I) of the Law of Nationality state that people can automatically qualify to become a Mexican citizen if their children were born in Mexico, if they're a Spaniard or a citizen of another Latin American nation, or if they're descended from someone who was born in Mexico. Don't fall under any of those categories, gabachos? Then live in Mexico continuously for five years and keep proof of it. No proof? Easy—bribe the immigration officials with some American *dinero*. After that, fill out a form, take some pictures, pay a fee, and turn in your American passport. Then wait a couple of months—but again, money goes a long way in Mexico, so fork over another *mordida* (literally, "bite," but signifying bribe in Mexican Spanish). Finally, renounce your previous citizenship. Congratulations—you're now a Mexican! But now comes the hard part—living in Mexico. Soon enough, you'll follow your new *paisanos* and head toward the border in the hope of a better life in *los Estados Unidos.*

What punishment could America give that would *finally* make crossing America's borders—repeatedly—unpalatable to Mexicans?

MAKE THEM STOP

Dear Gabacho: Easy. Show them all the Mexicans that already live in the United States and the mess they've made. Then they'll just wave *hola* to us on the way to Canada.

Why do some illegal immigrants bring their *familias* over but others leave them in Mexico? What are the advantages/disadvantages of each option?

ESPOSA NOSWIMO

Dear Gabacho: Have you tried sneaking your family across the border, Esposa Noswimo? Paid a coyote a minimum $6,000 per head? Fretted for days as they crossed *la frontera* stuffed in trunks or walking through deserts? And you have no way to know if your beloveds are alive until they show up at your door, exhausted? Then you have to take care of them on your illegal-immigrant salary? Makes leaving them back in Mexico easy, *¿qué no?* Nevertheless, a surprisingly large number of Mexicans do bring them. "Because unauthorized migration is driven primarily by the search for better wages," writes Jeffrey S. Passel in a 2006 Pew Hispanic Center study, "the undocumented migrant is commonly thought of as a young, male worker usually unaccompanied by a wife or children. In fact, the full portrait of the unauthorized migrant population is more varied." His report found single men and women account for only 3.1 million of the estimated 12 million illegal immigrants in the United States; by contrast, there are 6.6 million families where either spouse is undocumented. The obvious advantage in bringing over families is that they're—and say the following as if you're Edward James Olmos, *por favor—familia,* the spring from which Mexicans draw their strength and salsa. But some Mexicans don't want that. Part of the attraction of *el Norte* is the *absence* of family. Some Mexicans *want* to strike out on their own, leave home and family, and talk with the kids, spouses, and parents only during funerals or to bail them out of debt. Some Mexicans want to become Americans.

When can we expect Mexico to *officially* declare war on America?
MINUTEMAN MOLLIE

Dear Gabacha: Since when has the United States needed an official declaration of war to wage battle against a sovereign nation? It didn't happen in Vietnam, it didn't happen in Iraq, it definitely didn't happen in the various Indian nations we vanquished, and it sure as hell doesn't need to happen in Mexico. Besides, we've waged war against Mexico numerous times and lost. We took over half of Mexico during the 1846 Mexican-American War, only to allow Mexicans there to remain and sow the seeds of our eventual destruction. President Clinton and other free marketeers pushed the North American Free Trade Agreement forward, and millions of Mexicans lost their livelihoods and trekked to the United States in search of a better life. If we were to invade Mexico, we'd be faced with a reconstruction project that would make Iraq seem like a walk in the park. So be careful what you wish for: you just might get Mexico.

On the Mexican Government's Official "How to Sneak into the United States" Booklet; i.e., "Border Hopping for Dummies"

The Mexican government has never succeeded in anything except promoting Cantinflas and starving its citizens, so what makes people think it'll ever be different?

Consider its most literary solution to relieve Mexico's third-world conditions: getting Mexicans the hell out of Mexico. In late December of 2004, it began printing copies of *Guía del Migrante Mexicano* (Guide for the Mexican Immigrant), a thirty-four-page color booklet that advises Mexicans thinking of getting the hell out of their country on the best ways to do it.

The Mexican government has distributed millions of free copies to aspiring border hoppers in hopes it'll keep them from dying while they try to enter the United States. But anti-immigration advocates stateside charge that the publication is little more than a how-to manual and invitation to enter this country illegally, a claim Mexican officials deny.

"Unfortunately, immigration is a phenomenon that exists. We are not inviting or aiding that," a spokesperson for the Mexican consulate in Chicago told the *Chicago Tribune* around the time of the pamphlet's publication. "But the people who do desire to come here need to take certain precautions. Fundamentally, the protection of their lives—that's what drives this book."

The Mexican government should drop the charade. *Guía del Migrante Mexicano* is an invasion blueprint, pure and simple. And it does a terrible job of it.

Stylistically, *Guía del Migrante Mexicano* references the great comic-book tradition of Mexico. The cover of the booklet, a group of Mexicans looking in awe at the Mexican tricolor flapping outside a consulate, suggests the heroic masses of a Rivera mural. Inside the book, the illustrations are similarly bold. Men are muscled, mustachioed, or in jeans. Pasty Americans tower over cowering Mexicans. Nearly all the women featured are Russ Meyer fantasies, big-breasted with thick asses—we especially love the drawing of the fake-blond gabacha in the purple cat suit looming over a migrant on page 18. *¡Caliente!*

But as a survival guide for Mexicans seeking a better life in *el Norte,* *Guía del Migrante Mexicano* fails miserably. Most of the advice meted out is laughably apparent. One passage tells readers who plan to cross rivers that "thick clothes increase your weight when it gets wet and makes it more difficult to swim or float." Another warns, "If you cross [the border] by desert, try to walk in hours when the heat is not so intense." Really? Frankly, anybody who approaches the border and doesn't already know this deserves to be sent back by *la migra.*

Prospective Mexican migrants don't get any tips on how to successfully make it across *la frontera*—no phone numbers of reliable human smugglers, no locations of water stations in the desert, no fake passport and driver's license included to expedite the process. In fact, *Guía del Migrante Mexicano* denounces the things that might actually help illegals sneak into *los Estados Unidos.* It stresses that migrants should not assume false identities if caught by American authorities, since using a false ID "is a federal offense in the United States, for which you can be criminally processed and end up in jail" (as if the same weren't true for crossing illegally in the first place). Instead of resisting the unscrupulous Border Patrol, the handbook suggests that those captured should not resist and "be deported to Mexico." And the last ten pages of the pamphlet concentrates on what to do once the reader makes it across—mainly to "avoid noisy parties" and not sock their spouses.

Rest easy, Mr. and Mrs. Real American, any Mexican using *Guía del Migrante Mexicano* to cross the border won't get farther than El Paso.

Illegal Immigrants versus College Students: Who Has It Better?

For years, only coffin dodgers vented to newspapers that illegal immigrants posed the most ominous threat to the United States since the Irish. But if the growing number of college students rallying against illegals is any indication, it now seems college students also want in on the illegal-immigrant bashing.

We don't blame the undergrads for their zealotry—after all, college students only *wish* they had the same great lifestyle as illegal immigrants, a segment of the country that shares striking similarities to college students when it comes to housing, love for government financial aid, and propensity for travel. Consider:

- College students pay thousands of dollars to study abroad as a way to experience a new country and learn how to live away from home. But illegal immigrants are on permanent study-abroad programs—and they don't even have to wait in long attendance-office lines.

- College students frequently take weekend excursions but end up paying too much money for the right to get drunk under the stars alongside thousands of fellow inebriated scholars. Illegal immigrants never face such problems on their journeys—they're usually crossing through areas off-limits to the general American public. Plus, illegal immigrants don't pay thousands of dollars up front for the journey the way college students have to—they get to pay it off over decades.

- Many colleges still don't allow female and male students to share the same dorm room, prompting a mass exodus from campus housing once students enter their junior and senior years. Illegal immigrants get that benefit right from the start, frequently sharing apartments with men and women of different backgrounds and ages, usually four or five to a room. Talk about sexy hijinks!

- College students frequently complain about hard-ass RAs or campus security interrupting their fun. But other than their version of RAs—*la migra*—illegal immigrants have no such worries. Cops are so worried about offending immigrant activists if they deport individuals—which is a federal, not local, responsibility, after all—they generally leave illegal immigrants be.

So why the moaning about government aid for illegal immigrants who want to enter college, collegians? Ever heard of in-state tuition and FAFSA? The recent passage of state bills allowing illegal immigrants wishing to attend college to apply for aid merely puts them on the same financial footing as hundreds of thousands of other college students.

If you kids with your blue books and your toga parties and your Hacky Sacks really want to go after a group that's subsidized even more than you, we've got one word for you: corporations.

Live Like an Illegal Immigrant! Secrets of the Good Life from the Undocumented

You've been laid off from your expense-account job, and that dream of a split-level with an ocean view has suddenly been reduced to a duplex in the ghetto. The economy is tanking, your high-tech stock is squat, and career options now consist of daily Monster.com hits and calling about that greeter position at Wal-Mart.

When things were good, you read *Fast Company* and *Wired* and looked to people like Sumner Redstone and Jack Welch for guidance; you paid hundreds of dollars to sit in all-day "Winners!" seminars or $35 for poorly ghostwritten how-to-be-rich-and-successful books filled with big pictures, big type, and big promises of a good life that now seems far out of your reach. . . . Or is it?

Lemme ask you: Would you like a brand-new car? How about free child care? Care to party hearty every weekend or have people better looking than you fighting to take you out? Of course you would. But how, you ask, is it all possible?

Well, what if I told you that the good life is not only attainable but also being lived by millions of residents *right now*. What's more, *they're* willing to share *their* secrets of success *for free*.

Welcome to the world of the Mexican undocumented!

"Huh," you say. "You mean illegal immigrants? Why, they're just those stooped farmworkers and quiet old ladies who mop my bathroom floor."

Yes, but what if I told you that farmworker is the treasurer of his hometown benefit association, aggressively negotiating between the Mexican and American governments? Or that the maid tends an organic garden that produces enough to feed her family? What if I told you that undocumented workers get more for their food, clothing, and entertainment dollar and live in the kind of tight-knit communities that are the envy of master planners everywhere?

You see, insurmountable odds have a way of bringing out the best in humans. And it is the poorest of the poor—12 million of whom are illegal immigrants living in the United States—who not only survive in tough times, but also thrive.

It's about sticking together, looking out for one another, seeing one another—as another member of the Joad clan put it—as part of one big soul.

The good news: you don't have to evade *la migra* to live the fabulous life of an undocumented worker.

Here are the secrets of current and former illegal immigrants living the good life with little or no money. Just follow this easy three-step program and live the life you've only dreamed about. Just promise us the next time you see one of your mentors mowing your lawn or cleaning your bathroom, you'll stop and say *gracias*.

Step One: Getting Back on Your Feet

Food

There was a time when you considered it slumming to eat anywhere that didn't have finger bowls and warm towels. Now you're eyeing Dumpsters like hot-food trays in a smorgasbord. Does it have to be like this? No. Consider Irma. When her husband was deported a couple of years ago back to their native El Salvador, she had to make the family's already meager cash stretch even further.

"I couldn't even afford to go shopping for food at places like Northgate or La Rioja," she says, referring to Mexican supermarkets in Southern California that offer produce at vastly reduced prices.

Rather than approach the government or a social-service agency for assistance—and risk joining her husband in a San Salvador barrio—she scraped along on food donated by friends and family. Then, one day while shopping at a swap meet, Irma discovered a stand that sold supermarket food.

"There was everything: tortillas, diapers, granola bars," she recalls with wonder. "And the prices fit into my budget perfectly."

The prices would fit your current budget, too: 50¢ for a box of Lucky Charms, $1 for ten cans of corn. "I think the food was stolen from grocery stores, or something must have been wrong with it, because the canned foods were always bent out of shape and packages that were supposed to be sealed were open," she says. "But the food was good; we never got sick because of it."

But if even cents on the dollar for your sustenance is too much, you might consider growing your own food.

"It's hard to grow crops because houses here in the States don't have much open space," says Julia, whose backyard is filled with delicious corn, sugarcane, and cactus. "But it's better to grow your own food than to spend a bunch of money buying stuff that's covered in chemicals anyway."

You won't be limited to what you grow; Julia and her friends do almost no shopping by trading one another for the products that each grows. "One of my friends even raises chicken for our group," she says. "And we get our beef and milk from another friend in Riverside [California]."

Lesson: Food is life, and a successful life requires a good deal of risk. Embrace that risk, swallow it whole—as long as it has no obvious signs of taint. Also, it couldn't hurt to have a Riverside meat connection.

Shelter

The houses you once plotted after are now far beyond your price range; you'll be lucky to score an apartment these days. Moving in with your parents is not an option, and your friends are in the same financial straits as you. Time to start working the hometown-roots angle, as countless illegal immigrants have done over the years. Mario first lived in a two-bedroom apartment along with sixteen other people.

"Since I was from the same [Mexican community] as the owner of the apartment, I got to sleep on a couch by myself while everyone else slept on the floor."

He also got a discount: $100 per month as opposed to the $150 everyone else had to pay. But sharing cramped quarters—which were constantly visited by police responding to neighbor complaints—was a necessary nightmare.

"There was no privacy. I'd be eating my food, and right next to me would be a girl changing the diaper of her baby brother with the shit making me want to puke. And don't even get me started on how many times I was awakened by couples moaning during sex."

After finding a better job—he started as a *jornalero* (day laborer)— Mario now pays $200 per month along with four other men to live in a one-bedroom apartment in the backyard of a home owned by a family from Mario's *rancho*. "It's still cramped," he says, "but I get my own bed this time."

Lesson: Most Americans think of family as merely nuclear—mom, dad, siblings. When it comes to emergency housing, you've got to go post-nuclear.

Health

Lost your job and health insurance? Welcome to *my* world. When my mom was laid off in 1997, we had to plug into the same medical system that my father (who was an illegal immigrant until the 1986 amnesty) had used for years: the *curandero* and *sobadora* industry. Learned in the forgotten art of offering medical services at a cheap rate, these men and women will treat what ails you using a combination of folk remedies and Catholic and indigenous chants—not to mention pre-owned underwear for a sore neck.

If you insist on licensed doctors, take the trip to Tijuana's clinics. The border town's doctors can cure anything, even if it's not their specialty. Seek out the services of Dr. Emilio Vargas Huerta, a proctologist who removed tumors from my mother's breast, my father's stomach, and my cheek and has been attending to the needs of many illegal residents for the past fifteen years.

Lesson: Health is a state of mind. Baja is a state of Mexico. Tell Dr. Huerta that Lorenzo Arellano sent you.

Employment

As in any business, knowing someone is the best way to find work in the world of the illegal. Roberto got his first job at a carpet factory in 1979 from his cousin's friend.

"The guy was real close to the owner, who was always looking for new workers. Pretty soon, the owner promoted me to supervisor despite the fact I had no papers."

But he was let go after injuring his back, and because he was still undocumented, he was unable to collect workers' compensation or get sick leave. Later, Roberto got a job at another factory and became a citizen. Now he recruits for that firm by hiring recent arrivals from his *rancho* in Michoacán.

"Everyone in my *rancho* knows that if they need work, I'll give it to them," Roberto said. "You should always help the people from your town."

Use your own connections to try to find work. If you have none, street corners with equally friendless *jornaleros* await you.

Lesson: In life, it's not what you know or even whom you know but that you know people who appreciate what you know.

Step Two: Taking Control

Child Care

After years of seeing your children only when the nanny had major surgery in Tijuana, you're now stuck with raising them yourself, something for which you're completely unprepared. What's worse, you've just gotten a job by going through a friend—but can't afford a day-care center. Your parents wouldn't take the kids off your hands if your life depended on it, which it does. What will you do?

Create a *comadre* network, a method of raising children used by many Latino families for decades. Here's how it works: any stay-at-home female remotely related to you takes care of your child. This produces child care from someone you not only trust but who will also fatten your kid with homemade food and isn't afraid to discipline.

"Why should I let strangers take care of my kids when *mis comadres* can take care of them?" says Alicia. She drops off her children at six every morning with her sister-in-law before heading to her factory job. "A day-care center won't raise my kids right because they won't discipline them. But I can rest easy knowing that [my sister-in-law] will slap my son if he's *malcriado* [bad-mannered]."

The cost?

"I always try to give her at least fifty dollars, but she always refuses," Alicia says.

Lesson: It takes a village—and a short-tempered relation.

Wheels

The love of huge gas-guzzlers is not unique to you and your kind. You share it with your average illegal immigrant. For reasons known only to cultural anthropologists (status anxiety) and Freudian psychologists (compensation), many undocumented young men save their cash diligently over the years only to splurge on a *troca del año* (brand-new truck) or SUV. These illegal immigrants have been influenced by the SUV-driving elite in the belief that image is everything.

"Look, I work my ass off all week and have to share a bed with another man who I don't even like at night," says Jorge, a twenty-six-year-old native of Zacatecas who owns a 2001 Dodge Ram with a ten-CD changer. "So if I'm going to be suffering up here, at least when I go back home [to Mexico] or if I go to parties during the weekend, I'll have something to show off."

To save money to pay for the truck, Jorge works two nearly full-time jobs in addition to weekends cutting grass and cleaning pools. After saving diligently over five years, Jorge put down $15,000 to buy the truck (a friend with papers had to buy it for him) and now guards it zealously.

"I have no insurance, not even a driver's license," he says. "If a cop ever stops me, my truck is screwed."

Lesson: The most important thing in life is . . . a ten-CD changer?! Sweeeeeet!

Banking

You can't even afford the $2 ATM fee to access your life savings, and your IRA is down the drain. Do what illegal immigrants have done for years: buy tomato cans. You see, until Wells Fargo recently changed its policy, illegal immigrants were unable to open bank accounts, so . . .

"We couldn't save our money at a bank, but we had to keep it somewhere safe," says Angela. "So I'd get an empty can, and slit a small hole in it. I'd leave it with the rest of the food so if anyone robbed our house, they wouldn't even know all that money was there."

After years of making weekly deposits of $50 with every check, she and her husband saved a sizable nest egg. "We were able to pay our daughter's entire quinceañera with it" (about $9,000).

Lesson: Remember all that money you lost on Enron stock? You were investing in something called "electricity futures." At least a tomato can is something that won't tank.

Politics

Take a cue from illegal immigrants, whose political policy is extraordinarily libertarian.

"I don't care for the politics of this country because they're going to screw over everyone somehow, regardless of the party or immigrant status," says Benjamín, a forty-six-year-old native of Michoacán.

What have Benjamín and countless other individuals done to improve their lives in this country and the motherland? Prove to the Mexican and American governments that they are indispensable to the well-being of both nations. The governments need *them,* not the other way around.

Benjamín is an active member of his *rancho*'s benefit association, holding quarterly dances to raise funds for the tiny hamlet's modest infrastructural needs. The rest of the time, he washes dishes in a hotel, a member of the silent service-sector economy that keeps this nation rolling and is addicted to illegal immigrants.

"Both countries need us, even if they hate to admit it," Benjamín says with a hint of bitterness. He's right. Because of hometown associations like the one to which Benjamín belongs, Mexican politicians actively court the Mexican-immigrant vote. And before September 11, President George W. Bush openly talked of granting amnesty to the United States' most invaluable workers.

All this attention paid to people who don't truly belong to either country? Meanwhile, *your* member of Congress won't give you the time of day.

Lesson: "Show your government that it is unnecessary, and take care of yourself," Benjamín says. "Then they'll come back to you like the pendejos *they are."*

Step Three: Having It All

Fashion/Music

"I almost never shop at malls for clothes," boasts María. Instead, she frequents weekend yard sales and swap meets for many-times-used-but-still-wearable clothes for her family; an entire week's wardrobe can be bought here for less than $50. "If I really want to get fancy, I'll go to *la segunda* [thrift stores]," she says.

Don't wince in disgust at the prospect of buying already-worn clothes; María says you'd be surprised at what you can find. "One time, I was looking for clothes for my kids and found a beautiful dress that cost me twenty dollars. I thought it was expensive at the time, but when I wore it to a party, my daughter's friend saw it and said that she saw the exact same dress for several hundred dollars up in Beverly Hills!"

Like María, Lucas has only disdain for those who pay retail.

"Anyone who buys CDs or stereos from big stores deserves to be ripped off for their stupidity," says Lucas. He's a part-time DJ who got all his equipment and most of his five-hundred-plus CD collection from years of haggling with vendors at swap meets.

"They're always going to tell you that they can't go any lower on their prices," he says. "The vendors are always lying."

His advice for bargaining: "Give them a price, and when they refuse it, say forget it and leave. Come back later in the day—like in the afternoon, before they leave—and ask them if they've sold it yet. Most likely, they'll say no. Then tell them that you'll buy it, but only if they reduce the price to what you originally offered. They'll be so desperate to sell by then you'll have a good bargain."

Lesson: Cash will always be the most fashionable accessory.

Social Life

Ricardo's life consists of five days of strenuous labor, and weekends jam-packed with parties.

"There's always more than four parties I can go to any Saturday," he says. Ricardo has merely plugged into his *rancho*'s network of celebrations. "If it's not a wedding, then it's a baptism, quinceañera, a birthday party. Regardless, there's always great food and live music for dancing. Best of all, it's free!"

Of course, there comes a time in every person's life when he tires of parties and thinks about settling down. Joaquín was a loser with the ladies; he didn't have a car to pick them up or a place of his own, and the rigors of working sixty hours per week as an auto mechanic left him exhausted by Friday night.

"I still wanted a wife or at least someone to spend some time with," he says. Forgoing the women already here in the States ("They're too crazy for me," he says), Joaquín went back to his *rancho* in Guanajuato about five years ago and married a seventeen-year-old girl (he was twenty-four at the time). Their honeymoon: a trip back to *el Norte* with ten other immigrants crammed in a van that slipped unnoticed past *la migra*.

"Down there, there are no guys left, and all the girls are dying to get out of the *rancho*," Joaquín says. "They'll marry anyone, even an ugly guy like me, as long as it means moving to the United States."

Lesson: The most important thing in love is . . . a seventeen-year-old girl?! Sweeeeeet!

Going Out

"I try not to go out," says Susana. "I'm an illegal immigrant."

5

Music

Morrissey, Melodicas, and Ay Yi Yi Yis

Dear Mexican: I could've sworn I heard somewhere that the song "La Cucaracha" was originally about Pancho Villa's soldiers, and the lyrics had to do with them not being able to march without marijuana. I totally forgot where I heard it, man, but I also heard something about the U.S. cavalry tracking the troops, and how they would find joint butts strewn across the trail. Is this why gabachos from Hawaii to Ireland to Thailand refer to the end of a joint as a roach?

ALTO EN VIDA

Dear Gabacho: Next to "The Mexican Hat Dance" and "Livin' la Vida Loca," America's favorite Mexican song is "La Cucaracha." Even Carl Sandburg was a fan of the cockroach-citing ditty—the famed poet included it in his 1927 collection of folk tunes, *The American Songbag*. Sandburg wrote that he first heard it in 1916 in Chicago from two reporters who had covered the Mexican Revolution and "had eaten frijoles with Villa and slept under Pancho's poncho." Sandburg included eight stanzas of "La Cucaracha" in *The American Songbag*, but there are hundreds of variations. "'La Cucaracha' is the Spanish equivalent of 'Yankee Doodle'—a traditional satirical tune periodically fitted out with new lyrics to meet the needs of the moment," noted Cecil Adams, author of the syndicated column *The Straight Dope*, in his 2001 take on the song's meaning. Indeed, "La Cucaracha" is one of the oldest songs in Hispanic culture. There are lyrics that ridicule Pancho Villa, the French occupation of Mexico, the Carlist Wars of the mid–nineteenth century, even the Moors ("From the skin of the Moorish king / I have to make a sofa / So the Spanish captain / Can sit in it" goes one such version—and you think Europe hates Muslims today!). I'd never heard the "Cucaracha"/roach theory until you mentioned it, High on Life, but it wouldn't be the first time gabachos had appropriated Mexican culture to describe their sinful acts—"Dirty Sánchez," anyone?

I called the local sports arena for some tickets, and a teller said there's some kind of Mexican music awards show soon, hosted by a radio station. I thought the only types of Mexican music were mariachi and Los Lobos—is there more? And how the hell did Mexicans snag a spot at such a big arena? Are they sweeping it for a month afterward?

EARNEST LIBERAL

Dear Gabacho: Switch your radio dial off National Public Radio and hear the reality: Spanish-language radio *is* modern radio—has been since about a decade ago, when such stations first began topping the Southern California Arbitron ratings. And no station is as influential as KBUE-FM 105.5/94.3, the Los Angeles station better known as Que Buena (So Good). For the past four years, the Premios Que Buena awards show has highlighted the best Mexican regional musicians in various genres. And, yes, Earnest, there are more styles of Mexican regional music—execs created the catchall term *Mexican regional* to describe the music your car washer and nanny dance to every Saturday night—than rakes in your gardener's closet.

Que Buena usually honors the best acts in the following categories:

Norteño: The accordion-based mestizo polkas native to northern Mexico with a metronomic bass beat. *Norteño* musicians usually wear *tejanas* and frilly cowboy outfits that look like a combination of Jon Voight's character in *Midnight Cowboy* and Liberace.

Banda sinaloense: Ever drive through your local barrio only to hear what sounds like a Bavarian oompah band blasting from a Silverado driven by a cholo? That's *banda sinaloense,* a brass-band style replete with clarinets, trumpets, a massive drum, farting tuba, and even a French horn. Huge cast of musicians—usually eighteen members—that needs no amplification, even in a cavernous amphitheater: the rumble a full *banda* produces could disintegrate your spleen like nothing since Sunn O))).

Duranguense: Like *banda,* but faster and featuring a strange fascination with synthesizers and *mucho* use of the melodica wind keyboard. Refers to the central Mexican state of Durango but first became popular in Chicago (yes, Earnest: Mexicans live in Chicago. Even Alaska!). *Duranguenze* is the *reggaetón* of Mexican regional: wildly popular, incredibly annoying, and as addicting as mescal but without the little worm at the end.

Tierra caliente: Historically used to describe the Afro-Mexican rhythms of the southern Mexican state of Guerrero. Nowadays just another *banda* rip-off, this one is spruced up with harps, echo, and organs even chintzier than the ones pounded on in *duranguenze* music. The lamest Mexican music since the Frito Bandito theme song.

De la sierra: Related to bluegrass in that it's reliant upon nasal-voiced hicks backed by acoustic guitars, bass, drum kit, and the occasional fiddle for songs about murder, drugs, and murder. And murder!

Soloista: No Spanish translation needed. Just a guy or girl backed by any kind of regional Mexican music. While all the nominees in the Best Male Solo Artist category are *puro mexicanos,* perennial nominees on the female side include spicy señoritas Yolanda Pérez and Jenni Rivera, who are as American as a pastrami burrito.

Dueto: See? Spanish isn't that different from English—just knock off all those damn ending vowels.

And don't think the Premios Que Buena covers *all* Mexican regional music, Earnie. There are some genres too regional even for Que Buena. Take *son jarocho,* the twinkling, pounding, improvised music native to the Caribbean coastal state of Veracruz. Or the marimba music of Chiapas. Or Aztec conch jams. Or mariachi. Goes to show Mexicans can hate wetbacks as much as whites do.

I am a *güero* who considers himself fairly knowledgeable about Mexican culture, but there is one mystery that still eludes me: why does some Mexican music sound just like polka? What is it that Mexicans love about those wheezing accordions and that redundant "oompah-pah" rhythm? Is there some historical connection between beaners and Polacks? Also, since polka-type music has deep roots in both European and Mexican cultures, do you think gringos and Latinos could smooth over racial tensions with a giant Polka-palooza?

Tu Cuñado

Dear Gabacho: Few traits of the Mexican race perplex gabachos more than our love of Bavarian-style *banda sinaloense* brass bands and accordion-based *conjunto norteño* polkas. It's a question the Mexican gets all the *tiempo.* Faithful reader Whipped Beaners & Other Delights claims "that fucking German oompah music you guys listen to" is proof Mexicans "like Nazis," while Annoyed Citizen wonders why "Mexican hillbillies" love "that stupid polka music." But the answer *no es* that complicated: both *banda sinaloense* and *conjunto norteño* are testaments to what Americans lionize as the melting

pot but Mexicans know as *la raza cósmica*—the cosmic race. *Banda sinaloense* dates to the late 1800s, when Germans migrated to central Mexico and supposedly hired kids to play the oompah music of the Deutschland. *Conjunto norteño* also originated during this time in northern Mexico, thanks to the accordion-obsessed colonies of Czechs, Poles, and other Slavs who lived in that region.

So what's with the bewilderment and sneers whenever I blast Banda El Recodo as I cruise through a ritzy, *retre*-gabacho neighborhood? It's a misunderstanding: gabachos don't get that Mexicans keep the culture of ethnic white America alive with our happy mestizo polkas, mazurkas, and waltzes. We'd love to hold a Polka-palooza with *ustedes,* Cuñado, but the only gabachos who would show up are the octogenarian fans of *The Lawrence Welk Show.* And then they would call us wabs.

Do you know the name of the Mexican song that goes "Ay yi yi yi, ay yi yi yi yi"? I think it's a really famous *ranchera* song. I'm sure it doesn't come across quite so clear in the e-mail as it does when I belt it out.

Ya Llegó la Caderona

Dear Big-Hipped Gabacha: You mean every *ranchera* song? The song you're specifically referencing is "Cielito Lindo," which means "Beautiful Little Heaven," but gabachos know it better in its bastardized form as "The Frito Bandito Song." But you also reference one of the defining characteristics of *ranchera* music—songs of lament traditionally backed with mariachi—by typing out a glorious *ronca:* the shriek or soulful stream of consciousness a singer lets out during a song's emotional climax. Some of the more famous ones include Javier Solis's "¡QUE-A!," Pedro Infante's "¡AAAAAAAAAAAAAHAHAHA!," and Vicente Fernández's immortal "¡A-ha-ha-hai!" I'm sure it doesn't come across quite so clear in this column as it does when hombres belt the *roncas* out, Caderona, but they kind of confirm that stereotype about Mexican men being inarticulate, drunken divas, *¿verdad?*

"La Bamba": what is the song about?

MUSICAL MARAUDER

Dear Gabacho: Gabachos know only three Mexican songs: "The Frito Bandito Song," "La Cucaracha," and "La Bamba," first introduced to the United States by Los Angeles–area rocker Ritchie Valens (born Ricardo Valenzuela) in 1959, remade by Chicano punk icons The Plugz during the late 1970s, and repopularized in the 1980s thanks to a remake by East Los Angeles icons Los Lobos featured in a biopic of Valens. The song itself, however, is more than just the "Rapper's Delight" of Mexico; it's the crown jewel of *son jarocho,* the twinkly native music of the southern Mexican state of Veracruz characterized by small guitars, a consistent rhythm, and endless improvisations off the same rhythm. Like "La Cucaracha," "La Bamba" has thousands of lyrics, everything from "Yo no soy marinero / Soy capitán" (I'm not a sailor / I'm a captain) to "Para llegar al cielo / Se necesita una escalera larga" (To reach heaven / You need a tall ladder). Some historians claim it refers to a siege of the port city during the seventeenth century as well; some historians are better off teaching at community colleges. "La Bamba" is a sponge that's absorbed various lyrics throughout history, leaving us a strange, eminently danceable track that all Mexicans hate.

The other day, I switched through the Spanish-language station and I swear I heard a song that was a remake of an English song. Jeez—do Mexicans also rip off musicians along with the American taxpayer?

FURIOUS ELISE

Dear Gabacha: Ripping off American songs is a proud Mexican music tradition that dates to the time mariachi groups turned "Beer Barrel Polka" into "Los Barrillitos" (The Little Barrels). While that cover quickly became part of the Latin American songbook, tortured covers litter the highway of Mexican music history. The following are some of the more gruesome:

"La Noche que Chicago se Murio"

Cover of: Paper Lace's "The Night Chicago Died." **Artist:** Banda Toro. **Results:** Recorded at the height of the early nineties *quebradita* dance craze, this song continues to mystify musical scholars. How did a bunch of Mexicans come across this 1970s schlock? What motivated them to record it, lyrics intact, as a bouncy *banda* tune? And why is this song now more difficult to find on record than a bribe-free Tijuana cop? Disturbing footnote: Banda Toro also recorded a version of "Kung Fu Fighting," the ultimate case for shutting down the U.S.-Mexican border.

"Cosas"

Cover of: Bobby Darin's "Things." **Artist:** Los Bravos del Norte. **Results:** Darin's nostalgic weep turned into a gleeful two-step thanks to the infectious accordion of Los Bravos front man and *conjunto norteño* icon Ramón Ayala. But don't blame Ayala for the inappropriately happy tone of "Cosas"—the man could read "The Hollow Land" and get people to dance an all-night polka.

"La Plaga"

Remake of: Little Richard's "Good Golly, Miss Molly." **Artist:** Alejandra Guzmán. **Results:** "La Plaga" was originally recorded by the Mexican rock band Los Teen Tops during the fifties. That cover roared; the version by Alejandra Guzmán on her 1989 debut tried to match the fevered shrieks and sexuality of the Little Richard original but instead came off as the studio-produced faux rebel yell it was.

"Esta Luz Nunca Se Apagará"

Cover of: The Smiths' "There Is a Light That Never Goes Out." **Artist:** Mikel Erentxun. **Results:** Mexican *rockeros* have recorded great covers of gems such as Tijuana No!'s remake of "Spanish Bombs" or Los Abandoned's punky take on Selena's "Como la Flor." "Esta Luz," though, isn't one of them—an even whinier vow of romantic death, and without the double-decker bus! The honorary Mexican (Erentxun is Spanish) also sings a so-so "Everyday Is Like Sunday" in concert, primarily to please Morrissey: the Mancunian is known to frequent Erentxun's stateside shows.

"Angel Baby"

Cover of: Rosie and the Originals' "Angel Baby." **Artist:** Jenni Rivera. **Results:** We love the Long Beach, California, native when she's singing about courageous women who kick machismo in the *huevos.* We don't like Rivera when she butchers the "Ave Maria" of Chicanos by replacing the original's out-of-tune guitar with a burping tuba. But at least she didn't attempt a bilingual "I Think You've Got Your Fools Mixed Up"—that honor goes to Jessie Morales.

"Funky Band"

Cover of: Lipps Inc.'s "Funkytown." **Artist:** Banda los Lagos. **Results:** This midnineties track was recorded by various techno-*bandas,* the movement that fused traditional central Mexican brass bands with synthesizers and sequined suits. All versions kept the shuffling rhythm but chucked the vaguely sexual lyrics in favor of praising the writhing, Stetson-twirling dance form known as *quebradita.* Instead of the high-pitched "Won't you take me to / Funkytown!" we heard a man squeal "¡A todos bailar / La quebradita!"

"Tú y Yo"

Cover of: Shania Twain's "You're Still the One." **Artist:** Rogelio Martínez. **Results:** Martínez kept the gentle sway and wussy chorals of Twain's effort but added a new title (You and I), wussier lyrics, and a clarinet-heavy *banda* backbeat. Now a staple at many quinceañeras, the popularity of "Tú y Yo"—like that of the other examples—proves that moving to *los Estados Unidos* doesn't necessarily make Mexicans smarter.

10 Greatest Gabacho Mexican-Bashing Songs Ever!

The Kingston Trio, "Coplas"

There's really no rationale to this *arriba-arriba* recording, first performed by folkie pioneers the Kingston Trio in 1959. A Mexican peon asks an American in English and Spanish if he should pick green peppers and warns travelers to "not muddy the waters" since the town drinks from it. The song ends with a sleepless groom bemoaning that he spent "the whole night chasing a cat that had come in over the balcony." Yeah, we think they're referring to a different kind of pussy, *también*.

Loco lyric: "Ah, so! You are surprised I speak your language / You see, I was educated in your country / At UCRA."

Various artists, "Little Latin Lupe Lu"

A groovy garage growl covered by groups ranging from Mitch Ryder & the Detroit Wheels to the Kingsmen to even Bruce Springsteen. Locally, the Righteous Brothers went platinum with their 1963 version of it. While "Little Latin Lupe Lu" isn't inherently offensive—a guy boasts that his Mexican girlfriend is the best dancer around—the Righteous Brothers' rendition becomes suspect when you consider that the late Bobby Hatfield never visited his alma mater, Anaheim High School, in his later years—maybe because too many Mexicans such as myself—attended the school?

Loco lyric: "She's the best for miles around / She's my pretty little baby / Whoa—little Latin Lupe Lu."

Pat Boone, "Speedy Gonzáles"

With this 1963 novelty recording, Boone proved that blacks weren't the only minorities from which he could profit. Here, the King of Honky R&B assumes the identity of an American tourist who "walked alone past some old adobe haciendas" during "a moonlight night in old Mexico." Boone made no reference to the Warner Bros. cartoon star of the same name, but he did reference the mouse's refried take on life in spinning a yarn about a philandering, lazy, drunken Mexican man and his long-suffering wife.

Loco lyric: "Hey, Rosita, come quick / Down at the cantina, they're giving green stamps with tequila."

Jay & the Americans, "Come a Little Bit Closer"

Name the Mexican stereotype, this 1964 release lauds it—in the first stanza. Roy Orbison pretender Jay Black praises the American playground that is Tijuana ("In a little café just the other side of the border") and its hootchy-kootchy mamas ("She was just sitting there, giving me looks that make my mouth water"), while warning virile white bucks of macho men named José. When José challenges Jay to a duel, Jay runs away like a Mexican man from a condom. When the spicy señorita coos to José that she wants him to come a little bit closer, she confirms what gabachos have always known about Mexican women: they're nondiscriminatory whores . . . but nice.

Loco lyric: You mean you want more? Call your local oldies station—they spin the track about every *pinche* hour.

Frito-Lay, "The Frito Bandito Song"

Before there was the Taco Bell Chihuahua, there was the Frito Bandito, a crudely drawn Mexican that was little more than a sombrero, mustache, gold tooth, and bandolier. While the image itself enraged many Chicanos during the character's late-1960s introduction, what was probably more infuriating to them was the Bandito's trademark song— sung by Mel Blanc in heavily accented English to the tune of the mariachi standard "Cielito Lindo." The Frito-Lay Corp. vowed to use the character forever, but the Bandito mysteriously disappeared after 1971. Perhaps it was because television stations across the country refused to run the ads out of disgust?

Loco lyric: "Ay-yi-yi-yi / I am the Frito Bandito / I love Frito's corn chips / I love them, I do / I love Frito's corn chips / I take them from you!"

John Wayne, "Mis Raíces Están Aquí"

You remember John Wayne: American icon, expensive airport. Now remember John Wayne, recording star. In 1973, Wayne released *America, Why I Love Her,* ten spoken-word paeans to Old Glory and its inhabitants that finds a wheezing Wayne railing against multiculturalism, Vietnam War opponents, and feminists. Worst of the selections is "Mis Raíces Están Aquí" (My Roots Are Here), on which Wayne recounts visiting a destitute "*viejo caballero*" in the Southwest. "For hundreds of years, people with the blood of the Aztecs in their veins have lived and died on that harsh yet beautiful land," Wayne wrote in the accompanying book, "and names like El Paso, Las Cruces, Alamogordo, Santa Fe, Del Rio, and Nogales are perpetual monuments to their being there." Wayne strangely doesn't mention how Mexican-mowing flicks such as *The Alamo, The Searchers,* and *The Undefeated* were *his* personal monuments to their being there.

Loco lyric: " 'I have nothing for you, señores,' he said. 'My hacienda's empty now / There was a time . . .' He shook his head and gave a gentle bow."

Cheech and Chong, "Mexican-American"

Before Cheech Marín became a darling of the LULAC (League of United Latin American Citizens) crowd, the San Francisco native was a high-out-of-his-gourd comedian reviled by Chicano yaktivists for cholo depictions of Chicano life in film and sound alongside the equally stoned Tommy Chong. The duo's blazing achievement remains "Mexican-American," an improvised Cheech tune that Chong rejoins in 1980's *Cheech and Chong's Next Movie* with the equally self-explanatory "Beaners"—a two-note guitar strangle consisting of the screamed proclamation "Beeeeeaners!"

Loco lyric: "Mexican-Americans don't like to get up early in the morning, but they have to, so they do it real slow / Mexican-Americans love education, so they go to night school and take Spanish and get a B."

Genesis, "Illegal Alien"

Chirpier than a canary, the video for "Illegal Alien"—with members of the prog-rock monsters wearing sombreros and mustaches that make pasty Phil Collins look like Mexican Revolutionary martyr Emiliano Zapata—was the impetus for white bands to dress like Mexicans for MTV fun à la Weezer. The 1983 song's repetitive chorus—"It's a-no fun being an illegal alien"—is the most obviously stupid lyrical observation since Toby Keith's "I'm a Big Redneck Piece of Shit."

Loco lyric: "Got out of bed, wasn't feeling too good / With my wallet and my passport, a new pair of shoes / The sun is shining, so I head for the park / With a bottle of tequila and a new pack of cigarettes."

The Doug Anthony All Stars, "Mexican Hitler"

Further proof that Australians should stick to wiping out Aborigines. In this case, the misinterpreting musicians were the Doug Anthony All Stars (DAAS), an Australian comedy troupe notorious during the early nineties for crafting neo-Nazi parodies. While employing hatred as a pedagogical device is exemplary, mixing metaphors isn't, and the Nazi mass exodus to South America after World War II that "Mexican Hitler" ostensibly attacks soon devolves into the Fourth Reich "eating nachos in the sun" and meeting "a knee-slapping señorita who worked for a peso on Salon Kitty." Wallabies, take advice from the punk band X: when fighting skinheads, don't become one.

Loco lyric: "When you're low, where can you go? / *Where to?* / Mexico!"

Cherry Poppin' Daddies, "Zoot Suit Riot"

Take the worst race riot in Mexican-American history and gut it of meaning. Out comes "Zoot Suit Riot," blurted by the neo-swing Cherry Poppin' Daddies during the midnineties big-band revival. It starts off promisingly enough, with excerpts of police sirens backing lead singer Steve Perry and an ominous, accurate description of the 1942 mini-war between pachucos and navy nitwits: "Who's that whisperin' in the trees? / It's two sailors, and they're on leave / Pipes and chains and swingin' hands." The Daddies soon leave the social commentary for faux–Gene Krupa cool—that their fan base didn't give a damn speaks more about the failure of the American educational system than any high school exit exam.

Loco lyric: "Now you sailors know / Where your women come for love."

Why do Mexicans think they are such a powerhouse of music when in reality they are nothing but mediocre in that department? The best artists who represent Latinos in the United States are usually Puerto Rican, Colombian, Cuban, or of any other nation, rarely Mexican, if any at all.

CUBAN CONNOISSEUR

Dear Gabacho: If you're going to tell me Latin music artistry is defined by wabs such as Gloria Estefan, Ricky Martin, and Jennifer Lopez, I'll call *la migra* on you. No non-Mexican Latino musician in the United States compares to the earning power of Mexican artists in the United States. People like *ranchera* icon Vicente Fernández, the Elton John–esque Juan Gabriel, and many others fill up venues like Madison Square Garden and its other stadium brothers and consistently top the Spanish-language *Billboard* charts. Mexican regional music—the polka-and-waltz racket your gardeners listen to—accounts for more than half of all Spanish-language sales in the country. But the guardians of Latino culture have decided that the most popular Latin music genre in the United States isn't worthy of promotion because it might lead people to believe that all Latinos are Mexican. Frankly, I don't blame them: statistics prove that Mexican regional's primary audience is recent immigrants with little money—53 percent of adults who prefer it did not complete high school, and most who like it make less than $25,000 a year, according to a 2002 report commissioned by Arbitron. Why would Latinos want to promote Mexican artists when we can instead feature Incubus at the Latin Grammys?

I remember going to Metallica concerts and there being as many gabachos as *mexicanos*. But I thought Mexicans only liked mariachi?

I AM IRON HOMBRE

Dear Gabacho: Many gabachos get surprised when Mexicans profess to like a music form that doesn't involve accordions, tubas, or men on horseback, but one of the few places where Mexicans and gabachos exist in peace is the mosh pit. *Metaleros* boast a long history in Mexico's urban regions, especially in Mexico City, which boasts its own unique genre: *rock urbano,* a bluesy fusion of metal with stadium rock. See, gabachos? Even Mexico creates generations of young, disaffected youth whose only solace is to listen to eardrum-splitting music and crash into their neighbor's pancreas. If only gabachos could show the same love with our less assimilated Mexicans—or rather, something beyond the mariachi-loving music videos for Weezer's "Island in the Sun"—then this immigration debate would slide off the American consciousness as quickly as *The O.C.*

What do Mexicans think of Beck? He smokes a lot of weed and says a lot of gibberish in Spanish, so you'd think they would like him. Anyway, I'm just asking because I'm making a mix CD for a hot Mexican girl. You know what's up.

O MI AMORE

Dear Gabacho: We hate him. Beck had a chance to redefine American usage of Mexican Spanish forever when the Silver Fake hipster decided to name his latest album after a Mexican-Spanish slang word for a white person. Beck could've been the hombre to teach the world the wonders of *gabacho*. But Beck instead named his latest release *Guero*. Sure, many Mexicans use the term to disparage white people, but it doesn't have the pinpoint ferocity of *gabacho*—*güero* technically means "fair-skinned" and is used to describe Americans as well as white-looking Mexicans. More important, though, Beck forgot to put the umlaut (the two dots that hover above a vowel to indicate one vowel assimilating into another) over the *u* in *Guero,* rendering his album title meaningless. By the way, if you want to get into a Mexican girl's *chonis,* shore up on the Art Laboe and Luis Miguel comps. You know what's up.

I am originally from the South and resent country music. Are there Mexicans who are from Mexico and resent that trilling, wailing, accordion-blaring music the same way? Are there kids of Mexican immigrants who can't stand the crap their parents play, the same way me and my friends couldn't stand Ronnie Milsap? Are there Mexicans who think the music similarly reflects stereotypes of being rural, poor, and less educated?

ACHY BREAKY CORAZON

Dear Gabacho: The only Mexicans who hate Mexican music are *pochos* ashamed by Mexican music's peasant roots. Like country music, Mexican regional is the true music of a silent majority, because it reflects their day-to-day lives—violence, heartache, and poverty. The identification with this *chúntaro* music is so pervasive that the children of these immigrants—kids with no real ties to Mexico—end up becoming major Mexican recording stars in their own right. Consider the story of the Rivera clan of Long Beach, California. Dad Pedro was a struggling musician until he discovered Chalino Sánchez, a poor Mexican immigrant who was Johnny Rotten, Elvis Presley, and Woody Guthrie in one—a man who sang of violence and folk heroes and who died execution-style in 1995. After Sánchez, Rivera moved on to record his son Lupillo, who combined street smarts and thug life to popularize Mexican music among his generation of Mexican-Americans during the early part of the twenty-first century. But the most important figure in Mexican popular music might well be Lupillo's sister, Jenni Rivera, whose songs of empowered femininity coupled with a great voice makes her a Madonna for the *chúntaro* set. Wabby music isn't for wabs—it's for people who want to get ahead in American society.

Why is it that we Mexicans get teary-eyed and emotional when "Volver, Volver" is played on the radio, in concerts, or at weddings?
CHENTE CHUNTI

Dear Gabacho: If you want to render a Mexican helpless, play this tune of lost love, which translates to "Return, Return" and is sung by *ranchera* icon Vicente "Chente" Fernández, the guy you see on posters in your local music store's Spanish-language section: gold-embroidered *charro* outfit, ivory-white teeth, and mustache as thick as a folded wallet. "Volver, Volver" is all about the treacle, with a chintzy organ intro, plodding guitar chords, pussy lyrics ("This passionate love / Is all disturbed to return"), and Fernández whimpering throughout . . . until the chorus, when he roars, *"Y volver, volver, vooooooooolveeeeeeeer"* (And return, return, reeeeeeeeetuuuuuuuuurn). Psychologists have observed that overcompensation on one part of the psyche leads to unconscious manifestations of the other in a concept known as reaction formation, and "Volver, Volver" allows Chente—Mexico's ultimate symbol of *mexicanidad*—to reveal machismo's deep, dark secret: Mexican men, for all their bravado, are more emotive than Oprah. With "Volver, Volver," Fernández made bawling the ultimate proof of *huevos*—you're not a real man if you can't cry—and so Mexican men drunkenly howl along in unison in honor of the hombre whenever the song plays. Either that, or they're imitating Russians.

Why do Mexicans like Morrissey so much?

WEARING BLACK ON THE OUTSIDE

Dear Readers: This is one of the most asked questions in Mexican history, and a fascination tackled by all hipster music critics at one point in their careers. Fuck them: here's the definitive answer from a trusty *mexicano* written in 2002.

Their Charming Man:
Dispatches from the Latino-Morrissey Love-in

Yuma, Arizona

The crowd chants, "Me-xi-co! Me-xi-co!" in an attempt to get the singer to acknowledge that the majority of the audience is Latino. He does. "I'm going to sing a couple of more songs," he tells them, "then all of you can go back to Mexicali."

And the Yuma Convention Center explodes.

Only one white man in the world—and he's not the pope—can tell a group of Mexicans in the United States to return to Mexico and not only avert death, but be loved for saying so.

His name: Steven Patrick Morrissey, former lead singer of the Smiths, current saint among countless young Latinos.

The same convention-center audience demographic greets him

wherever he performs: Los Angeles, Colorado Springs, or this desolate desert town. So he always makes sure to yell out "Mexico" or perform some grand ethnic genuflection to his adoring fans, letting them know that *he* knows. They always respond in ecstasy, grateful.

By the time you read this, there will have been numerous television reports, radio interviews, and newspaper stories revealing that many Morrissey fans are Latinos. They will tell you that history—musical, cultural, transnational—took place at the Arrowhead Pond in 2002 when Morrissey shared the stage with Mexican rock *en español* titans Jaguares in the biggest crossover attempt since Drake burned the Spanish Armada.

And they will tell you that you should be surprised. You shouldn't. There's something logical in this Latino Morrissey-worship. Morrissey knows it, his fans know it, and even academics know it. What exactly "it" is isn't exactly clear except that it's there, as plain as the Morrissey tattoo on the left shoulder of the *muchacha* crying on the floor of the Yuma Convention Center.

New Wave's Sermon on the Mount

I received the call at about two in the morning: a weak, almost slurring cry for help. "Hey, Gustavo. It's Ben. Man, I need my Morrissey CDs back." [Long pause.] "I really miss them." [Longer pause, voice now quivering the slightest bit.] "I need them."

Ben follows up the next day with an e-mail: "Please get me those CDs as soon as you can. I am being deprived."

Ben is Benjamín Escobedo, a longtime friend. Across the back window of his car is the salute to Morrissey and his domination of the city in which the singer now makes his home, MOZ ANGELES. He let me borrow his Morrissey/Smiths collection (every CD, even the bootlegs, imports, and special editions) for only two days before sending those messages.

Ben's devotion to Morrissey is a lesser example of what Latino Morrissey fans feel for their god. They wear pins, patches, or tattoos with their charming man's face. They dress like him (rockabilly chic to British mod), carry around his favorite flowers (gladioli), and cite his songs as answers to every problem they might have. One particular favorite is ending e-mail messages with the line "It takes strength to be gentle and kind" from "I Know It's Over," New Wave's Sermon on the Mount.

Some fans, such as Patricia Godínez, go as far as visiting his house in the Hollywood Hills and dropping off stories they write about him. "His music is the sound track of my life," Godínez says. "He reaches my innermost thoughts and fears and aspirations and longing. For a long time, I felt isolated and alone. Only Morrissey comforted me."

Godínez wrote an article for a small publication discussing how Morrissey saved her life. "My friend Maggie told me where he lived and said I should go give it to him," she said. "Before, I never had the guts to do it. Even when we went to his house, Maggie put my story in his mailbox."

Ben has yet to visit Morrissey's home, but he knows the address. His love affair with the Manchester native began when his brother and friends introduced him to *Viva Hate*. "When I first heard the album, it blew my mind," Ben says. "Every time I hear him now, he impresses me more and more."

Morrissey plays such a big role in Ben's life that he has a death pact with his friend: whoever dies first will make sure that "Well I Wonder" ("Please keep me in mind / Please keep me in mind") is played at the funeral.

"Moz speaks to me," Ben says. "For almost any problem in life, I can think of a Morrissey song. For example, 'Hand in Glove' has that line"—and here Ben sings—" 'And if the people stare / Then the people stare / Oh, I really don't know, and I really don't care.' That taught me to not care about what others may think of who I love.

"From the very beginning, I knew that Latinos liked Morrissey,"

Ben remarks. "In fact, I cannot name one white person who likes Morrissey."

"A Heavenly Way to Die"

What is it about Morrissey that attracts Latinos? It may be that it echoes the music of Mexico, the *ranchera*. His trembling falsetto brings to mind the rich, sad voice of Pedro Infante, while his effeminate stage presence makes him a UK version of Juan Gabriel. As in *ranchera*, Morrissey's lyrics rely on ambiguity, powerful imagery, and metaphors. Thematically, the idealization of a simpler life and a rejection of all things bourgeois come from a populist impulse common to *ranchera*.

The most striking similarity, though, is Morrissey's signature beckoning and embrace of the uncertainty of life and love, something that at first glance might seem the opposite of macho Mexican music. But check it out: for all the machismo and virulent existentialism that Mexican music espouses, there is another side—a morbid fascination with getting your heart and dreams broken by others, usually in death. In fact, Morrissey's most famous confession of unrequited love, "There Is a Light That Never Goes Out" ("And if a double-decker bus / Crashes into us / To die by your side / Would be a heavenly way to die"), emulates almost sentiment for sentiment Cuco Sánchez's torch song "Cama de Piedra" ("The day that they kill me / May it be with five bullets / And be close to you").

"I see Moz as something like Los Tigres del Norte," Ben says, referring to the *conjunto norteño* legends who've graphed and broadcast Mexican sentiment for the past quarter of a century. "They can take you through the day—make you laugh, smile, and cry. And that's what Morrissey does."

Comparing Morrissey with Mexican music is an interesting game, but it's beside the point. Most of Morrissey's Latino fans, while growing up with *ranchera*, don't automatically relate Morrissey to anything Mexican. More immediate to them is the music of their Mexican-Americanized youth: 1980s New Wave, oldies-but-goodies, and the rockabilly rhythms that have been a part of Mexican culture in one form or another since the heyday of the zoot suit. It's natural, then, for

Latinos to find Morrissey appealing: he incorporates all of these styles into his music, singing their life.

"A lot of Latinos in Southern California grew up to oldies and *rancheras*," Ben says. "But everyone also listened to KROQ [the influential Los Angeles radio station], especially the flashback lunches. A lot of those artists on KROQ were English, and the one that really stuck to people was Morrissey. His music had the style of a lot of the music we were already accustomed to."

"I Wish I Was Born Mexican"

Morrissey once told a Las Vegas audience composed of (what else?) mostly Latinos that *"Mexico* is the only Spanish word I know. But it's the best word."

That concert was part of 1999's ¡Oye Esteban! tour. An advertisement for his concerts that year excitedly screamed, "*¡El cantante! ¡El concierto!*" (The singer! The concert!) On that tour, Morrissey performed wearing T-shirts and belt buckles emblazoned with MEXICO and at times even the Virgen de Guadalupe, the spiritual embodiment of Catholic Mexico.

Morrissey's most famous acknowledgment of his Latino fans, though, came here in Orange County during that same tour. "I wish I was born Mexican," Morrissey told an overwhelmingly Latino audience at UC Irvine's Bren Events Center. "But it's too late for that now." This is the Dylan-at-Newport moment of the Latino Morrissey crowd, the defining moment of the phenomenon, something that everyone attended even if he or she was somewhere else.

The argument can even be made that Morrissey's acknowledgment of his Latino lovers goes back as early as 1992's *Your Arsenal;* on "Glamorous Glue," he wondered, "We look to Los Angeles / For the language we use / London is dead / London is dead / Now I'm too much in love." Elizabethan English and its people have perished, he tells us; long live the Spanglish race of Nuestra Lady de los Ángeles.

Regardless of when Morrissey discovered his Latino worshippers, it's indisputable that he now tailors his career for them. He lives in Los Angeles, the second-largest city in Latin America, and attends rock *en español* shows in Huntington Park to see Hispanic troubadour Mikel

Erentxun sing Spanish versions of "Everyday Is Like Sunday" and "There Is a Light That Never Goes Out." His tours eschew the East Coast and Midwest in favor of Latino or nearly Latino enclaves in Arizona, California, and Las Vegas. Morrissey's participation in Jaguares' 2002 Revolución Tour is another show of solidarity with the people who've made him a king.

"It's no secret that he moved to Southern California where there's a huge Latino base," says Javier Castellanos, who's trying to get Morrissey to come to his Anaheim club, JC Fandango, and displays a smiling picture of the eternally dour Morrissey to prove it. "I told him, 'You know there're a lot of Latinos who love you.' And he just nodded his head."

Anyone attending Morrissey's show will most likely hear "Mexico," a new song he debuted on his 2002 tour. A slow ballad similar to the baroque horror of "Meat Is Murder," "Mexico" reads like a Chicano manifesto:

> *In Mexico*
> *I went for a walk to inhale the tranquil cool lover's air.*
> *I could taste a trace*
> *Of American chemical waste.*
> *And the small voice said, "What can I do?"*

Other stanzas are just as radical, with the most memorable passage observing that Mexicans in the United States face a situation in which "It seems if you're rich and you're white / You'll be all right. / I just don't see why this should be so."

After years of searching for contentment, Morrissey found it in the Mexican republic of Moz Angeles.

"Morrissey found us, and we bumped into him, and we fell in love with him," Ben says. "And he loved us back."

Turning Manliness on Its *Cabeza*

Despite such a devoted fan base, media treatment of the Latino Morrissey phenomenon is universally condescending, if not outright racist. Typical is the following passage from *Big Brother* magazine on one reporter's attempt to try to crack the Latino Morrissey obsession at a Morrissey/Smiths convention:

> *As much as I enjoyed hanging out with Edwin and his friends, I have to admit I had an ulterior motive. I wanted to exhibit their acceptance of me, as a gringo who's down with the southerners, to gain admittance into some of the other, more thuggier Mexican cliques that were scattered throughout the convention. I was fascinated with the monsters that filled their ranks, and I wanted to photograph them without arousing anyone's suspicion that I was just another white man exploiting the beaners for his own gain . . . which, in a way, I was kind of doing.*

Other articles on the Morrissey Latino phenomenon have called Latino Morrissey fans "an audience of East LA homeboys" (*Spin*) or "tattooed Hispanic LA gangs" (*Select*). They describe those fans as possessing "perfect Mayan features" and wearing "the standard barrio uniform of shaved head, baggy jeans, and short-sleeved plaid shirt" (*LA Weekly*). They describe Morrissey's divine powers to save Latinos from gangs (the British TV show *Passengers*). Or they'll sum it up easily by saying that Morrissey's Latino fans are "warm brown" (*Los Angeles Times Magazine*).

"It's hard to tell if the [press is] more upset with Morrissey for not knowing when he was finished," writes academic Colin Snowsell, "or with the audience for not respecting—or being unfashionably oblivious to—the tacit understanding that Morrissey was taboo."

Snowsell, a doctoral candidate at Montreal, Quebec's McGill University, has made a study not merely of the connection between Morrissey and his fans, but also of the media's perspective of both. He has presented his observations in major academic symposia and in his master's thesis, soon to be a dissertation, " 'My Only Mistake Is I'm Hoping': Monty, Morrissey, and the Importance of Being Mediatized."

A lifelong Morrissey fan, the Canadian discovered the Latino Morrissey phenomenon through occasional articles in the press and his interest in Latin American popular culture. "I was interested first in the fan base itself, but after reading a lot of articles on the subject, I became fascinated with how it was reported," Snowsell says. "The media seemed to delight in pointing out this phenomenon so they could mock him and Latinos. They're reporting it as a circus side story: the faded star appealing to nonmainstream audiences. But I say it makes perfectly good sense. I think Latinos have better taste than everyone else."

Snowsell theorizes that Morrissey's appeal to Latinos lies in that he represents for them the same hope that he offers to all: an opportunity to transcend your lot in life. "Morrissey was, in short, providing to lower- and middle-class Mexican-Americans the same dual utopian message that he had once provided a decade earlier to predominately Anglo fans in the United Kingdom," Snowsell writes. And what did Morrissey offer Anglos? "Escape from the injustices of a social order that confines them to the margin, but escape also from the limited identity options entrenched in peripheral, working- and middle-class culture."

Snowsell says, "There's something to the fact that the audiences that have liked him weren't rich. His original British fans were poor and lower class. With Latinos, they're certainly considered peripheral in their country. When they see someone who had a comparable experience, those themes of alienation and disenfranchisement come through. And Latinos pick up on those things and are drawn to him."

More intriguing for Snowsell, though, is Morrissey's subversion of gender and sexual roles and what that means for Latinos in a culture where everything begins and ends with machismo.

"Morrissey's macho, but in a different way," Snowsell says. "When you think of the archetypal North American male sex symbol, you think of rockabilly icons like Elvis Presley and James Dean. But he's taken this most masculine of identities and remade it as a fey, wimpy, cardigan-wearing, gladiola-loving singer. When you present that to Latinos, whose culture offers very rigid gender models, it appeals to them because he uses this to show through actions that there are other identity options available. There's no right or wrong way, and people can choose for themselves. They can be tough and sensitive at the same time."

Descent into Morrissey

My cousins and many of my Latino friends are Morrissey freaks, but they never introduced me to him. It's as if people must discover Morrissey on their own terms.

I saw the light in 2002. With Ben as my Virgil, I descended into Morrissey as we drove through the Imperial Valley to his Yuma show. The plan was to listen to every Smiths album during the four-hour journey out from Orange County and to Morrissey's solo work on the way back.

Ben was of no help; all he did throughout the journey was sing every lyric, mimic Johnny Marr's chiming guitars, and blurt from track to track, "This song, only *real* Morrissey fans understand," or, "This song is for Morrissey poseurs."

It didn't matter. I'm immediately enthralled by *everything* that is Morrissey—the gentle yet intensely morose instrumentation; the velvety voice that spoke to me, *only* me, and no one else; his (and my) sad tales of getting picked on in school, despising your environment; the nagging aspiration to be something much more—and in another place.

At the concert, it's more of the same; the man wins me over, his words come to life, and his acknowledgment of my culture is so beautiful. How could I *not* love Morrissey?

Morrissey sings to the disaffected, and God knows alienation is part of the assimilation tradition—the equal and opposite reaction of the immigrant's drive to blend in. We ache; Morrissey soothes.

Maldonado

It's 1999, and there's a hundreds-deep line around Tower Records in Hollywood, everyone hoping to meet and get autographs from Morrissey. José Maldonado is maybe No. 400, and when it's his turn to talk to the man, he begins mumbling some sort of introduction. But Morrissey doesn't allow Maldonado to finish even his first sentence.

"I know who you are," Morrissey snaps at Maldonado in a tone simultaneously accusatory and congratulatory. "You're with the Sweet and Tender Hooligans."

Indeed, Maldonado was. The Los Angeles County lifeguard founded the Smiths/Morrissey tribute band around 1996, and they had attracted worldwide media attention almost upon their inception. *Spin,* the *Los Angeles Times,* various British music mags, even the BBC, featured the quintet, using their majority-Mexican membership as an opportunity to explain why so many Chicanos continued to pray at the altar of an artist the Anglo press had long ago turned into a punch line.

But Maldonado was more bumbling fan than media phenom when he met Morrissey at Tower, and all he offered as a response to his hero's observation was an incredulous smile.

"After he identified me, he jokingly said, 'It's as if I'm looking at a mirror,'" Maldonado recalled over lunch, savoring that moment more than the nachos he was gobbling. "He then asked me about our show the Wednesday before his appearance. 'You heard about it?' I asked. 'Of course I did,' Morrissey replied. 'I hear about *all* your shows.'"

Finally, Maldonado had the approval he had long sought from the person of whom he says, "When I first got into Morrissey, I thought it was my life's goal to get as many people as possible to listen to the man."

There's an understood detachment between cover bands and their followers—the performers know they are mimicking a certain artist, *channeling* the artist, at best, and the listener focuses only on the output. But the Sweet and Tender Hooligans transcend this ontological limitation as the preeminent Smiths/Morrissey cover group, and one of the best tribute acts around, period. Seeing them in concert is like inhabiting a working-class English pub, circa 1985. When they're not storming the stage, fans at Hooligans shows liberally pass out gladioli in honor of the Smiths' fondness for the flower. Motivating them is the almost too perfect re-creation of the Smiths sound—David Collett's lead guitar twinkles with the same pretty rancor as Johnny Marr's original licks, while Joe Escalante's quartz-watch bass would make Andy Rourke jealous.

But the soul of the Hooligans is unquestionably Maldonado. Onstage and in real life, Maldonado exudes Morrissey—the whipping of the mike chord, the self-deprecating humor, and the affects of a masculine diva—"Don't list my age. Vanity reasons," Maldonado requests before our interview begins. He grooms the same fabulous pompadour that rises from Morrissey's forehead like a promontory, hosts the same sideburns that come to rest around the earlobes, projects the same falsetto that drips with confident pain. When Maldonado writhes across the stage, Morrissey/Smiths fans cry nostalgic tears.

"It's an honor when they want to hug me," Maldonado gushes, referring to the hallowed tradition of Morrissey fans eluding numerous security guards to rush their god. "What it's saying is that I'm doing my impersonation of Morrissey and they're doing their impersonation of loving Morrissey. Fans are as much a part of the show as we are."

The Hooligans' stunning Smiths simulacrum allows them to take their Morrissey love around the world. They've traveled throughout the United States and played in six different cities during 2001—including Morrissey's hometown of Manchester.

"Let me tell you, you had better have your A game on if you're a band from L.A. and you're going to play Smiths songs in Manchester," remembers Maldonado with a laugh. "Before the set, the crowd had an anticipating look that said, 'Let's see what you've got.' By the third song, we'd won them over. By the end of the set, everyone had jumped upon the stage at least once."

Acceptance by two of the most important arbitrators of what constitutes the authentic Smiths/Morrissey sound is important. But the Hooligans also must please hyperpossessive Morrissey fans that bawl if the group doesn't play *their* song. "That's the problem with sets—it's hard to narrow down what we're *not* going to do," sighs Maldonado. "We have to be sure to play the standards like 'Ask,' 'Big Mouth Strikes Again,' and 'There Is a Light That Never Goes Out,' because you don't have a tribute band and not play the famous hits. A Doors tribute band isn't going to forget 'Light My Fire,' a Zep band won't forget 'Stairway to Heaven.' But we still have to perform the songs that maybe only one person in the club likes but upon hearing it, makes their day.

"When it comes to other tribute bands, what separates the good ones is when there's fanship involved, when there's a personal investment," Maldonado adds. "That's why the Atomic Punks are such a good Van Halen tribute band. That's why Wild Child is a great Doors band. And we're all Morrissey fans. So, it's hard for us to play just the famous stuff—we all have our obscure gems too. Nevertheless, we might have done 'This Charming Man' five thousand times, but by the first five notes, we're doing somersaults along with everyone else."

And so, the Hooligans happily trudge on, bodhisattvas to the Morrissey cult, unconcerned that their career consists mainly of imitating and placating others at the expense of their own musical growth. "I haven't abandoned the idea of performing original stuff—there are twenty songs in my guitar case right now," says Maldonado. "Maybe they'll see the light of day someday. But as long as people ask us to play the Smiths and Morrissey, we'll always be happy to oblige. And if they don't, we'll be in a garage by ourselves doing this anyway."

Coda

Morrissey fans pack L.A.'s Knitting Factory and mouth every word that Maldonado sings. Perhaps it's because Maldonado sounds just like Moz, looks like him down to the pompadour and whipping of the mike wire. Or perhaps it's because Maldonado is Mexican.

There are non-Latinos in the audience. But the overwhelming majority cheers wildly when Maldonado introduces his new bass player, Joe Escalante, by revealing, "Tonight, the band is twenty percent browner!"

I tell Ben this story, and he smiles. He can. I had returned his CDs, and now I was a believer too. We stage an impromptu sing-along to "The Boy with the Thorn in His Side."

"I knew you were going to like Moz," Ben says, beaming. "All Latinos end up liking him."

6

Food

Tamales, Hot Sauce, and Testicular Avocados

Dear Mexican: I was always told Mexican children received tamales for Christmas so they would have something to open Christmas morning. Is this true?

WONDERING WITH CORN

Dear Gabacho: As a Mexican who annually receives misleading Christmas gifts (PlayStation boxes stuffed with swap-meet underwear and socks), I can unequivocally deem the tamale-wrapping barrio legend a lie. But the humble masa meal is a Mexican's most valued weapon come Navidad—it's our fruitcake, a fail-safe, universal present that also functions as an edible visa. For housemaids, a basketful of tamales ensures the doña will rebristle her broom; at the office Christmas party, the Mexican who brings luscious cactus-and-cheese tamales spares himself at least a month of whispered beaner jokes. Tamale diplomacy is so necessary for Mexicans that parents will force children—did I say *children*? I meant the *girls*—to stay up all night spreading masa over corn husks, crushing chili seeds into salsa, and glopping lard over the entire mess.

How is it that Mexicans can eat Mexican food three to four times a day, seven days a week, and fifty-two weeks a year? And can they eat anything without hot sauce? Are their taste buds that dull?

POZOLE PENDEJA

Dear Gabacha: You mean how can we eat American food, ¿qué no? The much discussed Mexican *reconquista* already happened—we took over American taste buds long before we did California. The cultivated tomato, the base for ketchup, salads, and Italian yummies, came from Mexico. The ancestor of turkeys was Mexican. Chocolate, vanilla, avocado, salsa—each one as Mexican as black caricatures on stamps. And we spray hot sauce over most of our meals, Pozole Pendeja, for health reasons. A 2001 *USA Today* article examined various medical studies and discovered that a steady diet of hot peppers or salsa helps digestion, fights heart disease, prevents tumors from spreading, acts as a calorie burner, and makes breathing easier. The only thing ketchup is capable of doing, as far as I know, is staining dashboards.

Is Chicago the best place for Mexican food east of the Mississippi? I live on the South Side, and there are almost as many Mexican joints as McDonald's.

AMANTE DE BURRITOS

Dear Burrito Lover: I work in SanTana, the capital of Mexico, and I usually sneer when residents of other cities claim their Mexicans do more than just clog up hospitals and public schools. But not only is Chicago the best place for Mexican food east of the Mississippi, it's a nexus of Mexican culture in the United States second only to SanTana. The Windy City is home to the second-largest Mexican community in the country, and the second-largest Mexican consulate serves the Midwest from there. Chi-town spawned Chicano punk icons Los Crudos (whose lead singer, Martin Sorrondeguy, lived for a time in SanTana) and *pasito duranguenze,* a frenetic *banda*-melodica hybrid. The country's premier high-end Mexican restaurants, the Rick Bayless–fronted

La Frontera and Topolobambo, are located in Chicago, as well as Homaro Cantú, the *pocho* genius who's wowing foodies worldwide with such exotic dinners as sushi-flavored paper and Caesar-salad ice cream. It's the home of the Chicago tamale, a cellophane-wrapped cylinder of masa and sugary chili. And Chicago also sparked the continuing wave of mass Mexican rallies when more than one hundred thousand people marched for amnesty on March 10 last year. Chicago is proof that not only are Mexicans everywhere nowadays, but that we're forward-looking: when the *reconquista* is complete, Chicago will be . . . well, Chicago to SanTana's New York.

I'm a bartender, and one of my customers told me MGD stands for Mexicans Getting Drunk. I take it there is a certain level of pride associated with drinking. Where does this originate in Mexican culture?

SPARE ME SOME CUTTER, HERMANO

Dear Gabacho: I dunno—let me go ask a Russian.

Can you tell me the meaning of the word *aguacate*? All I know about this delicious fruit is that it originated on this continent.

GUACAMOLE MAN

Dear Gabacho: *Aguacate* is the Spanish word for "avocado," but its Nahuatl meaning is more rustic: balls. According to Ana María de Benítez's 1974 classic, *Pre-Hispanic Cooking,* "The name *aguacate* (avocado) comes from Ahuaca Cuahuitl, *ahuacatl* meaning 'testicle' and *cuahuitl* meaning 'tree,' hence: tree of testicles." A Freudian might argue, then, that guacamole is castration gone gourmet. Women prepare it so they can symbolically crush the macho *huevos* that keep them repressed; Mexican hombres scarf it down in the belief that they'll become manlier. And the popularity of guacamole among gabachos—the California Avocado Commission estimates that consumers purchase 40 million pounds of their cash crop during Super Bowl weekend alone—is actually an American plot to de-ball the Mexican nation. Then again, an avocado might just be an avocado: a wrinkly—and sure, testicular—fruit.

I've noticed that areas with lots of recent Mexican immigrants have stores that sell nothing but water. I find this odd. Do people recently arrived from Mexico not know that tap water here is potable? How can these stores survive selling nothing but water anyway?

AGUA PA' LA RAZA

Dear Gabacha: Mexicans can never get far from the bottle, whether it's H_2O or Herradura tequila. In a 2002 survey, the Public Policy Institute of California found that 55 percent of Latinos in the state drink bottled water, compared with 30 percent of gabachos. It's definitely a custom smuggled over from Mexico, where tap water remains fraught with nasty viruses and bugs and crap. So it seems the Mexican affinity for Arrowhead is another case of assimilation gone dead, huh?

But another possibility is suggested by *Dr. Strangelove or: How I Learned to Stop Worrying and Love the Bomb.* In the 1964 Stanley Kubrick classic, Brigadier General Jack D. Ripper reveals that fluoride-contaminated tap water is a commie plot that's robbing America of its precious bodily fluids. Mexicans want no part of that. We want our *mecos* healthy and hopping, so when it comes time to repopulate the States after the bomb hits, we can turn all surviving *gabachitas* into baby mills.

Why does Mexican food always make me shit?

FUN WITH RUNS

Dear Gabacho: Because it wants to leave your gabacho ass as soon as possible.

Why do Mexicans steal fruit from trees that aren't theirs? At my job, a tree hangs over the wall, and they climb for the fruit.

WITH A CHIQUITA BANANA BETWEEN HIS LEGS

Dear Gabacho: Nothing—not walls, the brutal sun, or lack of bathroom breaks and potable water—will stop a Mexican from picking fruits and vegetables. It's Pavlovian, Chiquita Banana: if a Mexican sees an apple, he climbs the tree and picks it. Strawberries? Kneel down and pull. What you should be concerned about is the looming crop crisis predicted in the December 5, 2005, business section of the *Los Angeles Times*. A story that day reported that Western Growers, an Irvine, California–based trade group whose members grow 90 percent of the nation's winter crops, would only fill half of the fifty thousand field-hand positions they needed thanks to our country's tightening immigration policies. "Come January, we could see lettuce rotting in the fields because there will be no one to pick it," one El Centro grower fretted to *Times* reporter Jerry Hirsch. So make sure to thank the next Mexican who steals lemons or potatoes from your yard, Chiquita Banana: the fruit or vegetable that Mexican steals means one less illegal immigrant big business needs.

Why don't Mexicans tip decently? I labor as a waitress in a local upscale steak house where, unfortunately, many Mexicans eat, and the lousy tips are starting to piss me off! Even blacks tip better! (Although, I gotta say, Mexicans are much easier to wait on. No constant requests for "So' mo' ranch dressin'.") And, yes, I always give good service on the one-in-a-million chance the brown-skinned loser sitting at my table isn't a complete social retard. Could you possibly pass the word along so I can quit spitting in their drinks?

WAITS ON TOO MANY WABS

Dear Gabacha: Let's consult the findings of Cornell University professor Michael Lynn, the country's premier scholar on tipping. In a 2003 study titled "Ethnic Differences in Tipping: Evidence, Explanations, and Implications," Lynn examined the long-standing claims by waiters that minorities tip less than gabachos. He analyzed the responses of nearly two thousand eaters in Houston and found that not only did "Hispanics" (really Mexicans, since Houston's Latino community is nearly three-quarters Mexican) tip as well as gabachos, they usually tipped better. Mexicans, according to Lynn, "increased their percentage tips with service . . . more than did whites."

Lynn offered no explanation for his findings, but I will: Mexicans leave a little extra not out of a perceived social obligation but for a job well done—which includes how *caliente* the *chica* is. Most Mexican restaurants force their waitresses to wear skirts just below the *culo* and blouses with a neckline that plunges like the American auto industry. Mexicans tip accordingly—I've been to dives where Mexican men will tip three times their $40 bill if the waitress jiggles just a little bit longer. When Mexicans go to eateries where the waitresses dress more conservatively, the tips usually dry up. Want a little extra, Too Many Wabs? Bring us a bottle of Tapatío—not Tabasco—without prompting. And get some ass implants.

Waiters from across *la Naranja* wrote in after my column on whether Mexicans tip badly. The authors of the two finest letters on the subject work near the Happiest Place on Earth. Let's start with Arriba Anaheim:
I work at the Mimi's in front of Disneyland, where I get tourists from all over the world. Mexicans are extremely generous compared to other nationalities, although I do find something interesting: Mexican immigrants who live in the United States can be horrible tippers, because many are braceros who come to this country from *ranchos* or pueblos and aren't used to the fine-dining experience. But Mexicans who are tourists are some of the best tippers, because they have the money to come all the way from Mexico City, Monterrey, or Guadalajara to visit *el ratón Miguelito*.

Not as benevolent toward Mexicans was Fed Up in Fullerton:
I was a server at Downtown Disney for three years, and I have to say that Hispanics do not tip worth a shit. I was impeccable in guest and

service relations, so clearly it wasn't a case of my lack of service or inability to give prompt, efficient service. Not to mention that I'm half-Hispanic, but give me a fucking break. Mexicans would arrive fresh from Sunday mass, order the filet or lobster and a slew of souvenir $10 drinks. They would spend $275 and leave a $5–$10 tip and the extra incentive "Good job, my friend." They can take that compliment and shove it up their ass! Your answer is ridiculous, and we're not in Houston but in sunny California as far as your source goes. Straight up, this is what your readers were seeking as a response, not your sidestepped political response! Take that, you gold-capped bean!

Two points, Fed Up. First, you are a man, and unless an hombre is the bartender, owns the restaurant, or is related to the owner, Mexicans will think any guy waiting tables is a joto whose only tip should be a bitch slap and the advice to get a real job—such as busing tables or washing dishes. Second, you'd earn much more if you took my advice and got ass implants.

My boyfriend is Mexican, and when we're trying to decide where to eat, he almost always wants Chinese. Same with his family: when we recently visited some friends from Guadalajara, I was looking forward to some *tortas ahogadas,* but instead was served mu shu pork. Why do Mexicans like Chinese food so much?

CUISINE CONFUSED

Dear Gabacha: Mexicans are eternally fascinated with Chinese, and nothing piques our interest as much as the food. They eat what we eat: beans, pork, goat, turtles, rice, even dogs! But our interest in *comida china* boils down to economics, Cuisine Confused. Like Mexican food, Chinese is an ethnic cuisine where you can feast like a king on a day laborer's salary. I can go to any Chinese restaurant and order the three-item combo with fried rice, chow mein, and a drink for about six bucks. The value of Chinese food explains the popularity among Mexicans of instant ramen. According to the International Ramen Manufacturers Association, Mexicans consumed an average of

9.4 ramen servings in 2004, tops in Latin America and behind only the United States and Russia among non-Asian countries. Even the Mexican government distributes ramen to its poor ... what's that you say? Ramen is a Japanese dish? Don't tell that to a Mexican, who believes anything Asian is *chino* even when it's Japanese—right, Vietnamese readers?

Why do Mexicans cover their candies with chili powder? That's not candy—that's hell.

HERSHEY HONEY

Dear *Negrita:* Cultural food traditions originate from a region's native resources—what else explains America's affinity for tacos?—and the numerous types of chili peppers in Mexico mean we spice up *everything.* Soups. Beers. But especially candies, which range from fruit dusted with chili powder to chili paste that kids squirt directly onto their tongue. Chili candy love, like nearly all the knowledge I share with *ustedes,* comes courtesy of the ancients. In the 1996 book *The True History of Chocolate,* authors Michael and Sophie D. Coe described how Aztecs and Mayans enjoyed their chocolate drinks best by spiking them with chilis ranging "anywhere from mildly pungent to extremely hot." Going further, the Coes tried out an ancient chocolate recipe for themselves and wrote, "We ... can assure our readers that it is very good indeed." The Coes learned what we Mexicans know, but most gabachos refuse to accept: combining sugar with spice is the pinnacle of refined palates. The dual notes of heat and sweet open the taste buds and allow eaters to better appreciate both flavors. Besides, great cuisine involves contrasts in tastes—if you like your grub straightforward with no nuance, you might as well live in the Midwest. Or be Guatemalan.

MARGARITAS MEXICAN GRILL, MACON, GEORGIA.

Why is my local taquería named after a town?

TWO CHICKEN TACOS, HOLD THE BRAINS

Dear Gabacho: Many Mexicans nowadays don't identify themselves primarily as "Mexican" since there are so damn many of us here. Instead, we classify ourselves by the Mexican state or region of our roots, with fierce rivalries between groups (I remember epic PE basketball battles between *tapatíos*—people from Jalisco—and kids from Guanajuato), usually precluding any pan-Mexican unity. To make matters more provincial, many of us still associate with cities thousands of miles away that relocated virtually intact to the United States during the past three decades.

You can see these transplanted Mexican communities in the names of businesses like Zapatería Jerez (an Anaheim shoe store saving the soles of people from my ancestral city in Zacatecas), Sahuayo Tires, and Carnitas Uruapán. But if you want to experience these cities-within-cities without buying shoes or getting an oil change, there is an appetizing alternative. Many *ranchos* have gone into the taquería business as a way of creating a space where people can meet and eat meat. Two of the better ones in terms of hosting good community and food in Orange County are Taquería El Granjenal in Costa Mesa and Anaheim's Taquería Arandas.

Taquería El Granjenal is probably the most authentic taco stand in Orange County. The open-air, sit-down, no-frills eatery with a delightful pastel color scheme is located in the heart of Costa Mesa's barrio and close to the section of Santa Ana where many people from the Michoacán village first settled in the United States.

Although El Granjenal serves all Mexican fast-food staples (the *tortas* are especially noteworthy), stick to their exquisite tacos. The price may seem a bit expensive, but while most taquerías serve tiny offerings of their main dish, El Granjenal's rendition is titanic. The owners deviate from taco protocol by using full-size corn tortillas and pile on chunks of your choice of grilled meat. The salsa is also extraordinary, a dark red lava extract whose burn factor is unknown outside Paricutín.

Though the culinary side is splendid, the restaurant seems to have lost its community roots. Nothing other than its name suggests that thousands of people from El Granjenal now live throughout Orange County. When I asked the man working the counter why this is so, he told me that the taquería's founder sold the restaurant a couple of years ago, and a remodeling removed most vestiges of its roots (pictures and a map of Michoacán, etc.). However, the new non–El Granjenal–native owner didn't change the name out of respect for the community; too many people from El Granjenal still go there to remember their *rancho* through food.

Taquería Arandas' pride for its namesake is more obvious. I discovered this place after my *arandense* friends (all with homes in Anaheim and the city of about seventy thousand in Jalisco) started singing its praises last year. *Arandenses* are braggarts about their town, and this taquería shows it.

Before you even enter, a window painting of Arandas' landmark San José Obrero Cathedral (which also serves as the restaurant's logo) greets you. Inside, you'll find two pictures of the same church (one recent, another dating back to the 1900s) and another of the largest bell in Mexico, which lies within the church's premises.

The hole-in-the-wall's tacos are like those at most taquerías: minuscule, cheap, and tasty. But what distinguishes Arandas' version is its selection of rare-for-taco meats such as *buche* (pig stomach) and *tripas* (cow intestines). Regardless of which meat you choose, the restaurant uses down-soft tortillas as a base, cramming them with huge chunks of savory onions and cilantro and topping them with a salsa more tangy than spicy to make their humble specialty a gourmet meal.

It might seem weird for populaces to rely on taquerías to maintain civic unity; I mean, haven't they LA VIDA TAQUERÍA, SANTA ANA, CALIFORNIA.

heard of community centers? But El Granjenal and Arandas prove not only that it's important to maintain ties with your townspeople, but also that you can have a taco with them. I don't know about you, but great food would have me talking to my degenerate neighbors any day.

Does menudo really cure hangovers?

INTESTINAL BLOCKAGE

Dear Gabacho: Ah, yes, menudo. Its hangover-curing virtues are the only reason Americans take interest in this spicy tripe soup. Outside of this, it's nothing more than an edible donkey show: a horrific, disgusting artifact of a horrific, disgusting people.

But menudo is so much more than boiled cow guts or something to soak up the booze that fueled your previous night. Menudo is a sociohistorical lesson in a bowl: the fat, pale kernels of *pozole* have nourished Mesoamericans since time immemorial; the use of tripe and not the better parts of a cow is a testament to its status as a poor person's meal. Menudo is delicious, the trinity of firm *pozole,* chewy tripe, and fiery, bloodred broth producing a comforting, fatty flavor.

More important, menudo is *amor.* It's the soup Mexican women slave over for their hungry families on weekend mornings, the dish over which families unite and teens fall in love as they pitch woo while passing along a wicker of tortillas. Menudo nowadays exists in canned form, but that's heresy. True menudo is a difficult feat, taking hours to create, but it comes with a payoff that transcends taste buds and strives for the sublime.

Consider the menudo of my *madre.* Her menudo morning begins at Northgate González Supermarket in Anaheim, where Mom takes a number and waits patiently until the butcher calls it out from a tinny microphone. She tells the *carnicero* which slices of tripe she wants. Some people make menudo with only one of the four cow-stomach tripes; my mom uses three—firm honeycomb; smooth, flat tripe; and the feathery flaps of book tripe. Each has its own rubbery charm, and combining the three adds a fuller, more robust texture to the menudo.

Mami buys the tripe in pieces as large as letterhead, then takes it home and chops it into chewable slices. She washes the pieces in the sink, remembering to mix in lemon juice to absorb the tripe's ripe stench. She tosses the prepared bits into a steel pot angry with boiling water along with a piece of cow leg, tendons and all, to lend a beefier flavor.

Menudo is like a child; you must monitor it at all times. It takes at least two hours for the tripe to soften into a chewy, delectable meal. But *Mami* has other menudo chores even as it cooks. She fills up small bowls with the onions and cilantro my sisters are supposed to chop up but Mom inevitably does. She arranges the table, warms the tortillas, and calls her *comadres* to come over in about half an hour. She enters the garage and finds our massive bag of dried, hand-sized chilis from Caleras, Zacatecas, a region renowned for its smoky chilis. Tossing them into a blender along with garlic cloves (no *molcajete* for her: "Takes too long, and a blender is easier"), *Mami* creates the salsa for the menudo and throws it in the boiling pot along with the *pozole*. The salsa and *pozole* spread with the heat. She then lowers the flame to a flicker. At this point, the menudo's warmth radiates throughout the house, provoking a Pavlovian reaction from everyone: we awake from our slumber. Time to *comer*.

Mom used to make fresh menudo every Sunday, but that's no longer a certainty as the years have chipped away at her stamina. And even when we do feast on menudo, it usually comes from El Camino Real, a Fullerton restaurant that draws in gabachos and Mexicans alike with its safe Mexican menu of chiles rellenos, enchiladas, and chicken. There, *Mami* meets other moms who take the shortcut. Like in the butcher shop, they wait patiently in line, pot handles wrapped in foil to guard against the heat. El Camino Real fills the pots to the brim, yet the women lug it back home as if it were as light as *pan dulce*.

Will menudo cure a hangover? No doubt. But if that's all you eat it for, then you truly don't know love.

If Mexico was settled by Spaniards, why do Mexicans drink beer and not wine?

BARREL OF FUN

Dear Gabacho: Ever wonder why Spaniards drink sangria? Have you ever had Spanish wine? Clammy, bitter, vile muck. Barely gets you drunk, which means it's worthless for a Mexican. Mexico has its own indigenous boozes—mescal, and the great tequila. And then there's beer. In the United States, Mexicans largely eschew Mexican beers in favor of American beers. That Mexicans drink gabacho beer makes perfect sense: this is America, and the first things Mexicans pick up on the inevitable road to assimilation are bad habits like crappy beer (Budweiser and Bud Light rank *número* one and two, respectively, in sales among Mexican lushes in this country), conspicuous consumption, and flushing soiled toilet paper into the ocean. One possible explanation of the affinity for gabacho beer is the ubiquitous sponsorship of almost anything Mexican by American breweries—FIFA World Cup broadcasts on Univisión (brought to you by Miller Genuine Draft), the Mexican national soccer squad (Budweiser), the recent tour of *norteño* supergroup Grupo Intocable (Coors Light), and Cinco de Mayo (brought to you, according to Chicano activists, by a beer cabal intent on rendering Mexicans perpetually *pedo*—drunk off their asses). But be careful about romanticizing "Mexican" beer, Barrel. Sure, they come from Mexico, but it was Austrian immigrants who crafted the fine lager Negra Modelo in 1926. Bohemia's pioneer brewer was, as the name suggests, Czech (of Bohemia, John Steinbeck once wrote, "Ah, Bohemia beer and the Pyramid of the Sun; entire civilizations have created less"). Tecate's coat of arms looks suspiciously like a stylized version of Germany's heraldic eagle. And one of the founders of Cervecería Cuauhtémoc Moctezuma, the group that now brews Tecate and Bohemia, was a St. Louis immigrant named Joseph M. Schnaider. It's telling that the only major Mexican *cervecería* with no historic ties to Germans, Austrians, or Czechs is Grupo Modelo, which owns the Negra Modelo label now but started out with Corona and Modelo (a different beer from Negra Modelo)—and is now half-owned by Anheuser-Busch.

Whenever we go out to eat, my friend always reminds me when I order flour tortillas that no Mexican ever eats them. He does this within earshot of the hot waitress, presumably to embarrass me into jumping onto the corn bandwagon. Is this true?

TACO DEL CONGELADOR

Dear Taco from the Freezer: Unless you're eating burritos wrapped in Wonder bread, you've got nothing to be ashamed of. But I'll give your friend credit for noting the fight to the death between tortillas *de maíz* and *harina*. The Spaniards who conquered northern Mexico and the southwest United States first created flour tortillas because they were too stupid to learn corn-growing techniques from the vanquished natives and thus substituted wheat for maize. Flour tortillas subsequently

TIJUANA TACO, TACOMA, WASHINGTON.

became the flavor of choice in the borderlands, and gabachos quickly embraced the more familiar taste of flour over the corn tortilla's earthy Mesoamerican charm. According to ACNielsen Strategic Planner, sales of flour tortillas in the United States for the period between April 2004 and April 2005 were $653.2 million, while corn tortillas only notched $338.7 million. The pernicious spread of flour continues. In 1998's "Dietary Patterns and Acculturation Among Latinos of Mexican Descent," researchers Eunice Romero-Gwynn and Douglas Gwynn discovered that among the Mexicans they surveyed "while only 14 percent of the immigrants reported consumption of flour tortillas while in Mexico, 35 percent consumed these tortillas after immigration." Again, America: Mexicans pick up gabacho ways fast, so don't gasp when they start speaking English and discriminating against *tú*.

Is it true Mexicans eat crickets?

GRASSHOPPERS DO IT JUMPING

Gabachos love to malign Mexicans for their supposedly disgusting diet, delicacies such as cow innards, goat spine, sea-turtle eggs, and yes, crickets. But lemme ask you; have you actually tasted crickets? They're most popular in the state of Oaxaca, where women dry them, salt them, and usually put them in chili powder. The results are *delicioso,* taste crunchy like dried shrimp, and are absolutely fabulous when dipped in mole or cooked inside of a quesadilla. I never had *chapulines* until I was older, here in the United States, and that's the great thing about Mexican cuisines—while you can have Chicago dogs and Philly cheesesteaks almost anywhere in the United States, Mexican cuisine is still stubbornly regional, with foods usually available only in a particular Mexican region or in the United States. You might think eating crickets is vile, but it makes more sense than compressing leftover cow and turning them into patties. Plus, if we learn to capture them, we can be exterminators.

Why is your food so damn tasty and yet so bad for you?
PEPTO-BISMOL PATTY

Dear Gabacha: Mexican food is tasty because it's Mexican food, but who says it's bad for you? Sure, diabetes and heart attacks are endemic among Mexicans, but that owes more to the recent trend toward sedentary work rather than a defect in the Mexican diet. Mexicans ate Mexican food for millennia and turned out okay as the body's enzymes and digestive system adapted to best utilize the ingredients of a diet of corn and protein. When you introduce a new substance into your body, however, the body tends to react differently—in your case, apparently by getting the runs. Just keep eating Mexican food—diarrhea is but a temporary problem, a necessary penance for the greatest food on earth.

How and why have chipotle chilis been appropriated by gringo cuisine? I can think of no instances where *mexicano* cuisine smokes food, much less a jalapeño. I swear to you that the "real" chipotle pepper is not smoked. It's just a pepper that happens to taste smoked. I am tired of gringos correcting me with "It's a jalapeño smoked in banana leaves." Can you ask a botanist to put an end to the misinformation?
NATIONAL ASSOCIATION OF LATINO GOLF AFICIONADOS

Dear NALGA: Why all the *pedo* about the gabacho fascination with chipotle? Sure, Mexico has many better peppers—I prefer the serrano, a green pepper with the spice of jalapeño and the juiciness of a bell pepper—and eat chipotle only when enjoying a *cemita,* a glorious sandwich from Puebla. But chefs' use of chipotle flavors is a sign of respect, an acknowledgment that Mexican food belongs in the high-end cookbooks of the world. Gabachos like it precisely because it's so mild. So let them be pussies and let's keep the hot, best ones for ourselves. Besides, why should we claim a foodstuff as ours? Chocolate came from Mexico, went to Europe, and is now a worldwide favorite. Same thing with vanilla, maize, and many other of the foodstuffs that make great cuisine. All Mexican.

Why do real Mexicans love radishes? The authentic places always have them as condiments. I love them and always eat them.

BEETS ME

Scientific studies have shown that eating pickled products assists in digestion, and many world cuisines created pickled sides for their meals that go with everything—witness the Salvadorans with *curtido,* Germans with sauerkraut, Koreans with kimchi—really, most cultures except gabachos, who eat pickled products only at the ballpark. Similarly, Mexicans love their *escabeche*—a pickled-veggies dish that usually includes onions, cactus, radishes, tomatoes, carrots, or jalapeños. Mexican Mexican restaurants carry *escabeche*—American Mexican restaurants offer nothing and allow the farts to commence.

PEDROLAND.COM; SOUTH OF THE BORDER, DILLON, SOUTH CAROLINA.

Why does spicy Mexican food give *güeros chorro*?

DIRTY Q-TIPS

Muy popular question! One of the worst cultural insults you can throw at people is to say that their food gives you diarrhea, and that's why the English language has so many euphemisms for the thing—Gandhi's revenge, Gyppy tummy, Delhi belly, the Rangoon runs, Tokyo trots. But none has stuck better in the gabacho mind than Montezuma's revenge, named after the Aztec emperor who lorded over Tenochtitlán when the Spaniards came. Spanish accounts maintain that Ol' Monty loved to drink his chocolate laced with *muchos* chilis, and his digestive tract cleared out almost daily. Whether it's true or not is a matter of historical intrigue, but the stereotype was quickly gobbled up by gabachos eager to fulfill their critique of Mexicans as a dirty, ugly race whose food can cause that disgusting stuff. That's the gabacho way—blame their weak digestive tract on the natives.

What's the best tequila? I just point out my bottle of Gran Patrón, a 1.75-liter bottle of Cazadores, or my collection of red, white, and blue bottles of Corralejo.

TEQUILA TOM

Dear Gabacho: Trying to decide on the best tequila is like trying to figure out which grain of sand in the beach is the prettiest. But you mentioned two of my favorites, each with stories that illustrate the tequila industry in Mexico. The Cazadores label, founded in 1973, is distilled in Arandas, Jalisco, a city of about seventy thousand that's the main city in Los Altos de Jalisco (the Highlands of Jalisco). This region of agave farms, red-earth deserts, and stunning mountains is reputed to be the birthplace of mariachi and tequila; its claim to the prettiest and whitest women in Mexico isn't challenged by anyone. Cazadores makes three brands: Cazadores Reposado, which tastes like fire liquid; Cazadores Blanco, a slightly bitter libation better suited for cocktails; and the exceedingly smooth Cazadores Añejo, a smoky, woody thing that will make the afternoon melt away quickly.

My other favorite tequila is the aforementioned Corralejo, Mexico's oldest continuously produced tequila brand, since 1755. Corralejo is distinguished by its tall, colored bottles, and that it's produced in the southern-Mexican state of Guanajuato (Mexican law certifies all tequila produced in Mexico and requires it be produced in just three states: Jalisco, Tamaulipas, and Guanajuato). Most non-Jalisco tequilas are shite, but Corralejo features a sweet kick with its nectar flavor and even a hint of cinnamon. As for José Cuervo, the best-selling tequila in the United States? Just proof gabachos don't know anything about Mexico.

Why is Mexican weed synonymous with bad marijuana that's smuggled into the United States via spare tires? Can't Mexicans grow decent weed for a good price?

POCHO POTHEAD

Dear Wab: Bad Mexican marijuana has plagued the bongs and joints of North America since time immemorial—even the classic song "La Cucaracha" pokes fun at marijuana with the line *"La cucaracha ya no puede caminar / Porque le falta marijuana pa' fumar"* (The cockroach can't walk / Because he has no more marijuana to smoke). There was never much incentive to improve our crops—the drug of choice for Mexicans is tequila or mescal. But Mexican marijuana is improving as more of us realize that gabachos want to smoke their lives away. Telling are the comments of a Midland, Texas, police officer, who told a reporter with the *Midland Reporter-Telegram* in 2006 that Mexican marijuana "is better quality than it used to be and it's getting to be better quality all the time. It's not going to come anywhere near the quality of the hydro weed that's coming out of Canada that has a lot higher THC resin content and is a whole lot more expensive. But marijuana here, granted it is not as good quality as the hydro weed, but it's a lot stronger than weed from years ago." An FBI agent, meanwhile, added, "What is happening shows a growing degree of sophistication on the part of [Mexican] marijuana producers." Goes to show that when there's a gabacho demand for anything, a Mexican will show up and do it better and cheaper.

I see guys wearing hats or belt buckles with a marijuana leaf *all the time.* What's with the Mexican fascination with drugs?

STONED GABACHO

Dear Gabacho: Mexicans have always had a fascination with drugs. Some of the earliest *corridos* dealt with drug smugglers, and Chicano-music icon Lalo Guerrero extolled the virtues of Mary Jane in "Marijuana Boogie" around the time Cab Calloway was hi-dee-hi-ing his way through "Reefer Man." But over the past thirty years, thanks to Mexican economics, Mexico has entered the age of *narcocultura*—literally, the culture of narcotics trafficking—itself a by-product of the American war on drugs.

Like almost everything bad in this world, *narcocultura* can be blamed in part on American excess. During the drug-fueled seventies, entrepreneurs known as *narcotraficantes* introduced drug crops throughout rural Mexico, especially in the state of Sinaloa, where the major *narcotraficantes* have been based. In an effort to eradicate the emerging narco-economy, the Mexican army went after smugglers and growers with equal vigor. With a common enemy, *narcotraficantes* and townspeople united in a socioeconomic symbiosis: the narcos would give ailing *ranchos* financial aid, and the citizens would grow drugs.

The benevolence of *narcotraficantes* created cult followings for the cartels and their leaders, including Ámado Carrillo Fuentes, "El Señor de los Cielos" (the Lord of the Sky), who died during plastic surgery in 1997; Joaquín "El Chapo" Guzmán Loera, who escaped from a Guadalajara prison in 2001 and is still at large; and the Arellano-Félix cartel of Tijuana. Narcos became the modern folk heroes of Mexico, reported on breathlessly by the Mexican media.

With jobs and adoration, though, came gang hits and drug-related massacres throughout rural Mexico. The violence was exploited by a Mexican film industry that had been in decline throughout the 1960s and was desperate for a moneymaker. Thus the *narcopelícula,* the narco film. These were not Cheech and Chong farces but rather portrayals of the Mexican drug trade as a deadly but glamorous adventure. The men were almost stereotypically macho, the women either whores or virgins, and the movies violent even by the sanguinary standards of Mexican film. Shoot-outs were the norm—at weddings, while driving, in the mountains. The most famous actors of the *narcopelícula,* brothers Mario and Fernando Almada, were the good guys: fifty-year-old Dirty Geraldos massacring anyone who crossed their path. They became Mexican idols, and their films are still shown as if on an endless loop on Spanish-language television stations.

But the embodiment of *narcocultura* was the late Chalino Sánchez. Elvis Presley, John Lennon, and Johnny Rotten rolled into one undocumented Mexican immigrant, Sánchez helped transform the *corrido,* Mexico's traditional song structure, into a running commentary on the glories and terrors of drug running: the *narcocorrido.*

Sánchez sang *narcocorridos* not in Mexico but in Southern California during the late 1980s. He combined the violent imagery of the *narcopelícula* and the *corrido* form—with its emphasis on communicating history—and added his own ideas. Sánchez turned the *corrido* into something like journalism, singing about contemporary but otherwise anonymous people whose only claim to fame was their (usually violent) life story. If he was experimental, he was also traditional, writing songs on commission, transforming the invisible lives of immigrants into heroic songs of violence, hard work, and tragedy.

Soon, *narcocultura* had a sartorial style named for Sánchez himself, the *Chalinazo:* a cowboy hat, exotic-animal cowboy boots, gold chains, an ornate belt called a *cinto pitiado,* and silk shirts. After Sánchez's 1992 assassination in Sinaloa, his style and music became de rigueur for any Mexican who wanted to be *el más chingón,* the biggest badass around.

The music and clothes established, the official car of the *narcocultura* emerged from the suburban dreams of soccer moms and dads: the monstrous SUV. Much like *corridos* about famous horses in days gone by, new *corridos* hit the radio waves boasting about trucks—such as "El Cherokee de La Muerte" (The Cherokee of Death) and "El Suburban." These new ballads sing the praises of vehicles bought with drug money and emblazoned with symbols of the *rancho:* bulls, horses, and *la Virgen de Guadalupe.*

This love of materialism yielded the newest trend in *narcocultura: corridos pesados,* heavy *corridos.* They deal only peripherally with drugs and *narcotraficantes,* instead concentrating on trash talk. The protagonist in the *corrido pesado* has made his drug money; now he brags about what he owns as a result and vows to kick your ass if you have a problem with him. Most notably, singers of *corridos pesados* cuss—big-time. This created a dilemma for the Federal Communications Commission. During the birth of *corridos pesados,* around 1999, Spanish-language radio was awash in expletives. Perhaps FCC monitors spoke Spanish, but not the Mexican Spanish in which many swear words translated literally have no obvious vulgar content. For example, *Te voy a madrear* means "I'm going to mother you," but in Mexican Spanish more liberally translates as "I'm going to kick your fucking ass." The FCC seems finally to have captured the nuances of Mexican swearing; *corridos pesados* have been censored or outright banned on Spanish radio. With *corridos pesados* in one culture, gangsta rap in another, and *American Idol* as overlord, we can look forward to some interesting shit in the next couple of decades.

Is it true burritos aren't Mexican?

CHIMICHANGA CHARLIE

Dear Gabacho: Most of the cuisine that gabachos call Mexican—burritos, nachos, chili, and tortilla chips—aren't favored by real-deal Mexicans or even created by them. In his fascinating paper "Tacos, Enchiladas and Refried Beans: The Invention of Mexican-American Cookery," Andrew F. Smith delves into the history of these dishes. The burrito, for instance, "first saw print in America in 1934. It was sold at Los Angeles's famed El Cholo Spanish Cafe during the 1930s. Burri-

TEOTIHUACAN, HOUSTON, TEXAS.

tos entered Mexican-American cuisine in other parts of the Southwest around the 1950s and went nationwide a decade later." The tortilla chip, meanwhile, was created by Mexican national Rebecca Webb Carranza in Los Angeles in 1951. Fajitas come from Texas—some say the Rio Grande Valley, others point to Houston. I also direct you to *Houston Press* writer Robb Walsh's series on the history of Tex-Mex cuisine, which appeared in 2000; he tracks down the birthplace of nachos and fajitas (all Texas, baby). The popularity of "Mexican" food extends even to Mexico, where burritos and tacos are now common plates, which proves not even Mexico can stop Mexicans from invading anything and everything in the western hemisphere.

But with so many damn Mexicans in the United States, gabachos can finally experience a wider breadth of Mexico's food, one of the world's great cuisines. From the southern state of Oaxaca comes mole, an intoxicating thick sauce made with dozens of ingredients that simmer for hours. The coastal state of Sinaloa contributes *aguachile:* pickled cucumbers, onions, tomatoes, and shrimp served in lime juice in a *molcajete,* the mortar-and-pestle used by Mexican women to mush things up since forever. My state of Zacatecas likes *asadura,* boiled pig's blood, lungs, liver, heart, and many other goodies—Mexican haggis. Doesn't that sound better than the clammy taco-and-enchilada combo sitting in your fridge?

Can you trust a Mexican with your sushi?

SAYONARA, UNCLE SAM

Dear Gabacho: One of the unintended consequences of mass migration is the influx of Mexicans into kitchens and the preparation of the ethnic cuisines of other nations. I agree—it's somewhat disconcerting to sit at a sushi bar and have a dark-skinned wab shout *"Domo arigato!"* when you down a bottle of sake. But Mexicans are human chameleons, effortlessly adapting to the ways of the land, and pick up all the nuances of their workplace. Eat your sushi in peace, Sayonara—and don't act surprised if a sliver of jalapeño sneaks into your seared ahi tuna roll. We trust Mexicans with every other menial-but-important job there is—why not with our crunch rolls?

Why do Mexican men cook—but not in their own homes?

ANGRY MEXICAN HOUSEWIFE

Dear Wabbette: Simple: work is work, home is home. The Mexican man is an industrious species, but when he retires to the home, the last thing he wants to do is work. No man deserves to work in his home, so he enlists his wife to do everything—clean, unclog toilets, and especially cook. There's nothing demeaning about cooking, but women have been doing it for millennia, and hombres do it only as a way of making money. Besides, why bother to do anything when you have a broad dumb enough to do it? Which reminds me . . . Angry Mexican Housewife, can you slap together a quesadilla *pronto*?

7

Ethnic Relations

Chinitos, Negritos, Gabachos, and Wabs

Dear Mexican: I have very, very light skin because of my Scandinavian heritage. Around Halloween, someone asked me if it was whiteface makeup. Why is it that Mexican men find my pallor so fascinating?

FAIR MAIDEN

Dear Gabacha: *Because you're white.* Mexicans love gabachos even though you've fucked our country for five hundred years—literally (recall the maiden-raping conquistadors) and figuratively (ever tried walking a Mexican sidewalk during spring break without stepping in the puddles of yak left by frat boys?). Despite the boinking and barfing, Mexicans associate white with beauty and power—it's our national Stockholm syndrome. Check out our business elite—as white as those inbreds in the House of Windsor. Or the screeching fake-blond actresses in *telenovelas,* most of whom make Nicole Kidman look as dark as an aborigine. Whitey worship is evident even in our veneration of saints: when the Vatican canonized Juan Diego in 2002, Mexican

Catholic officials unveiled the official portrait of the man who first saw the Virgin of Guadalupe. Only one problem: the full-blooded Indian was now a light-skinned, full-bearded *broder*. So when Mexican men gawk at you, Fair Maiden, walk with pride: you are a goddess. That or you have a great ass.

What do Mexicans really think of Americans turning Mexico into Fort Lauderdale? Do Mexicans not care if gabacho college students embarrass themselves during spring break because they will gladly take our money? Would a Mexican stop it if he could? Am I giving Mexicans too much credit?

COAT CHECK GIRL AND HONOR STUDENT AT SMITH COLLEGE

Dear Gabacha: *Gracias* for the plug! The Mexican gave a keynote lecture April 6, 2006, at Smith College for their Latina Heritage Month festivities. It was right before Smith's spring break, so not that many *chicas calientes* remained to refry this bean—not even you, Coat Check Girl. They most probably joined the more than one hundred thousand students that the American embassy in Mexico says invade our southern neighbor each spring. Any student who wishes to join in the invasion, be forewarned: Mexicans will take only so much ribaldry. I refer you to *OC Weekly* Mexico correspondent Dave Wielenga, whose piece "Too Much Cabo Wabo" warned gabacho spring breakers that various gabacho pastimes such as public drinking, fights, and "corrupting a minor—even a sexy one—are very much against the law" and will earn offenders a stay in Mexico's hellish prison system.

These college students are a double-edged sword: on the one hand, Mexicans must wipe up their vomit, blood, semen, and piss—but that same effluvia funds jobs with billions of dollars. So what's a Mexican to do? Easy, move to *el Norte* and do the same damn thing. Let the gabachos experience the same conundrum—overtax their way of life, but reward them with slave labor and sweat instead of tits and beer bongs. And then make the Guatemalans clean up after us.

When I go to a party at a Mexican family's house, I sense they show a fake hospitality toward me with a strong underlining of disgust because I'm the ambassador from Crackerlandia. When I go grocery shopping at my local Mexican grocery store, I get dirty looks like I'm a black guy at a prestigious golf course. Mexicans always stare at me with a subtitle under their expressions that reads *pinche gabacho*. When did Mexicans assume the long-standing role of gabachos making people feel unwanted and alienated if they're not the same color?

TOKEN WHITE GUY

Dear Gabacho: The problem isn't that Mexicans are rude; the problem is you're the outsider. All minority groups exhibit an initial skepticism toward outsiders—they sometimes even kill them. I once attended the birthday party of a gay friend, and the dozen or so of us breeders initially sat together, politely but forcefully segregated by *los otros* ("the others," what polite Mexicans call homosexuals). We heteros didn't, however, resent *los otros*—we got that we were in a foreign environment, that we had to work for our acceptance, and that it wasn't anything personal. By the end of the night, we became part of their tribe and caterwauled to "It's Raining Men" as loudly as any homo.

I wish gabachos were as accepting of minorities, though. True story: I attended a mariachi show at a country club a couple of years back. While I was standing in line for a horrid Mexican buffet, a skinny, prissy thing approached. She asked if I could serve her some beans. I laughed. While I waited for the valet later that night, the same woman asked if I could grab her car. "Not unless you want it on cinder blocks," I replied. My Camry arrived. I paid the $5 charge and slipped the Mexican valet an extra $20.

Why do Mexicans hate the gays so much?

JUAN HOLMES

Dear Gabacho: There's a reason Dubya won 44 percent of the Latino electorate in 2004—*el presidente* preached the gospel of fag-bashing. He learned well from 2000, when Latinos in California voted for Proposition 22, the anti-gay-marriage initiative, by a wider margin than any other ethnic group. And Bush probably found the 2002 survey by the Tómas Rivera Policy Institute of the University of Southern California disclosing that 60 percent of Latino Catholics felt homosexuality is "always wrong," while 80 percent of Latino Protestants felt the same. In a community that's between 92 and 94 percent Christian, that's millions of votes. But although religion has much to do with Mexican *joto*-hating, it really goes back to two classic stereotypes that happen to be true: machismo and family. While English-speaking bros use the term *faggot* with ease, call an hombre a—take your pick—*fagote, hueco, joto, maricón, mariposa,* or *puto,* and you'll likely earn a Corona bottle in the face. More important, though, man love, in the Mexican psyche, threatens the family structure and doesn't produce babies—and without those features, you might as well be a gabacho.

I'm Polish/Italian, but nearly every time I encounter a Mexican, he or she asks if I'm Mexican. No other nationality ever asks me this. Why do Mexicans?

LATINA-LOOKING LADY

Dear Gabacha: I need more details, LLL. Were you wearing Dickies at the time? Cleaning a house? Maybe you're fat and/or sport a mustache? It could just be Mexicans think you're some distant cousin. Unlike their American counterparts, who wiped out the indigenous population, the various ethnic groups that migrated to Mexico over the centuries weren't ashamed to *coger* (fuck) the natives—and the natives *coger*-ed them right back. Thus, the phenotypical diversity of *la raza cósmica* is so dazzling many extended Mexican families include people who can pass for the darkest Nubian or the bluest-eyed Norse (and have you seen shots of Saddam Hussein? Doesn't he look like the Mexican janitor at your office building?). Conversely, our mutability means other ethnicities frequently assume we're members of their tribe. For instance, my large eyes, wavy black hair, and light olive skin lead people to believe I'm Persian, Filipino, Vietnamese, Japanese, Italian, Arab, Chinese, Indian, Lebanese, Greek, French, Croat . . . in fact, I've been called nearly everything but Mexican—and Guatemalan, thank goodness!

Why do my employees who are *chúntaros* (Mexican immigrants) seem to have a distaste for my employees who are *pochos* (Mexicans born in the United States) and vice versa? Is there any truth to this perception, or is it all in my deluded Italian-American brain?

DAMN ABRUZZESE GUINEA BUSINESS OWNER

Dear DAGO: You discovered what the Democrats refuse to acknowledge and the Republicans strangely refuse to exploit—the *pocho-chúntaro* divide. Mexican immigrants ridicule their *pocho* cousins for losing their *mexicanidad;* Mexican-Americans hate *chúntaros* because . . . well, they're Mexicans. But intra-ethnic hatred is not exclusively ours. Northern Italians spat on your swarthy forefathers, DAGO, when southern-Italian immigration to the United States began in earnest at the turn of the twentieth century. Similarly, the established Protestant Irish community of the mid-1800s brawled with the Catholic Irish (as aptly fictionalized in Martin Scorsese's *Gangs of New York*), while German Jews shunned their Eastern European *juden* brethren. The great thing about America is how quickly our tired, huddled masses become snarling, rabid immigrant haters— right, Arnold Schwarzenegger?

How does it feel to be known as America's new niggers?

MAMI, EL NEGRO ESTÁ RABIOSO

Dear Negrito: Look, just because Vicente Fox says something about Mexicans doesn't make it true. On May 13, 2005, Mexico's former *presidente* told a group of businessmen, "There's no doubt that the Mexican men and women—full of dignity, willpower, and a capacity for work—are doing the work that not even blacks want to do in the United States." African-American leaders rightly criticized Fox, who quickly apologized. But assuming that the words of the *pendejo*-in-chief reflect the sentiments of his people is like figuring all Americans are maladroits because Dubya runs the White House. Mexicans might be America's new underclass, the ethnic group that other minorities spit upon (Guatemalans, you're next!), but toiling in the fields and factories can never compare to shackles and *Soul Plane*. Fox's comments are reflective of his disastrous administration, which is the ultimate reason Mexicans continue to abandon their *patria* in droves—after all, who wants an inept leader like that? If only Americans were as smart . . .

I heard the Mexican on the radio recently, and it brought to mind one thing I'd been meaning to ask. The Mexican went on a rant some time ago about how hurtful the Taco Bell talking dog and the Frito-Lay Frito Bandito were (I start laughing just writing that; to think that someone would think twice about a cartoon character or a talking dog. Good God). But tell me, Mexican, why is the defamatory character that rides with the *¡Ask the Mexican!* column funny? Don't tell me it's a parody of the previous insults made by corporate America. If the Mexican were genuinely offended by the talking taco doggie, no doubt some Mexican-Americans that pick up the *Weekly* are equally hurt. Why don't you practice what you preach, Mexican? *¡Qué insultante!*

GEEZ, ÜMLAUTS ENRAGE YOUTH

Dear GÜEY: Gee, thanks a lot. How dare you say this column's logo is defamatory—that's a picture of me. Don't you know most Mexicans look like this? That's why the Taco Bell Chihuahua or the Frito Bandito are such affronts to the Mexican community—they're not authentic enough. When Mexican-American organizations protested the Taco Bell Chihuahua in the late 1990s, we weren't angry because he spoke like Mel Blanc's character on *The Jack Benny Show,* Sy the Mexican. We were angry because, in his most infamous commercial, the Taco Bell Chihuahua wore a beret. A beret! Where was the sombrero?! And where's the gold tooth, cactuslike beard, and evil leer on the Frito Bandito? That caricature is less Mexican than Ryan Seacrest. The authenticity of our *¡Ask a Mexican!* logo is what makes it funny, GÜEY—and if you can't laugh at racist depictions of wabs, gooks, or fags, then you, sir, are not human. Or are perhaps a Green Party member.

Isn't brown pride a PC adoption and morphing of white power?
SERAPES SCARE ME

Dear Gabacho: True, Serapes. And that's why events such as Hispanic Heritage Month are lame responses to centuries of gabacho oppression and exclusion. Hispanic Heritage Month is useful only to see how hilariously clueless gabacho administrators, newspaper editors—hell, the entire American power structure—still are about Latinos. Bake some *pan dulce,* throw in a salsa band, invite Edward James Olmos as a keynote speaker, and that's culture, right? Or run weepy profiles of Mexicans rising from nothing to barely something, as every daily newspaper does during Hispanic Heritage Month, and that pleases those pesky Latinos who clamor for positive, accurate coverage in the press, *¿qué no?*

What's worse is the litany of accomplishments recounted during Hispanic Heritage Month to show that Latinos are just like everyone else, but more so. Look—a Mexican astronaut! Golfer! Doctor! No gardeners here! And don't be surprised if you hear some MEChA student state some really out-there claim, like that Thomas Alva Edison was Mexican, that the Aztec empire went as far north as Michigan because the state name sounds like the central Mexican state of Michoacán, and that Mexican women take it up the butt to protect their virginity. All those cultural-pride *pendejadas* get tiresome after a while because it's nothing more than pandering and assumptions. Ask Mexicans what they're proud of, and they'll probably point to their shiny new Silverado.

My wife doesn't understand, and I'm not sure I do either. I'm a gringo, but all my friends are Mex. I eat Mex food almost exclusively. I watch Mex TV. I speak Spanish as much as possible. And I listen to Mex music. I have tried to make myself more gringo, but it doesn't seem to work. When I have time off from work, I often find myself flying to Monterrey or Mexico City to visit friends from high school. What should I do?

ONE CONFUSED GRINGO

How can a white girl like me become a *mexicana*?

WANNABE BROWN

Dear Gabacho y Gabacha: Both of you suffer from Edward James Olmos disease, an affliction caused when gabachos watch too many positive portrayals of Mexicans on film and television and thus think our life is one spent fighting racism, sharing a house with seventeen strangers, shooing a burro from the kitchen, and sweating through peso-paying jobs, but all of that is okay because we have *familia* and gabachos don't, so that's why Mexicans are such noble people, and shouldn't gabachos care about *familia* too? The remedy to this malady: live like a Mexican. Confused Gringo, rent an apartment in a barrio for a week—hell, even a day. I guarantee you the potholes, loitering cholos, and regular police-helicopter flybys will have you praising God for that *güero* skin of yours. And whoever told you being a Mexican *mujer* is great, Wannabe? From the day she is born, a *mexicana*'s life is war. Not only must she deal with a mom who thinks any daughter who returns from a date after 10 p.m. is pregnant five times over, but a *mexicana* must also live under the tyranny of machismo. A macho father. Macho brothers. Macho male friends. Macho boyfriends. Macho professors. Macho society. Macho strangers.

Macho columnists who don't bother to interview Mexican women in a column about Mexican femininity. That's why so many Mexican women try to be gabachas—explains the bleached hair, the light makeup, the successful white boyfriend. Besides, why do you think Mexican women are attending college in record numbers? Because of the homemaking classes?

Why do many Mexicans call themselves "Latino" instead of just "Mexican"? Are they ashamed of something?

COCONUT CARLOS

Dear Gabacho: What Mexicans are you talking to? Gloria Estefan? Self-appointed spokespeople for *la raza* such as your daily paper's "Latino" columnist and Dora the Explorer want you to believe Mexicans drop their nationality *en los Estados Unidos* in favor of the pan-hemispheric Latino. Well, that's a *pinche* lie. Only PC gabachos and Mexicans pining to be PC gabachos call Mexicans "Latinos." But you're right about Mexicans rarely calling themselves "Mexican," Coconut. Since there are so many damn Mexicans in Orange County, for instance, we more commonly identify ourselves by state—I, for instance, am from the central state of Zacatecas, Mexico. But since there are so many damn Zacatecans in Orange County, we usually branch off by *municipio*—the rough equivalent of a county. I'm from the *municipio* of Jerez, Zacatecas, but since there are so many damn *jerezanos* in Orange County, we then divide ourselves by *ranchos* (villages)—I hail from El Cargadero, Jerez, Zacatecas, Mexico. But since there are so many damn *cargaderenses* in Orange County . . . you get the picture. Provincialism is as Mexican as tequila and the illegal-immigrant cousin—there are multiple soccer and baseball leagues across the country organized around different *ranchos, municipios,* and states. In fact, the last thing a Mexican will call himself is a Mexican—and only to differentiate himself at work from that *méndigo* Guatemalan.

I'm a *pocho* and work with a Canadian and another Mexican. Every week when the Canadian and I read your column out loud, the Mexican never listens. He goes to the bathroom or doesn't pay attention. What's with our Mexican coworker's hate?

EL POCHO Y EL GABACHO CANADIAN

Dear Pocho y Gabacho: *Primeramente,* tell your *baboso* Mexican coworker *que se vaya a la chingada*—I'm *puro zacatecano* from the beautiful city of Jerez, Zacatecas. Second, all Mexican-on-Mexican bashing stems from class conflict—bone up on your Chicano studies, Pocho y Gabacho! Better-off Mexicans have always trashed poor Mexicans—look at the murder of Zapata, your typical *telenovela* plot, or the battle between assimilated Mexicans and those who just arrived. Similarly, loser Mexicans love nothing better than to pick on their betters. It's what one of my former professors used to call the crab theory—like crabs in a bag, loser Mexicans like to pull back those brave few who dream of a world free of Sunday-afternoon Raiders games and living with your parents until you're in your midthirties. But bringing down your race isn't exclusively a Mexican psychosis—Chris Rock once did an amazing monologue on how lower-class blacks derided their wealthier, smarter brethren for being "smarty-art niggers." Such squabbling helps keep the powerful powerful: the French pitted Hutu against Tutsi in Rwanda, Saddam Hussein did the same with Shiites and Sunni, and Cortés wrecked havoc with Tlascalas and Aztecs. So tell your *baboso* Mexican to stop hating you and me and turn his vitriol toward the true enemies: the Guatemalans.

I'm a gringo from Texas (or *Tejas,* as known to you) living in California. Are there any differences between a Mexican in California and a Mexican in Texas?

NOTHING BUT STEERS AND QUEERS

Dear Gabacho: The only things I know about Texicans are that it took more than six thousand of their ancestors to take back the tiny Alamo from one hundred and fifty or so gabacho intruders, and that the fan-club presidents of Texican musicians murder their idols. But in fairness to the undisputed wabs of the Mexican expatriate community, I forwarded your inquiry to the Daily Texican, a Seattle-based Tejano whose *Cholo Word of the Day* column on his eponymous blog is one of the Mexican's favorite Web sites.

"I don't know as many California Chicanos, so I may be way off," the Texican says. "But in *Tejas,* many Mexican-Americans would argue they have been accepted by the majority. Chicanos from California are much more militant than the ones from Texas but also seem much more rancho." Daily Texican went on to say Texicans dance to Tejano music—bass, accordion, and polka beats—and not *la quebradita*—brass band, synthesizers, and polka beats—like California Mexicans. "Both Texan and Californian Chicanos have kids with silver teeth and a mullet," Daily Texican adds.

Yet the Texican is way off. First off, California Mexicans call themselves Mexicans, not Chicanos. And our kids don't have silver teeth and a mullet—it's gold teeth (see my picture; they don't call me Gold-Tooth Gustavo for nothing) and a shaved head topped by a pink baseball hat worn at a forty-five-degree angle. More important, California Mexicans are a proud race of handsome, hardworking *gente;* Texicans smell like chili beans, have protruded foreheads, are lazy, eat their young, and don't put the cap back on the gas tank after filling up. Oh, and Alberto González will surely lead us to the gulags.

Unfortunately, the Daily Texan was deported.

I'm taking Spanish, and I'm wondering if Mexicans celebrate Hanukkah? We're researching religions and found nothing on Hanukkah, so I decided to ask you. Are there Jews in Mexico?

CHALLAH BURRITO

Dear Gabacha: Spanish class? In Washington? Did Vicente Fox suddenly become president of Canada? *Chula,* Jews own Mexico. That's why Mexicans are so anti-Semitic: a 2002 study by the Anti-Defamation League found that 44 percent of foreign-born Latinos hated

Jews, by far the largest percentage among ethnic groups in the United States. Mexicans don't even try to hide their hymie-hating. For instance, when a Mexican thinks someone is a slob, we call the person a *cochino marrano*—a dirty Jew. And don't believe your Spanish teacher when she pulls out the Webster's and reads that *marrano* means "pig"—Webster's doesn't know *mierda* about Spanish etymology. *Marrano* does mean "pig" but was also the term used to label Jews who hid their beliefs in order to survive the Spanish Inquisition. Oh, and Mexicans do celebrate Hanukkah, but we light policemen instead of menorahs.

As an Asian, would I be considered a gabacho? Or do I fall into the yellow bucket labeled *chinito*, even though I'm not Chinese?

NOT CHINESE!

Dear Chinito: Just as Americans assume all Latinos are Mexican, Mexicans think all Asians are *chinos*—Chinese. When I used to go out with a Vietnamese woman, my aunts would speak highly of *mi chinita bonita*—my cute little Chinese *ruca*. When I'd point out she was actually Vietnamese, *mis tías* would think about it for a bit and respond, "*¡Qué chinita bonita!*"

But just because a Mexican calls you a *chino* doesn't necessarily mean we think you're Chinese, Not Chinese. *Chino*, like so many of our swear words, has multiple negative meanings. In the colonial days, a *chino* was the offspring of a half-Indian/half-black and an Indian. This association with race also trans-formed *chino* into a synonym for "servant" and "curly." The term *barrio chino* (Chinatown) also became a euphemism for a town's red-light district. And a popular schoolyard refrain that all Mexican kiddies eventually chant at their Asian classmates is *Chino, chino, japonés, come caca y no me des* (Chinese, Chinese, Japanese, eat shit and don't give me any).

So why the Mexican *chino*-hate? After all, Chinese were the Mexicans of the world before there even was a Mexico, migrating to Latin America a couple of decades after the fall of Tenochtitlán. And our most famous native dress, the billowy, colorful costume worn by *baile folklórico* dancers known as a *china poblana,* was supposedly first worn by a seventeenth-century Mexican-Chinese woman. Bigotry is bigotry, though, and since Mexico's Asian population is still small and overwhelmingly Chinese, we lump Asians into the *chino* category—makes the racism easier, you know?

Why are Mexican activists aligning themselves with African-Americans? The same race of people the majority of Mexicans refer to as *pinche mayates*?

FIRMLY PLANTED WHITE GUY

Dear Gabacho: Because they're paying attention to the street. The *Christian Science Monitor* reported August 11, 2005, that the Reverend Al Sharpton and the granddaughter of César Chávez formed the Latino & African American Leadership Alliance in the hope that it "will help stop the two groups from undermining one another in competition for public dollars and programs." Sharpton and Chávez rightfully want to do something about the tension that keeps escalating between Mexicans and African-Americans in Southern California—witness the race riots at Jefferson High School in Los Angeles in 2005 and the furor provoked after Vicente Fox said Mexicans in the United States are "doing the work that not even blacks want to do."

But you're right, Firmly Planted: perhaps relations between African-Americans and Mexicans would improve if we didn't commonly refer to African-Americans as *mayates* (beetles). But that's probably the most polite racial slur we use toward blacks, considering many Mexicans also call them *negrito* (little darkie), *llanta* (tire), *sandía* (watermelon), *aguacate* (avocado, after the fruit's gnarled skin), *negro azabache* (wild Negro), *chango* (monkey), *Sorrullo* (after a black character in the *cumbia* classic "Capullo y Sorrullo"), *Memín Pinguín* (after the black comic-book character who appeared on those offensive stamps that caused such a ruckus in 2005), *Cirilo* (after the little black boy in the TV show *Carrusel,* the Mexican equivalent of the animated series *Recess*), *Cucurumbé* (after the title character in a famous song by the Mexican Raffi, Cri-Cri), and many, many more. With a Rolodex of racism like that, *mayate* is as inoffensive as Booker T. Washington.

How come you call yourself a Mexican? By definition, you're a Chicano, not a Mexican. A Mexican is a person that was born and raised in Mexico, not beautiful Orange County. A Mexican is a person that is proud of his country and appreciates and respects the Mexican flag even though he left the country years ago. A Mexican read the free textbooks provided by the Secretaria de Educación Pública during his school years and studied Mexican history. A Mexican is a person who sang the Mexican national anthem every Monday morning while watching six kids carry the flag around. Mexicans know the difference between the more than 150 chilis that exist in our country. Mexicans grew up eating candies with different chilis. Mexicans watch Televisa and Televisión Azteca, not Telemundo or Univisión. Mexicans speak fluent Spanish, not Spanglish. Mexicans came to this country to work hard and have a decent life, not to destroy this place like you and your people believe. Mexicans believe that family and religion are the most important values. Mexicans are not planning to take over California— we are too lazy to even think about it, and we do not believe in wars. I can go on and on describing the differences between you and me, but let's just leave it like that. How can you even describe our culture, values, or behavior if you don't have a clue about it? Eating burritos at Taco Bell, going to Mexican parties in SanTana, or having Grandma cooking some Mexican dishes doesn't make you a Mexican.

A REAL MEXICAN

Dear Wab: Let's run down your list: check (most of my parents' *rancho* had relocated to Anaheim by the time I was born); check, check (my dad's cousin was a history teacher in Mexico); check, check, check, check (where do you think Univisión gets most of its programming? Lifetime?), *por supuesto;* check, check, and too late. Add to this my mestizo heritage, the facts that *mi papi* was an illegal immigrant and I didn't speak fluent English until I was six or seven, and that I grew a mustache in the time it took you to read this sentence, and I'm more Mexican than Pedro Infante. Besides, who made you arbiter of *mexicanidad,* Real Mexican? National character is never static, and anyone who claims otherwise is as deluded as a Minuteman.

I'm fairly sure that your gibes against Guatemalans are mostly for comic effect, but, *entre broma y broma, algo se asoma.* What have you got against the true *raza cósmica?*

GUATEMALAN GUAPO

Dear Chapín: "Between joke and joke, something peeks out." Nice *dicho* (aphorism), Guapo! But you didn't ask a question about Mexicans, *pendejo.* I'll make an exception, though, since the United States, Mexico, and Guatemala are brothers in soccer futility.

Mexicans despise Guatemalans for many legitimate reasons. Your tamales are better—our puny corn variety doesn't compare to your wondrous *paches,* potato tamales stuffed with chicken, and just about the most filling, tasteful snack in the Americas. The Mayans contributed more to world culture than the Aztecs—did you know the Mayan calendar remains the most accurate in history? Your national bird, the long-feathered quetzal, is prettier than our golden eagle. In 1821, free from the yoke of Spanish rule, Guatemala joined the burgeoning Empire of Mexico—only to spurn us two years later for the United Provinces of Central America, a coalition of Central American nations created to resemble the United States but whose corruption and monocultural economics instead inspired the term *banana republic.*

But Mexicans hate Guatemalans mostly because of immigration, Guapo. Mexico can barely control its southern border with Guatemala because the Guatemalan government does *nada* to secure its side, leaving Mexico exposed to illegal immigrants, drug runners, and terrorists. Guatemalans top Mexico's annual list of the most deported. And the Guatemalans who do cross over dress funny, are darker-skinned than the average Mexican, and don't like salsa—some don't even speak

Spanish! Guatemalans are the Mexicans of Mexico—and who doesn't hate Mexicans?

Why is it that many (I won't say most) Mexicans don't bother to become U.S. citizens, buy homes, or get educated? So many things are offered here, and I don't see Mexicans taking the time to better themselves. I see other ethnic groups like the Asians and Cubans go a lot further to establish themselves in this country. I think it's the "*cangrejo* theory" myself.

CURIOUS MICHOACANO MEXICAN

Dear Wab: You're referring to the "crab theory," a train of thought popular among Chicano scholars that I mentioned earlier. It posits that Mexicans act like crabs in a vat by pulling back the brave few who seek a better life. The stats seem to prove it: a 2003 study by the Urban Institute showed only 34 percent of eligible Mexicans naturalized during 2001; by comparison, 67 percent of eligible Asians and 58 percent of other eligible Latin American immigrants became citizens that year.

But there isn't a cultural explanation for the phenomenon, Michoacáno Mexican. Most of the Mexicans in my life came to this country illegally, became legal due to marrying citizens (or the 1986 amnesty), bought their homes, and learned just enough English to vote for Hispanic-surnamed candidates every election. I know Mexicans who still aren't citizens but nevertheless own businesses, homes, and trucks large enough to cart a brass *banda* down the interstate. That they left the land of their ancestors for a country that despises them is proof enough the Mexicans here are those brave few who escaped the stagflating masses. Compare that with the gabacho citizens of this country, who get fat and watch *Dancing with the Stars* as Mexicans *reconquistan* the land.

Why don't Mexicans like being called Hispanics? The Spaniards conquered our ancestors—that's why we're Spanish-speaking Catholics. Why deny this?

HISPANIC DOESN'T MAKE ME PANIC

Dear Spic: Because Mexicans aren't Hispanic—Mexicans are Mexican. Besides, the history of *Hispanic* involves two attributes Mexicans despise: political correctness and a clueless bureaucracy. In 1975, Caspar Weinberger—then secretary of health, education, and welfare—created the Ad Hoc Committee on Racial and Ethnic Definitions to address the country's increasing diversity and to force bureaucrats to evolve beyond such antiquated, offensive terms as "colored," "Oriental," and "Guatemalan." According to a 2003 *Washington Post* article, the secretive committee—no minutes exist of their meetings—decided that the government would use *Hispanic* rather than *Latino* to describe the hordes that, then and now, swarm across our southern borders. Not all the committee members agreed, and the debate over whether to use *Hispanic* or *Latino* has raged ever since. Ultimately, though, neither side wins: a 2002 Pew Hispanic Center study discovered that 54 percent of Hispanics/Latinos/wabs primarily identify themselves by the country of their ancestry, while only a quarter of those surveyed called themselves either Hispanic or Latino. And contrary to Chicano urban legend, the Richard Nixon administration *didn't* institute *Hispanic*. Although Weinberger was the Orange County native's secretary of health, education, and welfare, the Dickster was far from Washington when Weinberger, then reporting to President Gerald Ford, created the ad hoc committee that settled on *Hispanic*. Sucks, doesn't it? I mean, wouldn't it have been swell if we could've included *Hispanic* alongside the Minuteman Project, *Mendez vs. Westminster,* and the Taco Bell Burrito Supreme in the Orange County Mexican-Bashing Hall of Fame?

How come niggers don't like Mexicans? It seems like they are welcome at our bars, but when you go to their bars, these motherfuckers act like you're trying to reinstitute slavery. Don't these *chanates* know that we don't think like the white man?

NIGGARACHI

Dear Wab: Time and time again wabs like you show why tensions between Mexicans and African-Americans are waiting for a match. To bridge this perilous racial gap, I urge wabs to consult Nashieqa Washington's *Why Do Black People Love Fried Chicken? And Other Questions You've Wondered but Didn't Dare Ask?* According to Washington, blacks don't like Mexicans because they feel Mexicans are slowly displacing them "socially, politically, and economically . . . with shifting ethnic demographics (i.e., more Latinos), I fully expect these tensions to extend beyond poor blacks into wider society." Washington is right—flare-ups between old and new communities in the United States are as American as jazz. But one thing Washington doesn't mention is how fiercely Mexicans dump on African-Americans, which gives them every right to want us deported. For chrissake, Niggarachi, you called African-Americans *niggers, motherfuckers,* and *chanates* (the Mexican-Spanish word for "blackbird"—and yet another slur in our Rolodex of Racism used against blacks) in your question—and you still have to ask why "they" hate us?

To order a copy of Washington's book, visit www.yourblackfriend.com.

Why, as a group sharing a common language, do Spanish-speaking peoples segregate themselves by nationality or culture and then complain that they are discriminated against by others?

MIXED-UP MESTIZA

Dear Wab: The segregationist answer is simple—that's how ethnic groups cope with living in a new land. What else explains the Chinatowns, Little Saigons, and Lower East Sides of the country? When streets turn into Little Mexicos, they're just following the natural progression of the immigrant experience. Gabachos do the same thing too—it's called the Hamptons. Your critique of Mexicans always crying discrimination is even easier to explain: the immigrants are still Mexicans, aren't they?

I'm a Mexican *güero:* light-skinned, green-eyed, and blond/brown-haired. I experience more racism from my own people than gabachos. Why so much hate toward Mexican *güeros* by my darker-

skinned *raza*? Do I remind the *pinches indios* too much of their Spanish conquerors? Are they just jealous that their horny *rucas* and sisters keep putting the moves on me? All of the above?

GÜERO AND LOVING IT!

Dear Pocho: The only thing Mexicans alternately love and hate more than *los Estados Unidos* are *güero* (light-skinned) Mexicans. Blame the Aztecs: when the light-skinned, bearded Spaniards showed up in Mexico in 1519, Moctezuma and amigos thought the conquistadors were manifestations of Quetzalcoatl, a light-skinned, bearded deity that oral tradition promised would return to save mankind in 1519—the very year the Spaniards showed up. The Spaniards quickly put that myth to waste by destroying the Aztec empire, but that initial reverence for *güeros* seared itself in the Mexican psyche. Light skin became synonymous with power, wealth, destruction. Dark skin meant *indio:* loser, poor, *estúpido* enough to believe that marauders were gods. Not even the efforts of Mexican intellectuals during the 1920s to popularize the idea of Mexicans as *la raza cósmica* (the cosmic race, made up of black, Indian, and white blood) could destroy the stranglehold *güerismo* has on Mexico. That's why you see light-skinned Mexicans on television, in the presidential palaces, and in corporate offices. Being a Mexican *güero* takes you only so far, though, Güero and Loving It: you're still Mexican, after all.

Why are Mexicans "proud" to be from Mexico when their country is such a filthy cesspool of lying, thieving, child-raping whores? I mean, especially once they make it to the U.S., why don't they say, "Whew! I may have been born there [Mexico], but I'm sure glad I got outta that shithole!"

MEXICANS SUCK RICK

Dear Gabacho: Calm down, Lou Dobbs. Nothing in this world is pure and sacred outside of the Virgin of Guadalupe and my sister, amigo, so take your patriotism with a nice dose of reality. Patriotism is the last refuge of a scoundrel, and Mexicans are notoriously jingoistic even though Mexico *is* such a fucked-up country. But really, what is there to be proud of with *any* country? Every nation has its skeletons—or have you already forgotten the millions of Indians the United States slaughtered so you could have the right to write your *estúpido* question? About the greatest national sin Mexico bestowed upon the world was Cabo Wabo tequila—and that came courtesy of a gabacho.

Why are Mexicans always categorized as nonwhite? Aren't some Mexicans white and some black?

BLACK BUMS UNITED

Dear Negrito: Mexican-American activists have historically fought to be classified as white. In 1936, for instance, the League of United Latin American Citizens convinced the Census Bureau to reclassify Mexicans as "white," a change reflected in the 1940 Census and that remained unchanged until the government re-reclassified Mexicans as "beaners" in the 1980 census. If you believe the Mexican government, however, Mexicans are *everything*. Black. White. Indian. Chinese. All rolled into one. The idea of Mexicans as constituting a unique race comes courtesy of José Vasconcelos, Mexico's former secretary of education. In 1925, Vasconcelos wrote *La Raza Cósmica*, one of the most influential works in Mexican history. Vasconcelos argued that the future of the world was that of mixed races, and since Latin America—specifically Mexico—was already at that level, Mexico would rule supreme. Mexicans and their smelly Chicano activist cousins have long celebrated the theory as proof of their racial superiority, but they should actually *read La Raza Cósmica*. Vasconcelos was a hypocrite—for all his rhetoric on the superiority of the mestizo, he still left a soft spot in his heart for Mexico's conquistadors, arguing, "We will not be great as long as the Spaniard of America does not feel as Spanish as the sons of Spain." This point invalidates his *raza cósmica* argument and shows why the terms *Mexican* and *intellectual* fit together as well as *Madonna* and *modest*.

Why do Mexicans hate Spain so much? The five hundred Spaniards under Cortés would not have been able to defeat the

Aztecs if not for how hated the Aztecs were by other Mexican indigenous people. The figure of 100 million people slaughtered by the Spaniards is not true, and many more were sacrificed by the Aztecs than by Spaniards, so what gives?

POCHO PENOSO

Dear Wab: Really—what's there to like about Spain? Tiny, timid country that couldn't keep its empire together for more than two centuries and helped invade Iraq. *Putos* whose sole contributions to world culture are Picasso, Dalí, and the party island of Ibiza, and who can't keep illegal immigrants from crossing the Straits of Gibraltar. And then there's their Conquest legacy. You'd hate a country too if it slaughtered your ancestors, enslaved them, raped them, and looted the country out of billions of dollars. More important, Spaniards despise Mexicans as half-breeds, so we have every right to dismiss them as fey Europeans. Besides, gimme a break. The Irish don't like the English; the Aborigines don't thank Britain for sending its criminals to Australia; whither the indigenous blacks of South Africa. You don't love the father who slapped your face, then raped you, and left you alone.

Why are Indians so hated in Mexico? Isn't most of the population of Indian descent?

GERONIMO!

Dear Gabacho: Few countries have a more complicated relationship with their indigenous than Mexico. Visit Mexico's major cities, and you'll probably find statues honoring the last Aztec emperor, Cuauhtémoc, renowned for his courage (and conveniently forgotten for getting killed by Spaniards). Aztec pyramids decorate the country's currency. But then there's the tricky problem of *mestizaje,* the mixing of European and Indian blood that created about 60 percent of the country's population. The Spaniards imprinted in their mixed-blood children that Indians were subhuman, and the resulting racial chaos left Indians at the bottom, where they remain today. Mexico's Indians are the poorest of the poor and a national shame—indeed, to call someone an *indio* is as bad as using the n-word here. But these *indios* might get the last laugh: the Mayan calendar, the most accurate calendar ever developed by man, mysteriously ends in 2012. If the calendar holds to form—and it's accurately predicted lunar and planetary cycles for over a millennia—those dirty Indians will have the last laugh.

My first North American ancestor was born a Spaniard in what today is Texas in 1729. I am the tenth generation born north of the San Antonio River. We became Texans and Americans by default. We have been in Texas nearly three hundred years and have never moved. My family lived under the Mexican flag less than fourteen years over one hundred and sixty years ago. Why do my Anglo friends and enemies call me a Mexican?

LONE ESTRELLA

Dear Wab: *Gracias* for exposing America's immigration secret. Despite all the racket about America and its indefatigable melting pot, America has never bothered to assimilate Mexicans even as Mexicans assimilate into America. The United States has a vested interest in not assimilating Mexicans: we need a racialized enemy. Hating the Other was crucial in forming this nation's national identity and proved a perfect fuel to power Manifest Destiny: consider our Indian wars and the justification of slavery. Now that African-Americans are a part of the American fabric and Indians are safely away on chunks of desert, America turns to Mexicans for their racial needs. They couldn't have asked for a better opponent: Mexico shares a border and engaged in two wars with gabachos. Pancho Villa invaded New Mexico in 1916 in the last incursion into American soil until Al Qaeda started their hijinks, and Mexico continues to send over its citizens by the millions each year. That sucks for the rest of us *pochos,* who might have all the money in the world but will ultimately never be anything better than a Mexican in the minds of millions of Americans. Accept your fate, Estrella—and chuck a taco at the next gabacho you see.

Why do all those Mexican cholos call us white girls *güera*? It obviously means "white girl" or something, but it's not like I go around calling them beaners or whatever. That goes for black girls too because they call them *negritas*. Why can't they just call us by our name?

MEXICAN GIRL AT HEART

Dear Gabacha: Those who throw stones shouldn't . . . look, you're whining about Mexicans calling you *güera,* and you call them Mexican cholos! Why can't you just call them wabs? Afraid they might jump you? But you can't blame Mexicans for being so obsessed with race—it's hardwired into our souls. While the United States never truly jumped into the miscegenation bed other than for the occasional slave-massa rape, Mexico owes its existence to everyone fucking everyone until most of its citizens became a mestizo glop. To justify their place in Mexican society, the Spaniards created what's called the *casta* (caste), with *peninsulares* (natives of Spain) on the top, followed by *criollos* (full-blooded Europeans born in Mexico), mestizos (Europeans with Indians), mulattoes (Europeans with blacks), and devolving through an incredible thirty others until you reached the bottom of the bottom: a *zambo,* a mixture of Indian and black. You improved your status in society by improving your racial classification, and Mexicans have obsessed over their blood mixture since. That doesn't excuse your Mexican friends' racism, but now you know why they call you a *güera.* Be happy that the Mexicans called you a *güera,* though, and not a *puta.*

Why do Mexicans hate *chilangos* so much? What do *paisanos* have against people from Mexico City? It seems to be a very long, deep-rooted bias. It's to the point that my husband does not want to admit he's from DF unless he wants to scare off any potential *sanchos* I may be lining up.

LA GÜERA LOCA CON ESPOSO CHILANGO

Dear Gabacha: A popular saying in Mexico is *Haz patria a México: mata un Chilango*—"Be patriotic for Mexico: kill a Chilango"—and few would disagree. Just as Americans hate New Yorkers, Angelenos, and anyone else from urban areas that think they're the epicenter of the universe, the Mexican nation despises the 25 million or so *cabrones* that live in and around *el DF* (Mexico City's official name in Spanish is México Distrito Federal—Mexico Federal District—or DF for short). But the hate for *chilangos*—the slang used to describe someone from Mexico City—goes deeper than a dislike for New Yawkers. Mexico City represents Mexico in all its terrifying, magnificent glory. It's the birthplace of modern Mexico, of impurity and endless sprawl, where the mestizo, overcrowding, and rampant pollution began. It stands on the former Aztec capital of Tenochtitlán, where the Spaniards first began their conquest of Mexico. It's one of the few places on earth where the contrasts between epochs come with every city block. Highrises stand within view of Aztec pyramids, majestic Catholic cathedrals are built from the ruins of the pyramids. And on top of that, *chilangos* speak a wonderfully vulgar argot that sounds like a monkey screeching while whistling that provides endless hours of mimicking fun for Mexican comics. "Together," Ruben Gallo wrote in his introduction to *The Mexico City Reader,* a fine collection of essays about *el DF,* "[Mexico City dwellers] form an unlikely cast of characters that turn the city into a vast stage for unpredictable everyday dramas: a chaotic, vibrant, delirious city." Mexico City, in conclusion, is modernity writ with tequila.

It's hard out here for a brotha! First we had to deal with those pieces of shit called the KKK and their supporters. Now we have to deal with the freakin' Mexican invasion. Now I see why whites fretted over seeing their neighborhoods turn dark when Cleophus and LaKeisha moved in. Now we're being overrun by Pedro and María and their carloads of kids and assorted *la familia* members. If you cruise the Dallas neighborhoods of Oak Cliff and South Dallas, you see greasy taco stands where there used to be a greasy catfish or fried-chicken place. We're being pushed to the suburbs, dude. We used to go to garage sales, but fat Mexican women are camping out overnight to get to them first—damn, they take garage sales seriously! Pretty soon schools will change their names from Carver High to Cheech Marín High. Shit, I better learn Spanish *el rapido*. Can't your people let us keep some semblance of our hood?!

CHITLINS AIN'T MENUDO

Dear Negrito: Why should Mexicans deviate from history? The American ethnic experience hews to a rigid trajectory that goes like this: Immigrants settle in the bad part of town because gabachos won't tolerate minorities near their homes. Said immigrants revitalize undesirable neighborhoods. The barrio/ghetto/hood is born. It flourishes for a generation. Gabachos visit solely for hole-in-the-wall restaurants, prostitutes, drugs, gambling, and cockfights. The immigrants sweat through life to get their children into college, only to see the kids repudiate their wabby parents and move to the suburbs. A new wave of immigrants living eight to a couch settle in the old neighborhood. The remaining pioneer immigrants despise the newbies for replacing the businesses, languages, and culture of their once familiar streets but can't stop the change. The old generation dies. The new immigrants prosper. And the circle of life begins again. You claim to understand this, Chitlins, so get over your lost catfish stands and join Cleophus and LaKeisha in scaring the gabachos out of the suburbs and back into their hipster downtowns. But don't get too settled in; in a couple of years, Mexicans will relocate to your suburban hood to get away from the Guatemalans, who are destroying our quaint barrios as we speak.

Why do spics and micks get along so well? Is it because both races are drunk, fornicating, degenerate Catholics?

DON MULLETINO

Dear Mick: Get your racial slurs correct—Mexicans are *wabs*, not *spics*. Otherwise, you nailed it on the *cabeza, cabrón*. And the similarities don't end there. The Irish were the Mexicans of the United States before the Mexicans. Millions of them migrated to this country destitute, as indentured servants (the precursor to the bracero program), and even as illegal immigrants. They were fleeing a homeland under siege by evil Protestants only to find similar treatment in the States. Gabachos here maligned the Irish for their Catholicism, their funny English, big families, and constant inebriation, stereotypes popularized by the mainstream press. The Irish fought back: they formed gangs and voting blocs, and—in the case of the Saint Patrick's Battalion—hundreds of soldiers defected to the Mexican side during the 1846 Mexican-American War.

But the Irish in America, to paraphrase Noel Ignatiev's famous 1995 book, eventually became white, while Mexicans will forever remain Mexicans in the eyes of gabachos. Nevertheless, the spic-mick connection continues. I know many children of Irish-Mexican heritage who call themselves *leprecanos,* a miscegenation of the words *leprechaun* and *Chicano.* Many Irish-American civic organizations support amnesty for illegals since about fifty thousand Irish immigrants have no papers. Mexico and Ireland have harsh laws against illegal immigration and must constantly deal with their idiot cousins across the border, Guatemala and Northern Ireland. And gabachos have warped our precious St. Patrick's Day and Cinco de Mayo holidays into bacchanals of booze and women—on second thought, that's a compliment. Our races are brothers in depravity, Don Mulletino, so let's unite and throw the gabachos down the well, *¿qué no?*

8

Fashion

Fake Blondes, Mustaches, and Swimming with Jeans

Dear Mexican: It can be ninety-five degrees outside and everyone else is sweating, but without fail, there is always a Mexican male walking around in a long—sometimes short-sleeved—plaid shirt with only the top two buttons buttoned. What does this mean?

FASHIONABLY PERPLEXED

Dear Gabacha: I haven't seen the buttoned-up Pendleton look in years—Mexican males nowadays prefer dress-long sports jerseys or ironic T-shirts with such slogans as "Powered by Frijoles" or "Indigenous Inside" styled as the Intel logo. If you still see Mexican men sporting the two-button look, then I refer you to UC Irvine professor James Diego Vigil's 1988 study *Barrio Gangs: Street Life and Identity in Southern California,* which scholars regard as the "Doing Fieldwork among the Yanomamo" of Mexican anthropology even decades after its publication. In *Barrio Gangs,* Vigil theorizes the Pendleton look is popular among Mexican men because "it conjures up the image of a group behind you, even if you are not what you represent. There is a certain amount of security created in that pause when an observer has to think about your social ties." So just like stuttering hipsters who wear a faded $30 Hall and Oates T-shirt, the hombres who still button up their Pendletons are sheer poseurs—except these poseurs can kick your ass.

What's the deal with Mexicans and Dickies?

DICKLESS

Dear Gabacho: "Ironically, and perhaps predictably," Vigil continues in his exemplary *Barrio Gangs,* the popularity of khaki pants such as Dickies among Mexicans "stemmed from public sources—military and penal." After World War II and the Korean War, according to Vigil, our fightin' brown boys returned in neatly pressed military-issue uniforms to the admiring eyes of their younger siblings. "[Wearing khakis] was the youngsters' way to identify with older brothers and relatives who had been in the armed forces," the professor wrote. *Barrio Gangs* also mentioned that kids picked up on khaki fashions from older brothers who did a different kind of stint—jail. And then there's the poverty factor: "As with other low-income people who try to stretch their dollars, the cholos have sought to find dependable, comfortable, durable, and reasonably priced clothing." Since jail and the military still remain the primary career paths for many low-income Mexicans, it's not surprising that Mexicans continue to wear Dickies. As for our young men's current fascination with pansy-ass white K-Swiss sneakers and the color pink? Blame metrosexuality, the biggest threat to machismo since the two-income household.

What's with those beautiful belts Mexican men wear?

BUCKLED UNDER

Dear Gabacho: With the decline of suspenders, Americans just don't care about what holds up their pants anymore. Not so the Mexicans. We like to use a *cinto pitiado*—a tawny leather belt embroidered with creamy white threads derived from the same plant that gives the world tequila. (It's the agave, stupid.) The *cinto pitiado* isn't some Wal-Mart castoff or the canvas strap with an initialized silver buckle that homeboys prefer for their Dickies—the *cinto pitiado* is honest-to-goodness wearable art. It's the most beautiful thing a man can wrap around his waist that doesn't have long, curly hair.

Each *cinto pitiado* features distinct ornate geometric designs spanning the length of the belt—abstract vines, geometric conundrums, elegant curves, all a legacy of the Moorish artistic influence over the Hispanic world. The carousel of shapes ends at the buckle with a singular logo—could be the wearer's initials, maybe a silhouette of a barnyard animal. With the recent rise in the narco business, some drug dealers are even adorning their belts with machine guns and marijuana leaves. Hell, I once saw a Calvin pissing on some Mexican soccer-team logo—but better you stay away from that auto fashion faux pas.

Buying a *cinto pitiado* reflects on how much pride you take in dressing splendidly. You can visit your local Mexican clothing store and come out looking sharp in a $50 imitation *cinto pitiado* produced in some Los Angeles factory. But to get the real deal, the kind that takes months to produce and costs about a month's worth of cleaning houses, talk to your neighborhood Mexican from Jalisco or Zacatecas, where the art of *cinto pitiado* reaches cubist levels. If a Mexican man visits these states, it's almost inevitable he will return with a couple of belts for his friends. Take note, Homeland Security: the *cinto pitiado* smuggling business is the best contraband since turtle soup.

How come Mexican men wear belt buckles that look like wrestling belts?

R.I.P. EDDIE GUERRERO

Dear Gabacho: Think utility, vanity, and Freud. A massive belt buckle ensures that our sturdy belts won't burst under the double strains of the tools we hang from it—whether they be wrenches, cell phones, or revolvers—and the bellies that rise from our middles like Kilimanjaro in the Tanzanian plains. It's a Mexican man's most cherished accessory after the *tejana* and alligator boots, so of course he'll glam up his buckles with engravings—names, arabesque designs, and pastoral scenes are the most popular. But owning a *bonito* buckle isn't enough for Mexican men. As Freud points out, anytime men flash abnormally large possessions—whether it's goateed gabachos flying the American flag from their Ford F250s or the military with its missiles—it's a stand-in for our cocks. In an hombre's case, however, the buckle is a stand-in for our less-than-stellar members (most sexology surveys rank Latinos third behind blacks and gabachos on the large-*pipi* scale). So, ladies, the larger the buckle, the teenier the weenie.

Why do Mexican men always wear cowboy hats and boots?
WETBACK MOUNTAIN

Dear Gabacho: Americans would *love* to believe Mexicans will never assimilate into this great land, but the sartorial style you describe is the perfect counterevidence. Each region in Mexico has its own traditional headgear, from the fabulously embroidered sombreros of Jalisco to the massive straw canopies immortalized by Emiliano Zapata, and all points in between for humility or ostentatiousness— but always big. As with all clothes, the sombrero serves the primary purpose of protecting against the elements—in Mexico's case, the unforgiving sun. When Mexicans sneak into the United States, though, they adopt the American hat best suited for working outside: the Stetson-style cowboy hat, which is native to the regions once owned by Mexico—hence their name in Mexican Spanish: *tejanas* (Texans). Why don't we keep the sombrero as we do our language, machismo, and taste for chili-coated, lead-based candy, you ask? Because we're smart. Sombreros are so damn huge that they function as bull's-eyes for immigration authorities. Wearing a sombrero here screams POR FAVOR DEPORT ME. As for the cowboy boots? Then and now, on this side of the border and *el otro lado,* comfortable and pointedly perfect for kicking ass.

The current clothing trend is for ladies to wear low-cut jeans and belly shirts that expose their midriffs. That looks great on a hard-bodied woman, but why do so many fat Mexican *mujeres* insist on dressing like this? I can't believe they look in the mirror and think they look attractive!

FAT IS MALO

Dear Gabacho: American men might prefer boinking skinny things, but the wisdom of the ancients still informs the male Mexican mind, and the ancients loved fatties. Many pre-Columbian codices and statues depict women as *gorditas*—plump *chicas*. Obesity meant wealth, fertility, what Groucho Marx called "an armful of fun on a cold night." But it wasn't just the Aztecs or Mayans who loved their ladies large. Carl Jung and other psycho-mythologists point to the Earth Mother, found in almost all societies, as one of the most powerful archetypes of the collective unconscious. Most artistic renditions of the Earth Mother depict her as *retre*-voluptuous—think of the Venus of Willendorf, the famous prehistoric statue of a fertility goddess with massive breasts, vulva, and stomach . . . come to think of it, this Venus bears an uncanny resemblance to those Mexican women you so hate, Fat Is Malo. A bad diet also explains the endemic obesity among Mexican women, but all that a massive *mujer* does when she squeezes into those low-cut jeans and belly shirts is transform into the Earth Mother and invite males to partake of her eternal fecundity. And, judging by the litters of kids Mexican women produce, more men take up the invitation than not.

Why do Mexicans swim in the ocean with their clothes on? I mean, denim?!

VICENTE FOX'S MUSTACHE

I know this might be a seasonal question, but why do Mexicans like swimming in their clothes? Is it a Catholic thing? I remember as a child growing up that my *pocho* Catholic cousin even bathed at home

in his T-shirt and underwear through his adolescence. He claims the nuns told him it was a sin to be naked.

BABOSO

I am half-Mexican myself but just don't understand—why do Mexicans wear their clothes when swimming? They are the only people at a beach or public swimming spot who do it. Very bizarre—please explain!

HALF-MEXICAN

Dear Pochos: This is by far the most-asked question in *¡Ask a Mexican!* history. So, to *todos ustedes,* I have my own question: are you all brown chubby chasers? As with gabachos, an alarming number of Mexicans are out of shape. According to a 2003 study by the Organization for Economic Co-operation and Development, 24 percent of Mexico's population is overweight. That's the second-highest obesity rate in the world following—wait for it—*¡los Estados Unidos!* Unlike gabachos, Mexicans respect the public when it comes to flashing our flabby *chichis, pompis,* and *cerveza* guts—so when we're out near the pool or by the beach, we cover up. It ain't Catholicism, machismo, or an homage to our swim across the Rio Grande. It's good manners.

Why do Mexicans put on their Sunday best to shop at Wal-Mart, Kmart, Target, and the swap meet?

FLAT-HEELED MEXICAN

Dear Pocha: You gotta love our moms and aunts, *¿qué no?* Despite living in abject conditions, never having enough money to purchase vaccines for the kids—let alone save up for a Prada this or Manolo that—Mexican women always primp themselves for something as simple as buying tortillas. It's a remnant of *rancho* life, where market day is more a social event than an exercise in the unfettered exchange of commodities. Free from their homes, women catch up on life with their *comadres* while warily eyeing their sexually repressed daughters, horny *hijos,* and drunken husbands gamboling around *el mercado.* So, since almost everyone in town will see you, of course you'll wear the nicest outfit available. It's classy, it's sexy, and it's a thousand times better than the plague of middle-aged gabachas shopping in sweat suits, spaghetti-strap tank tops, fanny packs, Volcom baseball caps, low-rise jeans, and other clothing items pulled from their slutty daughter's closet.

Why do some Mexican girls dye their hair blond? It looks so fake! I hate seeing a dark-ass Mexican girl with nasty dyed-blond hair. Whom is she trying to fool? Where is the pride in having dark hair?
MÁS CÁBRON QUE BONITO

Dear Wab: From the broom-thick mustaches Mexican men sprout to the penciled-in eyebrows of our women, the world remains transfixed by the follicle follies of Mexicans. And nothing provokes more sneers than the insistence of some Mexican women on dyeing their hair blond. The easy explanation is to claim fake-blond Mexicans so hate their roots that they literally bleach them into oblivion in the effort to assimilate, a phenomenon feminists and Chicano studies professors call internalized colonialism. But the fake-blond Mexican woman, like the Chinese railroad laborer and the Slovak steelworker before her, is an archetype of American immigrant tenacity. The fake-blond Mexican knows everyone will laugh at her look—and still she dyes. No one will deny her the right to look as flashy as a peacock—not Americans, not Mexican men, not good taste. The fake-blond Mexican is a strong woman. She's a survivor. She looks like a Swede who has just returned from the Sahara. Dyeing your hair blond while Mexican isn't a fashion faux pas, More Badass than Cute: it's a Randian display of individuality no gabacho would dare attempt. And for that, fake-blond Mexican *chicas*, we raise our peroxide bottles in honor.

Where does a Mexican's "sense" of color scheme come from? I have seen trucks that are teal, maroon, and yellow—all on one truck! Is this something *ustedes* do on purpose, and do *ustedes* know it looks like crap?

BLINDED BY THE BLIGHT

Dear Gabacho: Alan Burner doesn't think that the Mexican love of vibrant colors is crap. Burner is a professor at the Art Institute of California, Orange County, and one of the country's premier color theorists; his textbook, *The Dynasty of Light,* is required reading in art schools nationwide. "Color is very spiritual and symbolic of one's inner nature," the *bueno* professor told the Mexican. "Worldwide, if you view ethnic people with a rich heritage, you'll find vibrant colors, because they're energized. You look at Mexicans, they're passionate at what they do. When they work, they work hard. When they play, they play hard." That translates into the retina-searing trucks, houses, and hair that offend you so, Blinded. Burner adds that gabacho criticism of bright colors is "just singing sour grapes because we don't have the guts to do what Mexicans do. [Bright colors] are a very brave approach to life—it shows you're not afraid of emotions. Americans, we're lazy and lethargic. We're stuffy. We're colorless. We're too busy building facades and not being genuine. We'll say, 'Bright pink is not a sophisticated way to paint your house,' but that's only because we want everyone to be as phony and plastic as we are." Translation, Blinded, you're as cowardly as a Guatemalan.

What's up with all the elaborate wrought-iron fences in the Mexican parts of town? It almost seems like everyone is trying to outdo each other with these amazing displays of metallurgy. Is it just another way to try to protect the cars parked on the lawn and keep the livestock from wandering off, or is it a pathway to instant respect and envy among the neighbors?

WHROUGHT IRON TO ENVY (WHITE) GUY

Dear Gabacho: This is a question that fascinates even sociologists. The Mexican was a senior fellow at a 2005 weeklong seminar held by the University of Southern California Annenberg School for Communication titled "The Latinization of American Culture." There, University of California, Los Angeles, professor David Hayes-Bautista showed pictures of wrought-iron fences to describe what gabachos can expect when Mexicans move into their neighborhoods. But you can find the answer on the United States–Mexico border, WHITE: fences. Miles and miles of American-made fences. Triple-layered. Jagged. Deadly. That's our introduction to American society when we illegally enter *los Estados Unidos*. All Mexicans want to assimilate, so fences are usually the first thing we erect once we buy a *casa:* pointy, menacing bars wrapped with organic barbed wire such as bougainvillea or roses to keep the damn Mexicans at bay. And still—as evidenced by the lemons stolen from my front lawn every night—Mexicans jump them.

My question is two parts: why do Hispanic women pluck out every eyebrow hair, and why is that attractive to the guys?

BROW BEATEN

Dear Gabacho: Eyebrow plucking is as old as civilization itself— archaeologists excavating Abraham's hometown of Ur found tweezers in a tomb carbon-dated to about 3500 BC. Sexologists link male attraction to thin eyebrows and other depilated female regions to an obsession with the younger female form. But seriously, Brow, be glad Mexican women trim their eyebrows so finely. If they didn't, the natural hirsuteness of our *mujeres* would sprout forth, and all would resemble Frida Kahlo, whose unibrow and light mustache remain a Mexican hombre's ultimate cold shower.

Why do many Mexican men wear mustaches? Is there a history behind this?

BIGOTE BILL

Dear Gabacho: I am not well-endowed—not even close. I need braces, a personal trainer, and LASIK. But none of this matters—I can grow a mustache.

It sprouts almost from the instant I shave in the morning, becomes a five-o'clock shadow around noon, and transforms into a sharp, jagged line spanning my mouth within two days. After a week, the mustache is worthy of Cesar Romero; after a month, Emiliano Zapata. In a year? You can smuggle a migrant family inside it.

I don't usually grow a mustache, primarily because modern American society banishes nongoatee facial hair to the domain of the fags and Arabs. Indeed, almost all gabachas who have seen me with a mustache loudly voice their objection. "Oh my gosh!" one Hawaiian hottie once gasped after not seeing me for a couple of weeks. "The mustache makes you look like a Mexican!"

That was the point, *chula*.

Mexicans are different. They treat the initial dark hedges that spread across my upper lip like the first seedlings of spring. Murmurs of "You look good" and "You should keep it" greet me at social events. Men share their mustache envy, lamenting they can't grow something as thick and lengthy as mine. Without one, they think I look like a woman.

And the ladies? I've only had two Mexican girlfriends in my life—met them when I was clean-shaven. Both requested within days of our initial bedding that I grow a mustache.

Ladies, tongue piercings flicked toward the pudenda don't match four days' of lip growth. Imagine a mustache gliding down your neck, across your back, past your abdomen toward the sweltering Promised Land; a mustache brushing your breasts, your thighs, your everything; not quite a kiss but even more so. Like that? Let's just say there's a reason I'm known as the Mouth of the South.

But Mexican mustache love isn't just predicated on sexual sensation—it's rooted in something deeper, something more primal to the mestizo labyrinth: machismo. The mustache is power, commands respect, wins elections. Archimedes said he could move the world with a lever and a place to stand; some political observers say Vicente Fox's magnificent black *bigote* catapulted him into the Mexican presidential palace in 2000.

As with almost everything inexplicably retro in Mexican society, we can thank the Conquest for this follicle fetish. When the Spaniards arrived in the early sixteenth century, the Aztecs marveled not only at their iron armor and deer (actually horses) "as tall as the roof of a house," but also at the bizarre growths on the faces of these fair skins. One Aztec codex of the period dramatically noted the troops of Hernán Cortés wore "long and yellow [beards], and their mustaches are also yellow." This obsession wasn't trivial: the Aztecs—who could only grow pitiful wisps on their cheeks and chins—thought of the Spaniards as gods because of their facial hair. Cortés happened to arrive in Mexico in the exact year that, Aztec mythology said, the bearded god Quetzalcoatl promised to return to save his people. To the Aztecs, a full-blown mustache meant power, salvation, a chance encounter with the heavens (of course, it ultimately became genocide, but that's another story).

Nearly five hundred years later, Mexican culture still maintains the cult of the mustache. Our dads wear them; in official photos, our greatest leaders—Pancho Villa, *ranchera* legend Vicente Fernández, the Frito Bandito—brandish them like guns. Any self-respecting man grew a mustache—tellingly, the only segments of the Mexican male population that don't wear a mustache are the indigenous and the Americanized.

And so, I grow my mustache. When I told a friend about my plans, her eyes enlivened—became fearful, even. "Wow, you could look really tough—respectable, but also dangerous at the same time," she exclaimed.

I know.

I've tried to get my Mexican wife to trim her pubic hair down to a landing strip, but I couldn't convince her. I was once able to get her to shave it completely, and it looked great, but now she won't even trim it! I don't even ask anymore. Is trimming the pubic area taboo in Mexican culture?

PANOCHA PAUL

Dear Gabacho: The hairy Mexican pussy existed until a generation ago, when feminine grooming was still the—what shall we call it?—

bailiwick of slutty gabachas. Times have changed: a recent survey from the bushmasters at Remington shows 67 percent of ladies under forty-five shave their hoo-hah. The study doesn't break down the numbers by ethnicity or class, but one lady at the local beauty salon where the Mexican lives can vouch for Mexican gals pampering their *panocha* (she refused to be named because her boss doesn't want national attention and thinks more Mexican women will come if she gives the name of the location). "I'd say a third of my clientele is Mexican," she says. "I get Spanish-only speakers, little chola girls, rich women, older ladies—all kinds." Although she subscribes to the theory that many immigrant women were taught to "not touch themselves down there," the grooming gal says the most guilt-ridden ladies are actually Indian and European. "The main reason women wax nowadays is they like to feel clean and it makes them feel pretty," she adds, "and that applies to all races." If your wife allows her rose to bloom too much, Panocha Paul, she either isn't interested in you anymore or she's auditioning for the *Hirsute Honeys* porno series.

I just don't get Mexicans and their grooming. The men slick their hair with baby oil, gel, or Vaseline or just shave it all off. The women wear it in ponytails with a neon green hair band or in pigtails or wear bangs created with the biggest curling iron in the world. Do they see themselves in the mirror before leaving home?

TOMMY TOUPEE

Dear Gabacho: Not only do we stare at our hair in the mirror, but we also blow kisses to our reflection and whisper, "*Ay, papi chulo,* you're *más bonito* than those gabachos *feos.*" If there's one body feature that Mexicans can boast about—besides the glorious guts of our men and the asses *grandes* of *mujeres*—it's follicles, repositories of the world's hair DNA. Kinky, straight, curly, or wavy, the Mexican head is pregnant with possibility, and Mexicans do everything possible to draw attention to what humans can do with a comb and three pounds of gel. Some hairstyles are utilitarian: the Mexi-mullet protects the neck from the brutal sun, while bangs allow our ladies to hide switchblades. Other styles, such as indigenous pigtails or Zach de la Rocha's frizzy 'fro, sing the body Mexican. But the best Mexican hair involves Three Flowers brilliantine, the lightly scented petroleum jelly revered by generations of Mexicans for its tight hold, pleasant smell, and a shine that rivals a flashlight; women use it to slick their hair into buns, men to sculpt Morrissey-esque pompadours. Class, thy name is *mexicano*. Oh, and contrary to popular belief, no self-respecting Mexican man shaves his head; that's the domain of *pendejo* cholos and their Chicano cousins.

What's up with the bull stickers on the truck doors? Is this a secret business, something earned at some unmentionable contest south of the border, or a brotherhood of sorts? I thought about taking Spanish lessons so I could politely ask one of these guys.

NATIVE CALIFORNIA WHITEY

Dear Gabacho: The bull sticker is no cloak-and-dagger marker. *Toros* on trucks are just cultural archetypes, a manifestation of Jung's theory that recurring characters, festivals, and monuments in society represent a shared memory from its collective unconscious. Americans decorate their lives with such motifs: lawns (reminder of—take your pick—the savannas of our African roots, English manors, or the open prairie from the frontier days), Thanksgiving (ceremony honoring our Puritan forefathers), and the continued popularity of Mickey Mouse (signifies our fascination with the Trickster). Likewise, Mexicans consider the bull a reminder of the *rancho* they left behind, of the life that will never return. Besides, as cultural archetypes go, a bull sticker is one of the best. Consider the attributes of the animal on display: Ferocity. Virility. Protection. Horns. It's everything a culture wishes its members could be—and so much better than the fruity shamrock or American flag decal on your Scion, no?

What's with the memorials on the back windows of Mexican cars? Some days, driving through the Mexican side of town, I feel like I'm navigating a cemetery.

MUERTE MAN

Dear Gabacho: Ruminating on the Mexican obsession with death is as hack as a reporter rolling with gangsters. Yes, Mexicans embrace death—we laud it in song, codify it with holidays, and, *sí*, plaster the names and dates of birth and death of our deceased beloveds on car windows, ornate back tattoos, and even sweatshirts. "In Mexican homes across Aztlán, an altar is usually present," notes La Pocha, a SanTana artist who specializes in Day of the Dead lore. "In this modern age, spending more time in our cars than our homes, resourceful Mexicans have placed mini-mobile *altares* in their vehicles. Now you can honor your dead homies while cruisin' in your Chevy. That's progress!"

"Death is present in our fiestas, our games, our loves, and our thoughts," wrote Octavio Paz in his 1950 classic, *The Labyrinth of Solitude*. "To die and to kill are ideas that rarely leave us. We are seduced by death."

But before you cite Paz—along with Aztec human sacrifice, cockfighting, bullfighting, and the front pages of Tijuana tabloids—as proof of our inherent bloodlust, Muerte Man, consider this: Isn't there something honorable about living in the presence of death, something valuable, even, in remembering our mortality? Why relegate death to cemeteries as gabacho Protestants do? Why forget those who passed before us? Again Paz: "The cult of life, if it is truly profound and total, is also the cult of death, because the two are inseparable. A civilization that denies death ends by denying life."

Why have Mexicans traded in their 1960s Impalas and 1970s Monte Carlos for 2000s Toyotas? Does *Toyota* mean something in Spanish, or is it symbolism like the Aztec Thunderbird emblem on those Ford T-birds you guys no longer drive?

LOWRIDERS UNITE

Dear Gabacho: You're mixing up your brownies. It's the cholo cousins of Mexicans, Chicanos, who own tricked-out Monte Carlos and Impalas. You're right to note, however, that Mexicans are loco over Toyotas. According to automotive research company R. L. Polk

& Co., the number of Latinos who registered Toyotas increased 45 percent from 2000 to 2004, while the total vehicle registration figures among Latinos for other brands during that same period grew by a mere 15 percent. And Toyota was the top seller among Latinos during the first quarter of 2004. Industry watchers give much of the credit to Steve Jett, Toyota's national truck advertising and event promotions manager, who aggressively pushed for such inventive Mexican-themed ad campaigns as a commercial where a soccer goalie protected a truck from oncoming soccer balls. But the real explanation is that Toyota offers eight types of trucks, vans, and SUVs, second only to Ford among the major automakers. Toyota understands that Mexicans need big vehicles to ferry around the *familia,* to load up with tools, or just to roll down to Mexico and show off their wealth. And, yes, Lowriders Unite, *Toyota* means something in Spanish: "cheap, efficient, and not gabacho-made."

Why do Mexicans drive trucks that cost more than their homes? You drive through barrios, and Lincoln Navigators are parked outside tenement slums!

STUCK WITH MY KIA

Dear Pocha: You say it as if it were a bad thing, Kia, but rejoice: if Mexicans spend more cash on their cars than their *casas,* that's just further proof we're assimilating into American life. A telltale trait of gabachismo is conspicuous consumption, the phenomenon identified by American economist Thorstein Veblen in his 1899 classic, *The Theory of the Leisure Class.* Veblen theorized that commoners buy the most expensive and ostentatious products in the name of achieving social status—keeping up with the Gonzalezes, if you will. Conspicuous consumption, not thrift, is the true American way. Look at our government, for instance, which talks about fiscal responsibility yet spends more and more on war follies without care for the health of his nation. No one cares about ballooning federal budgets or having to rent out the garage to five perverts from Guerrero to make rent as long as you can show off the *chingo* bling.

Why do Mexicans traditionally like Chevys? Did Chevy once target the Mexican consumer base for some reason and it worked?

POCHO IN A PONTIAC

Dear Pocho: An urban legend suggests that Mexicans don't like Chevys (pronounced with a harsh *ch* as in *chicken* and *chupacabra, gracias*) because the auto giant named one of its 1960s-era cars the Nova—which translates to "doesn't go" in Spanish. But General Motors' stats show that the Nova did well for the company, even in Mexico. And not just the Nova. Mexicans consume Chevys like mescal and, come to think of it, sometimes together. In the 2003 report *Market Trends: Hispanic Americans and the Automobile Industry,* author Raúl Pérez found that Chevrolet ranked at or near the top of the list for Hispanic (the PC *pendejo* term for "Mexican") first-time, used-car, and general buyers. Pérez doesn't go into the *porqués,* but according to *Lowrider* magazine's book *Lowrider* (2003), the Bible of *ranflas* and *rucas* (that's hot cars and hotter chicks), the Mexican affinity for Chevys "was an economic consideration" dating back to the 1930s cruising culture. Chevys were quite simply "cheaper and more plentiful" than other brands.

Nowadays, Mexicans purchase Chevy's expensive trucks and SUVs (Chevy hasn't manufactured a *mexcellente* car since the 1964 Impala) as useful status symbols: nothing smuggles your family like a gleaming Suburban the size of a small-apartment living room. Sure, Mexicans should invest their money in better things than Chevys equipped with spinning hubcaps and built-in flat-screen televisions, but dig this, gabachos: while more and more of youse ditch Detroit in favor of jalopies pieced together by goldfish farmers, Mexicans buy American. So who's patriotic now, *cabrones?*

Where did the guayabera shirt originate? I see that Mexicans and Filipinos both lay claim to these shirts.

SLAVIC PRINCE

Dear Gabacho: The origins of the guayabera—the translucent, embroidered shirts worn by Mexican men on hot days—are lost somewhere between Mexico, Cuba, and the Philippines, where it's known as a *barong*. Some legends point to Cuba's Yayabo River, where a rancher supposedly invented the shirt. Other fashion historians note the guayabera is also known in Mexico as a *filipina*. Mexico lies between the two countries, so it's more likely that the shirt originated there and was then exported to the two nations. On the other hand, the Mexican propensity for theft suggests Mexicans are as likely the originators of the guayabera as gabachos.

On the Imitation *Simpsons* Shirt

The swap meet is the communal graveyard of Southern California, where our consumer culture banishes its former fads to the bazaars of smelly tarps and gaping vans. But for one brief, inauthentic moment during the early 1990s, swap meets were the Rodeo Drives for the season's fashion statement—the imitation *Simpsons* T-shirt.

At the time, *The Simpsons* was still considered a passing phenomenon, rather than the American cultural landmark it eventually became, so Fox swamped stores with *Simpsons* action figures, T-shirts, and music albums. Kids and adults alike bought reams of *Simpsons* T-shirts, visually announcing to the world their hipster ratings.

An adroit clothier—his or her identity is lost to history, but he or she probably ran a Malaysian sweatshop—must've taken notice because imitation *Simpsons* T-shirts soon popped up in swap meets. The telling factor was in the signature: Fox-sanctioned T-shirts bore the autograph of *Simpsons* creator Matt Groening; knockoff producers didn't bother with that final detail. No matter—the much cheaper imitations became as popular as the real McClure.

Then things got strange. Swap-meet sellers began hawking *Simpsons* T-shirts that imagined the clan as Rastafarians; lizards; and even Mexicans wearing ponchos, smoking pot, and playing guitars. Most of the *piratería* ("pirated goods" in Mexican Spanish) T-shirts, though, focused on Bart Simpson, who was then the show's focal point. One genre of *piratería* T-shirt depicted Bart assuming the identity of the era's popular sports stars: Michael Jordan, Joe Montana, and baseball/football machine Bo Jackson. Other T-shirts—Bart stuck between the ass cheeks of an obese sumo wrestler, with the legend CRACK KILLS; Bart karate-chopping his cartoon competition the Teenage Mutant Ninja Turtles into bloody bits—defy categorization.

Still, the most infamous *Simpsons* T-shirt mutation remains the "Can't Touch This" series. You'll never see Bart like this again: black, with red fingernails, flipping off the world via the chest of the shirt's wearer, the legends "Can't Touch This" and "Fucking Bart" buttressing Bart's head. Bowdlerizing teachers at my elementary school forced kids wearing this T-shirt to turn their shirts inside out. Shows what little principals know: the bird continued to brightly offend through the T-shirt's flimsy material.

The T-shirts largely disappeared once the show transformed into an institution and manufacturers focused their factories on *Mighty Morphin Power Rangers* and Pokémon. But the legacy remains: in the classic episode "Behind the Laughter," the faux narrator notes that the *Simpsons* became so popular their faces showed up on crappy merchandise. The corresponding animation shows a store rack hung with T-shirts that feature a smiling Bart uttering such non-Bart maxims as "You Bet Your Sweet Bippy, Man" and "Life Begins at Conception, Man," trademark licenses be damned.

I used to work at a neighborhood center that serves the Latino community in San Francisco. I noticed that a large number of the Mexican and Central American people I met smelled strongly of laundry detergent. Additionally Mexican guys love their stinky cologne. Can you explain this?

STINKIN' SAMMY

Dear Gabacho: There's a reason why the slur *dirty Mexican* has stuck to us for so long—since Mexicans are the James Brown of the American economy, we sweat like boxers and get caked in enough dirt to grow corn on our jeans. Sometimes, the shower isn't available because the fifteen other roommates already used the hot water, so Mexicans either spray on *mucho* cologne or draw up an impromptu bath by using laundry detergent, wetting it in the sink, and lathering it across their body. Maybe it's not the most sanitary of procedures, but better a clean Mexican than a dirty Mexican, no?

Why do Mexican parents dress their daughters in frilly dresses?

LACY LAURA

Dear Gabacha: Ever see the various apparitions of the Virgin Mary in Mexico? The Virgin of Guadalupe? Of San Juan de los Lagos? Of Zapopan? Of the Rosary of Talpa? Of Izamal? They all wear dresses that block everything but their faces and hands. This is the model that all young Mexican girls must follow, and parents help out their daughters by dressing them in the most stultifying layered dresses since *Petticoat Junction*. It's an effort to cool the libidos of men, to keep the girls as pure as the driven snow. But modern Mexican women are revolting against those dresses by targeting the very Virgin Marys that inspired the lace. In her 1996 essay "Guadalupe, the Sex Goddess," famed Chicana author Sandra Cisneros wrote, "When I see La Virgen de Guadalupe, I want to lift her dress as I did my dolls' and look to see if she comes with *chones* [underwear], and does her *panocha* [vagina] look like mine, and does she have dark nipples, too? Yes, I am certain she does." Amen, sister.

It seems that every Mexican infant girl I see has had her ears pierced. Some of these babies appear to be only minutes old and still wet. The nurses must be poised and ready with a needle the second the baby pops out. Is there some cultural significance?

BUBBA

Dear Gabacho: Piercing a girl's ears from birth dates to the days when Mexican women were little more than chattel. Patriarchs provided the women in their clans with fancy earrings so the rest of society knew of the family's wealth. Rather than just purchase simple diamond or pearl studs, though, many Mexican men had their daughters wear *arracadas,* gorgeous earrings engraved with fanciful designs borrowed from the Moors. The more intricate the design, the wealthier the family, the better chance a daughter had of getting married to a rich man. In their 1963 study, *Mexican Jewelry,* authors Mary L. Davis and Greta Pack also mentioned that most Mexicans didn't consider a woman eligible for marriage until her ears were pierced—so, Mexico being Mexico, the earlier the piercing, the more chance your daughter has of getting married. Gabachos might call this cradle robbing; Mexicans say it's getting a head start.

Why do Mexican females wear so much eye shadow?

MYOPIA MARY

Dear Gabacha: In nature, animals display extravagant colors or body parts to show off their sexual attraction in a phenomenon known as biological fitness. Similarly, women do the same with their eyes. But Mexicans overdo it because, frankly, their eyes are prettier than those of any other race of women on earth—luminous saucers that come in every color imaginable. Check out the peepers of Salma Hayek, of Eva Longoria, of any spicy señorita—almost all have gorgeous eyes. So why would we ever try to not draw attention to them?

Why do so many Mexicans have silver teeth?

GAP-TOOTHED GRINNER

Dear Gabacho: Few stereotypes ring more true than the Mexican with metal in his teeth—gold in my case, silver for all other wabs. It's all about the bling, baby: Mexicans know what hip-hop artists are just discovering: nothing says menace like a silver tooth. It might fill in our cavities, but just a glimmer strikes fear into the heart of any gabacho—and in a country where we face discrimination at all times, any little advantage we can get we'll take.

Why do Mexicans consider Charles Bronson the most fashionable gabacho ever?

DEATH WISH 1000

Dear Gabacho: Ask a group of twentysomething Mexican-Americans if they grew up watching Charles Bronson movies, and heads hang low. Eventually, someone shamefully allows that, yes, his parents rented all episodes of the *Death Wish* series, that a family night out on the town during the mid-1980s involved watching the latest Bronson bloodbath on the big screen, and that his mother thought the helmet-coiffed actor was the handsomest screen Adonis since Ricardo Montalbán. Relieved not to be alone in embarrassment, everyone soon sheepishly admits the same, and conversations shift toward the sharing of favorite Bronson bits.

The grim-faced performer maintains an earnest following throughout the world even after death because of his career-long portrayal of expressionless psychopaths. Bronson-love in Mexico and her American colonies, however, approaches the hagiographic—and not just because the actor's crumpled mug allowed him to half-believably portray Mexicans or half-Mexicans in such movies as 1960's *The Magnificent Seven* (Bernardo O'Reilly) and 1968's *Villa Rides!* (Rodolfo Fierro) and *Guns for San Sebastian* (Teclo). The Bronson canon's gallery of urban warriors enraptured the Mexican cinematic imagination like little else during the late 1970s and early 1980s and persists today despite the rise of stars even more ethnic and violent.

The Mexican cult of the man born Charles Buchinski is everywhere. Spanish-language channels broadcast such Bronsonian symphonies of mayhem as *The Valachi Papers, Mr. Majestyk,* and *The Evil That Men Do* during prime time almost weekly. Video stores in heavily Latino neighborhoods know to shore up the Bronson catalog and *still* find themselves constantly out of stock. And if there aren't any Bronson flicks around, many Mexicans will settle for the next-best approximation and rent a *narcopelícula*. This geysers-of-blood film genre that emerged during the mid-1970s—not coincidentally the same era that Bronson established himself as a major film draw throughout the world—is Mexico's most popular type of movie, consisting of little more than Mexican actors assuming Bronson's shoot-first, shoot-later wrinkled archetype. In fact, *narcopelícula*'s most famous presence, eighty-four-year-old Mario Almada, has a career trajectory similar to Bronson's. Neither man hit his box-office stride until his fifties, and both made the same gleeful-vengeance film again and again even when the plot had the septuagenarians mowing down men a third their age. A bonus: both had the same fabulously sagging mustache.

So why the Mexican obsession with Bronson? One can approach the question via a psychocultural perspective and argue that Bronson embodied a sort of hypermachismo embedded in the Mexican male mind that determines an hombre's worth by how well he protects the women in his life. Mexican men are attracted to the Bronson characters, then, because his roles involve the failure and redemption of such a philosophy. Remember, Manhattan businessman Paul Kersey in the *Death Wish* films became a trigger-zealous guy only after the murder of his wife and the rape of his daughter, which stained his honor. Kersey regained his testosterone by killing man after man after man.

But let's cut the grad-student babble. When I was a child, my parents took me to the drive-in to watch Bronson flicks, their hands covering my eyes during the most violent scenes. Watching Bronson zip down opiated thugs was one of the few times my parents and their Mexican friends ventured into the English-speaking world—rains of bullets, after all, don't need subtitles.

9

Work

Oranges, Day Laborers, and Lazy Kentuckians

Dear Mexican: I'm sick of gabachos mangling the pronunciation of my name, César. Should I just change it to Caesar?

CÉSAR THE WEATHER GUY

Dear Wab: Lose the name, period. Gabachos tend to associate the name César with the late labor leader César Chávez, but that name is forever slimed thanks to his heirs. The *Los Angeles Times*' 2006 four-part series on Chávez's old union, the United Farm Workers, describes its devolution from the conscience of the Chicano movement into an organization whose legacy is likely to be nepotism, broken promises to migrant pickers, and exploiters of the Chávez legacy. Chávez doesn't come off so great either: *Times* writer Miriam Pawel opens the third segment of her opus with a creepy account of Chávez forcing UFW leaders to participate in a psychological browbeating called the Game; it sounds a lot like a Maoist reeducation camp, with friends profanely skewering one another in front of the group. After this, Pawel writes, Chávez turned into a brown Howard Hughes, purged dissidents in the UFW, studied "mind healing," and surrounded himself with sycophants, ensuring his organization's slow, sad demise.

Why couldn't blacks cope with Katrina, yet Mexicans affected by similar natural disasters are always able to rebuild on their own without the help of the government? They reorganized without shouting, "We wan' food. People iz dying. Help us, Mista Bush."

¡QUÉ CHOCOLATE CITY NI QUE CHINGADA!

Dear Readers: This wab raises three interesting issues. First is his blatant racism—his use of Stepin Fetchit dialect shows why many African-Americans don't back Mexicans in the current immigration debate. *Segundo* is the wab's wonderfully idiomatic pseudonym. The literal translation is "What Chocolate City nor What the Fuck?!" However, *¡Qué* [insert noun here] *ni que chingada!* is a Mexican-Spanish turn of phrase that means "Don't give me any of that bullshit!" And weird but true, the polite form of this saying is *¡Qué* [noun] *ni que ocho cuartos!*— "What [noun] nor what eight rooms?!"—a phrase that makes as much sense as a Mexican vegetarian.

But never mind the bigotry or the cleverness with the language: the third point this wab raises is the *más interesante*. Mexicans long ago learned that government won't bail your *culo* out of anything, whether it's a devastating earthquake, howling hurricane, or tanking economy. So we learned to be self-sufficient in a way that makes libertarians look like socialists. Mexico's infrastructure markedly improved in the past couple of decades because Mexican migrants in the United States raised funds on their own; the Mexican government assisted them (by matching remittances on a federal, local, and state government level) only when they realized the money would save Mexico. Americans, on the other hand, still expect elected leaders to help in times of need. That's not a bad thing: that's the ostensible role of government. But Katrina victims and all Americans should know this: not only is the border between the United States and Mexico gone, but our government has assimilated into the ineptitude and corruption that marks all Mexican presidential administrations. In this age of globalization and mass people movements, government won't do a single damn thing for you: salvation will come only via Mexicans.

How come so many Mexicans send their money to Mexico?

GÜERO POWER

Dear Gabacho: Gabacho, gabacho, gabacho. You have at your service a Mexican who can answer any question about his country—from why Mexican men beat their wives (same reason white men do) to which local restaurant makes the best spiced crickets (El Fortín in Fullerton) to where you can find the cheapest fake driver's licenses (visit Santa Ana's Centennial Park Saturday in the evening and ask for "El Kennedy"). And this is the best you can do? Come on, *pendejo, ¡usa tu cabeza, cabrón!* But you want an answer, an answer . . . remember what George Mallory said about the Himalayas? That people climb its mountains because they're there? Same thing with Mexicans and their cash. The Mexican government offers a *tres-por-uno* (three-for-one) program: for every dollar a migrant invests in hometown municipal projects, the government matches it on a federal, state, and local level. Given the chance to improve a third-world country, Mexicans have responded enthusiastically—according to Banamex, Mexico's largest bank, Mexicans in the United States sent back an estimated $14 billion in 2005, making remittances the country's second most important source of income after oil. Such altruism is unsurpassed in human history, so I have to ask you, Güero Power, why not make like a Mexican and offer your money to Uncle Sam in the name of better schools, highways, and infrastructure? Oh, right, because you're an American.

I detect a strong anti-American bias in the local Spanish-language media—or is it my imagination?

VIVA LOU DOBBS

Dear Gabacho: I forwarded the above *pregunta* to Pilar Marrero. She's a nationally syndicated columnist and features editor for the Los

Angeles-based *La Opinión,* the nation's largest Spanish-language daily.

Why is the Spanish-language press anti-American?

Who says the Spanish media is anti-American?

Some gabacho. So why do you think so many Americans are afraid of the Spanish-language press?

Many Americans don't even know the Spanish-language press exists. . . . I don't know for a fact that Americans, like you say, are afraid of the Spanish-language press. I think many Americans are misled by their leaders to fear foreigners and immigrants because it's human nature to fear that which is different. And the leaders use it to manipulate people for political reasons.

Do you get e-mails from gabachos accusing you of being anti-American?

No, I never get e-mail from "gabachos" calling me or [*La Opinión*] anti-American. Gabachos, as you call them, rarely read *La Opinión.* I thought you knew that.

For the record, gabachos have historically distrusted America's foreign-language media since immigrants used newspapers and radio programs to espouse radicalism—for instance, the Industrial Workers of the World (the infamous "Wobblies") published their daily in Finnish, while Jewish socialists used Yiddish-language papers such as the *Forward* as mouthpieces. But don't worry about today's Spanish-language media, Viva Lou Dobbs—with the exception of *La Opinión,* it's just as devoid of news as the gabacho media, but with more dwarves and big-breasted *chicas.*

Why is it that Mexicans call all cereal "cornflakes"? They even say, *"¿Que tipo de cornfleis quieres—*Fruity Pebbles, Cheerios, *o* Wheaties?" Please explain.

CONFUSED ABOUT CORNFLEIS

Dear Gabacho: César Chávez's heirs know something of the Mexican fascination with *cornfleis* (Mexicans pronounce it that way because the letter k doesn't appear in Spanish outside of words borrowed from English, such as *kilometer*). The *Times* reported that the César E. Chávez Foundation accepted a $25,000 donation from the Kellogg's Company, makers of such wabby breakfast faves as Froot Loops, Rice Krispies, and the aforementioned Corn Flakes. In return, the foundation allowed Kellogg's to release a limited-edition Kellogg's Corn Flakes box during Hispanic Heritage Month featuring a picture of Chávez and salsa legend Celia Cruz. They're no longer available at supermarkets, but you can visit any SanTana produce truck and buy a box for $6—double the retail price. If that's not official enough for you, Cornfleis, the César E. Chávez Foundation resells Chávez Corn Flakes boxes autographed by Chávez's widow, Helen, with the slogan "Viva la Causa!" for $20—$5 more than the price just a month before the *Times* story hit. In other news, Coretta Scott King refused an offer by Uncle Ben's Rice to place the face of her martyred husband on its product during Black History Month on the grounds it was tacky.

Why are Mexicans always selling oranges on street corners? Is that like the national fruit of Mexico?

A. HOT TAMALE

Dear Gabacha: What do you want them to sell—Steinways? Oranges are easy to carry, in demand year-round, and earn vendors great profits. According to Dolores, who sells oranges off the 91 freeway, Euclid Strect, on-ramp in Anaheim, she can earn almost $100 per week hawking the fruit. That averages out to more than $5,000 per year—and since it's the underground economy, she doesn't pay taxes! But, no, oranges aren't Mexico's national fruit—it's our most secret of assault weapons. Ever see the movie *Born in East L.A.*, a 1987 Cheech Marín vehicle that is Mexico's *Nanook of the North*?

Marín's character, Rudy, sells oranges in Tijuana to earn enough cash for his passage across the border. Rudy ends up giving most of his inventory away, though, to a destitute family. That same family eventually saves Rudy from a beating when they chuck oranges at his assailants. If cops are smart, they'll arm residents with five-pound bags of oranges. Betcha that'll do more to stop violence in immigrant communities than the PD's current crime-stopping strategy of deporting immigrants.

Why do none of the Mexicans in Louisville have jobs?

BLUEGRASS GABACHO

Dear Gabacho: We take after Kentuckians.

Why is it that Mexicans can be put into two working classes: those who work their asses off while everyone else takes a siesta, and those who take a siesta while everyone else works their asses off? The MexiCAN and the MexiCANT?

PERSON UNDERSTANDABLY TICKED OFF

Dear Gabacho: PUTO, you have to realize it's the parents who never take the siesta—it's their children who slag off and become the stereotypical lazy Mexican gabachos so relish. In a 1993 sociological study, ethnographers Alejandro Portes and Min Zhou found that the more assimilated a Mexican-American youngster was, the worse his lot in life would be. "Seeing their parents and grandparents confined to humble menial jobs and increasingly aware of discrimination against them by the white mainstream,"

Portes and Zhou wrote, "U.S.-born children of earlier Mexican immigrants readily join a reactive subculture as a means of protecting their sense of self-worth." Translation: Mexican kids see their parents sweat and toil to move out of an apartment and into a dingy condo only to see gabachos dismiss them as wetbacks—and then resign from life. While the parents continue to work eighteen-hour days to make the rent, the kids leave for college, join an activist group such as MEChA, wear a Che shirt for a couple of years, and travel through Central America to "find themselves." They return as shiftless, lazy *flojos* who become vegetarians and talk of revolution while bouncing from collection job to collection job. In other words, they become Americans.

My respect for the Democrats plummeted when they let Alberto González get confirmed. Jeez, Mexicans will steal your car and your civil liberties. They will ruin your neighborhood *and* your Constitution. Why do Mexicans fuck everything up, whether they're working for a strawberry grower or the president?

A FORMER MEChISTA

Dear Pocho: You seem disturbed that González became the country's first Latino attorney general; follow the lead of such Latino advocacy groups as LULAC, the National Council of la Raza, the Hispanic National Bar Association, and the Mexican American National Association and be proud! If you can say one good thing about the Bush administration, it's that it doesn't reserve the monumental, national, security-threatening fuckups solely for the gabachos. Look at Condoleezza Rice, the country's first female African-American secretary of state and a woman who single-handedly could start World War III. Consider Colin Powell, son of Jamaican immigrants, the man who spun Dubya's WMD lies before the UN. Then there's Korean-American John Yoo, who wrote the memos for the Bush administration justifying torture of terrorist suspects and assisted González in the latter's defense of said memos. And Orange County's own Viet Dinh was the author of the USA Patriot Act. Now, just as Mexicans are finally going to have the same chance to destroy our freedoms, you want to take it away. *Pinche pendejo,* haven't you ever heard of the Land of Opportunity, a magical place where any hardworking immigrant has the opportunity to rise to a position where he or she can limit the opportunities of others?

I have never been able to figure out how a Mexican working for minimum wage can afford multiple children, a brand-new gas-guzzling American truck, pay California rent, *and* still have money to spend on clothes and entertainment. What a crafty race! Can you share the secret?

MONEY-CHALLENGED GRINGO

Dear Gabacho: Simple. Live five families to a house and charge them rent. Make your kids work at the expense of an education, then force them to hand over three-quarters of their paychecks. Create a hometown benefit association, then embezzle the hell out of its treasury. Work three minimum-paying jobs, and garden or clean houses on the side. Barter for all goods. Dump the kids on the grandparents. Sell the land in Mexico that belonged to your family for generations. And since everything is under the table, no taxes! With profit margins like this, it's amazing more gabachos haven't figured a way in.

When I was in the Marines, Mexicans comprised most of the nongabacho jarheads. I served with Gunny Ramírez, Sergeant Major Sánchez, Captain Guzmán, and so forth. In the midst of anti-immigration sentiments, why do the armed forces run Spanish-language recruiting ads? Do Mexicans make better soldiers and marines?

IGNORANT IMMIGRANT MARINE

Dear Pocho: Uncle Sam *loves* poor boys or girls, especially if they're immigrants—and no *inglés* is necessary! "Immigrant soldiers have always been an important sector of the U.S. military, going all the way back to the U.S.-Mexico War, when Irish immigrants made up a large part of the American army," says Jorge Mariscal. He's a Vietnam War vet, literature professor at the University of California, San Diego, and editor of the 1999 collection *Aztlán and Viet Nam: Chicano and Chicana Experiences of the War.* "Today is no different. Immigrants have limited economic and educational opportunities, and many have a desire to 'prove themselves' as patriotic citizens." Mariscal told the Mexican that the Department of Defense devotes about $27 million of its $180 million recruitment budget to Spanish-language ads and bilingual personnel; these ads use the double-edged sword of *familia* and machismo to convince Latino recruits that a life of death is for them. The strategy is working: according to a February 9, 2006, *New York Times* article, the number of army Latino recruits rose 26 percent in the past four years, while the number of Latinos in all military branches rose 18 percent. And it doesn't matter whether the immigrants are legal—remember that Orange County's first Iraq War martyr was twenty-one-year-old Costa Mesa resident José Angel Garibay, a former illegal immigrant who received American citizenship only after his April 2003 burial.

Why do Mexicans keep livestock (mostly chickens and goats) in their yards? Are the animals raised for a more economic supply of food? Is it safe and/or legal?

LA VACA GORDA

Dear Gabacha: Many municipal codes in urban areas allow people to own limited amounts of livestock given a house's dimensions and proximity to other houses. Never mind the laws, though. Don't you want fresh milk and eggs daily, Fat Cow? Or a monthly feast of goat cooked in an earthen pit? How about still steaming chorizo? Mexicans like their food fresh, free of preservatives, and free-ranging. Put us and our barnyard in Napa or Chiapas, we're "organic farmers." Put us in an American neighborhood, we're "wetbacks."

I constantly hear that Mexicans send billions of dollars back to Mexico. So why isn't the country getting better?

FOOTING THE BILL

Dear Gabacho: You're not paying attention—those billions are Mexico's salvation. Mexicans in the United States send billions by organizing into hometown benefit associations, groups that hold fund-raisers to raise money for infrastructure projects in their hometowns. The groups are nothing new to America—many immigrant groups created such organizations to assist individuals with funds and culture (read the University of Minnesota's 1981 pamphlet *Records of Ethnic Fraternal Benefit Associations in the United States: Essays & Inventories* for more information). What's remarkable is how the Mexican government—historically hostile to Mexicans that left the *patria*—has responded to these groups. In 1993, the state of Zacatecas began a program called Dos por Uno (Two for One), where the government matched immigrant remittances on a local and state level. Seizing on that success, the Mexican government expanded it to twenty-six states, adding federal money to the pot. Those billions are just remarkable—in the Mexican's home village of Jomulquillo, Zacatecas, we now have potable water and working toilets! And instead of just one phone for the entire village, we have two! Be glad this is happening, Footing. If Mexicans weren't sending all those billions of dollars back, I guarantee the Mexican government would find a way to make Americans give billions of dollars in relief to Mexico. And while the government might provide services to illegal immigrants here, at least gabachos get goodies like cheap labor and tacos in return.

Why do Mexicans litter so much? In other words, why are they such pigs?

OSCAR EL GROUCH

Dear Gabacho: Don't you watch television? Mexicans aren't pigs—they're burros. No, wait—Chihuahuas. Excuse me—rats. Mexicans are Yosemite Sam–evading rats. And many rats make their living cleaning up the garbage of others. After a day of wiping the feces-laden *culos* of gabacho babies, washing cars, digging up weeds, mopping floors, or carting out the El Torito dinner buffet, you think Mexicans want to come home and plan how to tidy up their hous and streets? Do carpenters call it a day and carve boxes in bed? You shouldn't expect us to keep our *casas* spick-and-span—that's what the Guatemalans are for.

Why do Mexicans commit so many crimes? I've noticed police pursuits on the news, and the chase always turns up a Latino male.

LOOKING FOR A NEW JOHN WAYNE

Dear Gabacho: Look, just because Mexicans celebrate and romanticize violence and murder in film, song, art, television, popular culture, and marriage doesn't mean that Mexicans are more prone to violence than, say, Iraq-invading Americans. In fact, it's quite the opposite: a Rand Center paper, *Social Anatomy of Racial and Ethnic Disparities in Violence,* found that rates of violence for Latinos as compared with gabachos are actually 10 percent *lower.* Similar conclusions are found in 2002's *Latino Homicide: Immigration, Violence, and Community;* in it, author Ramiro Martínez examines homicide rates among Latinos in the preceding five years and finds that they're markedly lower than the national rate. I understand the misconception, since Mexicans or Hispanic-surnamed criminals usually get bragging rights on the eleven-o'clock news. Besides, crime has always been rampant among the poor—recall the similar glorification and high rates of violence in the Old West, the South, and among African-Americans.

So what's with this constant gabacho obsession with Mexicans and crime? You referenced it: the media, in a partnership with the Minuteman Project and NAFTA, have fostered a Mexican-crime conspiracy as loony as the fake moon landing. "The immigrant criminal has always projected a violent image in the public imagination, but the creation of a 'Latino bandito' formed a new caricature and gave life to a new ethnic stereotype," Martínez wrote. He dates it to the Mexican Revolution, which occurred right as silent films were revolutionizing

...rica. "Newspapers documented the actions of Mexican revolutionaries on the battlefield, depicting bloodshed on the field between troops, translating real images of violence into fictional images of banditry, and in turn transforming the bandito into a criminal bent on violence. The stereotype of a bloodthirsty Mexican bandit became embedded in the public imagination. Mexicans were violent on the battlefield and off of it." America: you're so concerned about the 25 percent of jailed criminals who are supposedly illegal immigrants, what about the 75 percent who are not?

Why do Mexicans work so much harder at construction (pure labor) than blacks? I have had to hire temporary labor to assist me in completing some pretty rough jobs over the course of my life, and the times the agency has sent blacks, it's like watching a movie in slow motion. When they send Mexicans, the job is always done much quicker and better, more thoroughly. *Way to go!*

GRACIAS, HOME DEPOT

Dear Gabacho: What do you expect? Put a Mexican on the lawn, in the boardroom, or in the snoop-happy Attorney General's office—*anywhere*—and Mexicans will outwork everyone else. Construction is a great example. I can tell you why African-Americans aren't great construction workers—they're Americans, and the country has always relied on immigrants to construct the infrastructure of the country—think of the Chinese railroad layers, the Italian skyscraper monkeys, and now the Mexican stucco sprayer. According to the Pew Hispanic Center's *Latino Labor Report, 2004,* although Latinos made up about 20 percent of the total construction workforce, they accounted for 40 percent of the total addition to workforce in 2004. Even as we speak, Mexicans are invading New Orleans to do hazardous jobs and brave the muck and humidity to rebuild that great city. Construction is the perfect job for the Mexican—toil that takes every part of your body to succeed in. Leave the specialty jobs involving typing to gabachos—Mexicans are proud working the jobs of real men.

Why do Mexicans stand on the side of streets trying to get jobs? Wɪ
can't they just get real jobs!?

WELFARE CHEESE

Dear Gabacho: I take it you refer to *jornaleros*—day laborers, who battle with each other for the right to work that day while gabachos hold
signs claiming that they're Vietnam War vets or need one dollar of gas
to get them home. The only other Mexicans who stand by the side
of the road are people waiting for the bus and those selling oranges,
roses, strawberries, fake CDs . . . but I digress. Real jobs? Like sitting
in a cubicle and updating your MySpace account so it features
that picture of you puking? In *The Economic Transition to America,*
researchers with the Pew Hispanic Center found that two-thirds of
Latino immigrants that responded to their December 2005 survey
worked in the agriculture, construction, manufacturing, and hospitality industries: the realest of the real jobs. Manual and self-labor are the
trademarks of the American immigrant experience; it's the children of
Mexicans that get the easy jobs, the jobs whose only toll on the body
are carpal tunnel syndrome and expanded asses. Besides, the real jobs
of Mexicans promise upward mobility—after all, you can only go
upward when you start at the bottom.

My son attends medical school in Guadalajara. I keep sending him
stuff, but he never gets it. Why is it so difficult to mail a package to
Mexico?

NEXT DÍA DELIVERY

Dear Gabacha: Gotta get the right service, Next Día. Drug runners
and immigrant smugglers can transport bulk goods safely and effi-
ciently but charge thousands of dollars for their services. American-
based shipping companies such as DHL or UPS have to deal with
pinche customs. But even those options are better than dealing with
Sepomex, Mexico's national postal service and an object of world-

e ridicule. According to *Latin Trade* magazine, a 2003 survey by exican polling agency Parametría revealed 29 percent of Mexicans nadn't even heard of Sepomex, while nearly a third used private delivery agencies instead. *Latin Trade* pointed out that Sepomex still hasn't recovered from a devastating 1986 Mexico City earthquake that destroyed key facilities. In the meanwhile, Mexicans created courier services for their delivery needs, ranging from the multimillion-dollar Houston-based Estafeta USA to your local Mexican regional restaurant (ask for Pablo). The rise of Mexican courier services proves again that Mexicans are natural Republicans—believers in smaller government, self-sufficient, and perpetual harassers of gays and Guatemalans.

Which comes first: the low-paying, so-called jobs that Americans won't do, or the Mexicans who are willing to sleep three and four to a ten-by-twelve-feet room so that they can afford to work those jobs?

VIVO CONTONTOS

Dear Gabacho: You're presenting us with a Rorschach test—our answers reveal our position regarding the Mexican Question and say more about us than the actual effects of Mexicans on the economy. Whether Mexican immigrants drive down wages, improve the economy, or have no effect (or are part of a triple alliance with Islamofascists and the Chinese to take over the United States) is a topic so complicated that you can easily find an "expert" and "stats" to support any "position." The July 9, 2006, *New York Times Magazine*, for instance, featured battling economics professors who fought round after round until coming to no decision. This Mexican's take: Mexicans will continue to take the jobs Americans won't do until Big Business pays a living wage across the board or Americans are willing to pick strawberries at the minimum wage. Don't bet on the former; if Americans do the latter, they're either stupid or desperate. Or Mexican.

Why do Mexicans protest against the police department whe_ the boys in blue shoot some cokehead or gangbanger?

CURIOUS WHITE GUY

Dear Gabacho: You're lucky, you know that? The only time gabachos worry about the police is when they burn couches or drink beer on front lawns during Independence Day. But Mexicans and Salvadorans and blacks and Asians—hell, anyone poor and colored—get to fret about trigger-happy cops daily. That's why Latino activists are always furious whenever a Mexican gets killed by cops. I'm not defending the victim or demonizing the officers involved—haven't read the police report—but you gotta ask at some point, what's with cops and dead minorities? And would you ever see police rain bullets on a millionaire's house if there was a domestic dispute? Just asking.

But tell you what, White Guy, take a drive to my hood, Orange County. In the city of Huntington Beach, there's a historic Mexican barrio called, alternatively, Oak View or the Slater Slums. Put your question to residents there. They'll tell you the story of Antonio Saldivar, an unarmed eighteen-year-old who was killed by Officer Mark Wersching in 2001 because he vaguely fit the description of a gang member Wersching was pursuing. Two years later, a federal jury awarded Saldivar's family $2.1 million for the unprovoked death; Wersching remains on the Surf City force (he was cleared of wrongdoing in three separate investigations by law enforcement). Saldivar's sin? A shaved head and brown skin. Yep, the cops are always right.

Having traveled all around the world, I see tourists of all nationalities—except Mexicans. I know they have the means, what with their buying of all those gas-guzzling Chevy trucks and gold chains to go with the tooth. I love to travel. Where are my compadres?

CHICANO MALINCHISTA

Of all of the places in the world I've visited, I've never met a Mexican traveler. When I talk to my Mexican coworkers, their idea of travel is

oad-dust tacos, drinking tequila, and getting harassed by the
les in Rosarito Beach. Is that why they have such a narrow-
_aded view of the world?

WINNEBAGO GÜERO

Dear Pocho and Gabacho: What are you _cabrones_ talking about? Mexicans are the ultimate travelers—why do you think gabachos call us border-hoppers? But we don't backpack across Europe like you, Chicano Malinchista, because Mexicans view traveling differently. When we travel, it's to the _rancho_ so we can show off said gold teeth, chains, and Silverados large enough to rival anything the United States has deployed in Fallujah. Anywhere besides _la patria_ is a luxury affordable only to those with secure jobs and disposable income—traits few Mexicans can boast. This Mexican, for instance, hasn't taken time off since spring 2004—I'm afraid management will hand my rake to a younger, less expensive Mexican while I'm gone (or maybe a Guatemalan!). Perhaps this limited vacation experience leads to a narrow Mexican worldview, Winnebago, but you're one to talk: while the number of passports issued to Americans increased dramatically from 7.3 million in 2003 to 8.8 million in 2004, that hasn't translated into a broadening of the gabacho mind—we're still in Iraq, aren't we?

Diary of a Day Laborer:
A Human Drama in Five Parts

Prologue

I once worked for a World War II vet who'd lost his leg in combat. Everyone always has these stereotypes that old white people are the most racist, but he was the best employer I ever had. He paid good, treated me and my friends with respect, bought us hamburgers for lunch, and even let us eat in his air-conditioned office so that we wouldn't have to bake in the sun. He suffered a lot through life, and although I never lost a limb, I think he could relate to us. People who have suffered throughout life relate very easily.

—"TÍo," 53

No matter what you're doing, you run. It doesn't matter if you're o
hundred feet or just two feet away, you run. Your life depends on it
Your life depends on a random stranger who could kill you, will probably disrespect you, and will most likely pay you much less than you
deserve. But even those prospects are better than the ones you used to
have. This is the life of *los jornaleros*—the day laborers. Best known for
standing around on street corners looking for work, their life actually
consists of running, figuratively and literally. Running from a life of
poverty toward the promise of America that comes in the form of the
bluest blue-collar work. Running from the danger of *la migra* and
toward employers who are absolute strangers with a car, some work,
and some cash.

Even if the bulk of the *jornalero*'s day is sedentary--i.e., hanging
around a street corner, waiting for work—he must always be prepared
to run. His day is constant anticipation. As I discovered over three days
as a day laborer, not running fast enough is the difference between a
day of work and a day of painful waiting.

Day 1: The Chinese Mexican

*I worked for a couple of years at a factory, but they paid badly,
and the conditions were horrible. You do the same thing over and
over, get paid shit, and break your back for the same fucking wages
regardless of how you do the job. Here, you can make much more than
in a factory or in a restaurant. Yeah, it's hard work, but I do something different every day. But I have to do it good. If not, I don't
work.*

—MIGUEL, 31

I arrive around 11 a.m. outside a Home Depot in a shopping plaza on
Brookhurst and Crescent. It's one of Anaheim's main gathering places
for day laborers. Some of the few men remaining—maybe twenty alto-
gether—have been waiting for work since 6 a.m.; by 10 a.m., most of
the hiring is done; by 11 a.m., waiting for work is hoping against
hope.

It's obvious I do not belong here, no matter how hard I try to fit in.
I have the right outfit: shoes caked with dust, the thinnest T-shirt I

...n, battered work pants, and a hat that will be my only protection against the unforgiving sun. But I wear glasses. My hands are smooth and show no sign of hard labor. And my skin, while somewhat dark, owes its tan to indoor lighting.

Which explains what happens next: as I approach the day laborers, they think I'm looking for workers, not for work. A man wearing a soccer jersey approaches.

"You need one worker?" he asks me in English.

"*¿Mande?*" I ask—What?

A perplexed look crosses his face. He wasn't expecting Spanish.

"Are you looking for workers?" his friend asks me, this time in Spanish.

"No," I reply, again in Spanish. "I'm looking for work. You guys think I'm some *pinche* gabacho?"—a fucking white guy?

Everyone laughs. The tension is erased.

"Nah," he replies. "We thought you were Chinese."

"I knew that you were born here," one man tells me proudly after I reveal that I was born in the States and, yes, graduated from high school. "Ever since you first walked over here. You can tell if people were born here by the way they walk." People "from here" walk more stiffly—supposedly. The men I speak to—all in their midthirties—are curious: why would an American-born Mexican with a high school education have to stand on street corners to find work?

I don't tell them I also graduated from college and am on my way to grad school. I act the way they do. I don't use English at all, instead employing the singsong Mexican Spanish of the *rancho* punctuated with graphic swear words to make my points.

I also ask questions that establish me as naive. An older gentleman, noting my inexperience, offers advice. His name is Julian. He's a forty-seven-year-old immigrant from Guerrero who has been working without papers for more than twenty years and is still looking to improve his life. "I'm going to computer classes to learn how to use a computer," he tells me proudly. "I recently bought a computer for my daughters who are in college to do their homework, but I also want to learn how to use it."

Julian shows me the finer points of getting a job in an environment

in which work comes to those who run. He talks to me offhande
almost out of the side of his mouth, as he scans the street.

"You have to present a certain self-image," he says. "A lot of these
guys"—he indicates the others talking in small clusters—"they want to
work, but it doesn't seem like it to prospective employers when they're
standing around talking to one another. You have to be on the lookout
all the time for work. Every person that passes by, every car, is a
prospective employer."

"But how do I know which people are actually looking for workers
and which ones aren't?" I ask.

Julian looks directly at me, as if he is about to impart ancient wisdom. "Sometimes, the people are shy, and you have to approach them.
Other times, they'll be more direct. Regardless, when they come, you
run toward them like a motherfucker."

I stick around until two in the afternoon. No one comes, and by
then I am one of the last *jornaleros* remaining. Men are returning from
a full day of work, dirty but grinning. I notice that most pick up their
transportation at the bicycle rack at the nearby Carl's Jr. As I drive
home in the Camry that I parked far away, I feel spoiled.

Day 2: The Manic Hispanic

*People who hire us don't care about legality or who has papers—and
neither do the cops. All they want are people who can do the job at a
much cheaper wage than a professional. They want to save the most
money possible. That's why the police or the companies around here
don't care. They're in on it too.*

—Anonymous, 18, Mexicali

A Silverado enters the parking lot and is immediately surrounded by
about fifteen men. Just as quickly, one man climbs into the truck and
shakes hands with the driver, an older white man who apparently
knows him. There's nothing special about the worker, a guy with a
scruffy beard and a hat that says SPICE GIRLS. The men surrounding the
truck begin yelling "How many workers?" and "What kind of work?"
But the driver waves them off. "Sorry," he says. "I don't need anyone
else. Maybe tomorrow."

I arrive at 8 a.m. Around forty men occupy what they refer to half-jokingly as their *oficina*—their office—a sidewalk across the street from Home Depot. By unwritten agreement among the *jornaleros,* the police, and nearby businesses, the sidewalk is the only area where men can look for work in the shopping center. No wandering around the parking lot. No hanging around inside the stores. The sidewalk is about four feet wide and a parking lot in length. But all the men gather on the first one hundred feet next to Brookhurst, where vehicles bound for Home Depot—and therefore the possibility of work—first enter.

The *oficina* operates like any office tower. For lunch, the men avail themselves of the Chinese restaurant or Carl's Jr. or the father-daughter team that comes around 11 a.m. selling peanuts, pumpkin seeds, and CDs. Someone has tied around trees plastic bags that serve as trash cans to make sure no one litters. Bathrooms are located inside the Carl's Jr., which also serves as an air-conditioned haven—if you have the money—from the brutal heat that is just beginning.

Most of the men spend most of each day waiting. To pass the time, they chat among themselves or just stare intently at the street. Everyone tries to squeeze into the minimal shade cast by a large sign and a few scrawny trees. Even in the early morning, the sun burns us all.

The minute a car passes, everyone employs the same tactic: each rushes to the edge of the sidewalk and lifts their hands, trying to catch the driver's attention. They shout out their specialty or just "Work!" The negotiation lasts two seconds as a car passes or stops to pick up someone. But mostly, the cars drive on. When they do, the *jornaleros* go back to waiting for the next prospective employer. Sometimes that could be hours away.

Friends who've worked in retail say humans—or at least consumers—are tied together like some multicelled organism, that we all show up in theaters and grocery stores or whatever en masse, leave together, and then return. Crowds flow. So does work. At 11:30 a.m., a line of cars pulls in looking for workers. I rush each car, but work goes to the swiftest. This is proved again and again. As soon as he picks a worker, the driver tries to leave, but all the men surround the vehicle, begging the driver for work. The drivers usually say courteously that they don't need any more workers. But sometimes, they delight in bringing more misery to the life of the *jornalero.*

Case in point: A van stops in the middle of the street. The driver is a Latino—a conservative one, judging by the copy of *National Review* on the passenger seat. We swarm the van, but he angrily tells the laborers to go away.

"Is there a Manuel around?" he asks. "I'm looking for a Manuel." He speaks in English that is only slightly better than that spoken by the workers.

"He's not here—hire us," one guy tells the driver.

"No, I want Manuel. He does a good job."

A younger man forces his way through the crowd to the passenger-seat window and boldly proclaims he could do better than this Manuel, whoever he is.

"Oh, yeah? What can you do?" the driver asks him in Spanish.

"Anything," the boy confidently replies.

"Can you drywall?"

"Of course I can."

"What's drywall, then?"

The boy begins to explain, "It's when you put stucco inside the house—"

But the driver rudely cuts him off, "Sorry, you put stucco outside the house."

Manuel finally emerges from the mass of men, gets in the van, and leaves.

The young boy knew what he spoke of. But the driver was listening for terms that only someone professionally trained would use, and most day laborers have probably never been professionally trained. Or perhaps he just delighted in tormenting someone.

I talk to the rejected worker, a nineteen-year-old whose name I never catch. The men here care more about what Mexican state you're from, and I find out he is from the city of Toluca, just outside

Mexico City. He has been here one week and has no relatives or friends in Orange County. The only thing the *tolucense* has done besides search for work is pay $175 per month up front for the right to sleep on a woman's couch.

Although he has just arrived, he already understands the rules of this workplace. "You have to be the first person to talk to the [employers] or you're screwed," he says bitterly. "Every time a car comes, people circle it, and the driver cannot pick someone based on true talents or work ethic. He usually picks whoever came first. There's no order, and we end up screwing one another because we surround cars." What's worse, he says, is that he knows no one.

Day labor is pretty much like work anywhere in at least one respect, though: the more people you know, the better your chances.

"A lot of people that come looking for workers want someone who has already worked for them," the *tolucense* tells me. "And if that worker has a friend, the employer will pick the friend based on his word. If you don't have a friend here, it's nearly impossible to find work."

I have no blue-collar skills, nor do I have any friends here who can hook me up. This explains why I am unable to find work and probably explains his bad luck. He is I—although I am just pretending to do what he depends on for his survival. His backpack, filled with various impressive-looking tools, suggests he has real skills.

Watching him close up his bag and turn back to the street, I think, If I were really in his situation, I would probably be homeless. That thought has not left my mind.

Day 3: White People Rule

You have to be there constantly. I go there from eight in the morning and am usually the last person to leave. Some people start leaving at the lunch hour; I leave at 4 p.m. Maybe I didn't get work today, but maybe somebody saw me standing there for a long time and they'll remind themselves, "That person wants to work, and next time I see them, I'll hire them just because they stood there for such a long time."

—UNNAMED IMMIGRANT, 29, JALISCO

"They sure know how to enjoy life," an older man says sarcastically as four Anglo men run around the block with their shirts off. Day laborers do not enjoy the luxuries of fashion, health-consciousness, and other problems unique to middle-class life. Their lives depend on waiting, outstanding—literally standing longer than others—and running fast. According to a 1999 study by Dr. Abel Valenzuela of UCLA's Center for the Study of Urban Poverty, about twenty-thousand day laborers operate in more than ninety sites in the Los Angeles/Orange County area. Almost all of them—98 percent—are from Mexico or Central America, and about 95 percent of these entered the country illegally; most of them remain without papers. Half the workers surveyed said employers had abused them at least once, usually in the form of nonpayment or insufficient payment. Fully half of them have been doing this for more than ten years. The other half have been doing it for less than one year, suggesting that a large portion of the workers are recent immigrants living lives as tenuous as that of the *tolucense*.

These men are workers, plain and simple. They might have personal lives, but their existence revolves around finding work, no matter how long it takes.

"You can never lose hope," says one gentleman, whose choice of a Mighty Ducks hat and a Kings T-shirt attests to his unconcern with sports rivalries. "I was once underneath the shade, the only person left, and was about to leave until I heard a honk. 'You want to work?' the guy asked me. Of course I did. I worked for five hours and received sixty dollars for an easy job."

His story is interrupted. As he's speaking, everyone starts pointing toward the street. I have let my guard down; a truck has arrived. I rush to find work. I can't see the driver, but the men start shouting, "¡Es un chino!"—he's Chinese.

What difference this makes does not occur to me until a guy tells me afterward, "White people are the best [to work for] because all they ask is that you do the job right and they'll pay you." Chinese, the catchall phrase in Mexican Spanish for Asians, "are more demanding, and they pay cheap."

Prospective employers usually act nervous. They'll slowly drive down the street, probably debating whether they should stick to their anti-immigrant rhetoric or hire cheap help. Then they'll pull into the parking lot after making a couple of circles, still debating their hypocrisies.

But the *chino* manifests authority, as if he has done this many times before. "I give eight hours, eight dollars," the man says in broken English. "Three workers. Construction."

A clamor breaks out among the men. "Ten dollars, two workers," one man shouts.

"No, eight," the Asian holds steadfastly. "Eight hours, I guarantee."

He picks a guy with a ponytail, who immediately asks the old man to hire his two friends. "Who are your friends?" the old man asks. Everyone shouts, "Me, me!" but the ponytail guy picks his friends and they get in the truck.

Those who remain try to shrug off their disappointment. "Eight dollars? That's too little," one says. "I'm sure I can find someone who pays more later on."

Though the rejected men are devastated, the chosen are transformed. It's an amazing and heartbreaking contrast. The faces of chosen *jornaleros* are full of life, and they always start small talk with the person who selected them. Although the job will probably be backbreaking and they will no doubt be paid badly, anyone who remains on the sidewalk would kill to trade places.

There is no such thing as an "unskilled worker" here. Everyone has a specialty—drywalling, construction and its myriad requirements, gardening. Some can do everything. But woe to the man without a skill. He is never picked.

I am never picked. As I leave the sidewalk for lunch around 1 p.m., the irony does not escape me: I am college-educated, young, and sound of mind and body. But in this world, any of these men has more to offer a prospective employer than I do.

Epilogue

I always try to help others out. Sometimes, a person will come with a job that I cannot do. But maybe I know someone there that can do it. I'll yell out to the person that they have a job there. Sure, there's competition for work here, but I'd rather make sure that others get a job I can't do than leave that job unfilled and deny someone their day's wages.

—"EL PANSÓN" (THE GUY WITH THE HUGE GUT),
NO AGE GIVEN, MICHOACÁN

"So do you want to work or not?"

Leaving for lunch put me in a perfect position to get to a truck before anyone else. I immediately ask the lady driver what type of work she has. She is looking for people to pull weeds in her garden, something even I could do.

Here, at last, is an opportunity to work eight hours at $10 per—a king's income here. I flash through the advantages of saying yes, but I refuse the job. It wasn't the weeding; I've been pulling weeds all my life and know the basics of front-yard horticulture. But I can't bring myself to take the job. I would be robbing these men of money they need to survive, especially one that pays this well. I walk away as others crowd around, a few of them winners in this rudest lottery.

Sure, it's a hard job, but I suffer through it to show my children what type of life not to have. Lots of Americans, they've been here forever: their parents, grandparents, great-grandparents, and so forth. They're used to a life of luxury. If a little kid breaks his toy, he just waits until his parents come home so they can buy him a new one and throw the broken one away. We immigrants, on the other hand, come from a life of hardship. We appreciate the United States more than gabachos. All of us here, we just want to work.

—ENRIQUE, 38

It's long been a stereotype that Mexicans are lazy and shiftless. Could that be why you have problems answering my questions?

DOUCHE CHILL CHOLO

Dear Gabacho: Patience, gentle gabacho, patience. I have so many questions in queue it looks like the checkout line at the border. *¡Ask a Mexican!* has grown from an excuse to print the immortal curse *pinche* *puto pendejo baboso* (fucking stupid-ass asshole) into the world's primary font for all things Mexican. The questions arrive daily via burro, e-mail, or plopped out from the *culos* of drug mules—like my wabby cousins, they keep coming. If the Mexican hasn't answered your question yet, that probably means your *pregunta* isn't that racist, sexist, or scatological or doesn't include enough mustache references. My advice: work harder. Or ask a Mexican to ask your question for you. He'll do it better *y* cheaper.

Got a spicy question about Mexicans? Ask the Mexican at themexican@askamexican.net. And for those of you who do have questions, include a hilarious pseudonym, or we'll make one up for you!

Acknowledgments

Dear Mexican: Why are your families so damn big?

Dear Readers: That's one stereotype I won't try to debunk—hell, I have more than one hundred *first cousins*. And that's just the biological portion of *mi familia*. Like all good Mexicans, I have hundreds of members in my extended family, all whom I owe a thousand *gracias* and tamales for making this book possible:

Theological family: A shout-out goes to my four patron saints: the Virgin of Guadalupe (patron saint of Mexico), the Santo Niño de Atocha (patron saint of my parents' home state of Zacatecas), St. Boniface, and St. Jude Thaddeus, patron saint of lost causes. *Gracias* for answering my prayers; I'll try to attend Mass soon.

Biological family: *Mami y papi,* who showed me that you can speak bad English and still be more American than John Wayne. My siblings, Elsa, Alejandrina, and Gabriel, who never let me get away with anything and who make my parents and me proud. My grandfathers—*mi Pepe y Papa Je*—both former orange pickers in Orange County who look down on me from heaven; *ojalá que sean orgullosos de mi*. My *abuelitas* Angelita *y* Mama Chela. All my cousins who have made something of themselves and showed those *pinche gabachos* that Mexicans are not always losers. To my *media chica,* who showed me that second acts are sometimes better than the first. And Sweetpea!

Work family: I'm the man I am today thanks to Will Swaim. Not only did this quarter-wab give me the idea for *¡Ask a Mexican!,* but he also started my journalism career and continues to demand the best from me week in, week out. Guillermo, I never believed in real-life heroes until I met you. God blessed me by having our lives cross. And I feel the same way about everyone whom I've been lucky to work with at the *OC Weekly*—a *very* short list includes Nick (I'll dominate you in tennis yet), Rebecca, Steve, Theo, Dave, Ellen, Tom, Vickie, Scott, Matt, Anthony, Stacy, Rich, Chris, Patty, Tenaya, Jenn, Ofelia, and all the interns who have fact-checked my articles; the various receptionists—Nadia, Sarah, Erin, Leslie, Kevin—who I bugged when suffering from writer's block; all the production, classifieds, and advertising freaks. Hey, America—this is the best damn newspaper in the country after *Weekly World News*. Visit us at www.ocweekly.com.

Syndicate family: Thank you to all the papers that carry *¡Ask a Mexican!* for having the *cojones* to publish it. As of my writing these acknowledgments, the list includes *OC Weekly, LA Weekly, La Prensa San Diego, Alternate 101, Las Vegas CityLife, Salt Lake City Weekly, Phoenix New Times, Flagstaff Live!, Tucson Weekly, Seattle Weekly, Jackson Hole Weekly, Weekly Alibi, Houston Press, Dallas Observer, Urban Tulsa Weekly, Wichita City Paper, The Pitch, Westword, Nashville Scene, The 11th Hour,* and tiny *Coastal Beat* in Naples, Florida. Any publisher interested in picking up *mucho* readers can pick up the column by e-mailing me at GArellano@ocweekly.com.

Corporate family: Yes, Virginia, I am an acolyte of the barbarians from Phoenix, otherwise known as Village Voice Media, formerly known as the New Times Corporation. Thank you, Jim Larkin, for letting me keep all profits from this book. Thank you, Scott Spear, for allowing me to syndicate the column. Thank you, Andy VandeVoorde, for spreading the gospel of The Mexican to our sister papers. And Mike Lacey, you drunk Irish *cabrón*—when are we downing that bottle of tequila?

Professional family: Rubén Martínez, Sam Quiñones, Yvette Cabrera, Lalo Alcaraz, and Tony Ortega, for taking the e-mails of an aspiring twenty-two-year-old journalist and providing him with great career advice; Daniel Hernández, for writing the *Los Angeles Times* profile that forever changed my life; Al Rantel, Tom Leykis, and Joe Escalante, for allowing me to take questions about Mexicans on your radio shows to hilarious results and higher ratings for *ustedes;* The *AirTalk with Larry Mantle* gang, for allowing me to be the lefty wacko every other week for over two years; Nick Goldberg and Matt Welch, for allowing a writer from a rival publication to become a contributing editor to the *Los Angeles Times* op-ed pages; Ben Quiñones, for always being a phone call away—*LA Weekly* doesn't know what they're missing, *'mano;* Kevin Roderick, for always posting my stuff at laobserved.com; and Rick Reiff, television genius.

Scribner family: My hillbilly editor, Brant Rumble, his boss, Nan Graham, and *their* boss, Scribner publisher Susan Moldow—*gracias,* all of *ustedes,* for having faith in me; my publicist, Kate Bittman, for whoring me out to the national media; and all the other geeks at the best damn imprint on Earth (we originally published *How the Other Half Lives,* suckers!).

Promotion family: David Kuhn, my agent, for not being insulted when I gave him five minutes to tell me why I shouldn't hang up on him the first time we talked. Billy Kingsland, for patiently answering my questions. Jason Corliss, for whoring me out on the speakers' circuit.

Amigos family: Art, Victor, Plácido, and Danny (remember how I told you I'd put you in the Acknowledgments for burning my DVDs? *Aquí te va*); the Gonzalez sisters, Javier, and Pelos; Sali and Carla, Mateo and Adriana; the Midnight Club; Ben, Sarah, and Mike; all the Centro Cultural de México and Calacas peeps; Los Abandoned; Drs. Apodaca and Ortiz-Franco at Chapman University; Messrs. Cross and Logan, Misses Spykerman and Sinatra at Anaheim High; the Librería Martínez group of MacArthur geniuses—I love you all.

Miscellaneous family: Jim Gilchrist, who showed me you can think the exact opposite of what I think and still be a gentleman; the readers of my column, both those who love it and loathe it—without your readership, I'd be just another overworked Mexican. The people who call me a *vendido* and/or *reconquista* apologist—your diatribes against me always bring a laugh to my day. Mark Dancey, for his gorgeous drawings. Robert Diefenbach, martyr for the Mexican.

And, finally, a special thanks to my homeland: Orange County, California, the most Mexican-hating county in the country. It's your xenophobia toward my parents and my culture that allowed the column to explode. Be warned, *naranjeros*—I get to write about us next.